WHEN COUNTRIES TALK

The American Enterprise Institute
Trade in Services Series

COMPETING IN A CHANGING WORLD ECONOMY PROJECT

Deregulation and Globalization: Liberalizing International Trade in Air Services — *Daniel M. Kasper*

Global Competition in Financial Services: Market Structure, Protection, and Trade Liberalization — *Ingo Walter*

International Trade in Business Services: Accounting, Advertising, Law, and Management Consulting — *Thierry J. Noyelle and Anna B. Dutka*

International Trade in Construction, Design, and Engineering Services — *James R. Lee and David Walters*

International Trade in Films and Television Programs — *Steven S. Wildman and Stephen E. Siwek*

International Trade in Ocean Shipping Services: The United States and the World — *Lawrence J. White*

When Countries Talk: International Trade in Telecommunications Services — *Jonathan David Aronson and Peter F. Cowhey*

International Trade in Services: An Overview and Blueprint for Negotiations — *Geza Feketekuty*

WHEN COUNTRIES TALK

The American Enterprise Institute
Trade in Services Series

COMPETING IN A CHANGING WORLD ECONOMY PROJECT

When Countries Talk

International Trade in Telecommunications Services

Jonathan David Aronson

Peter F. Cowhey

An American Enterprise Institute/Ballinger Publication

Ballinger Publishing Company, Cambridge, Massachusetts
A Subsidiary of Harper & Row, Publishers, Inc.

"American Enterprise Institute" and ⬤ are registered service marks of the American Enterprise Institute for Public Policy Research.

International Standard Book Number: 0-88730-284-X

Library of Congress Catalog Card Number: 87-37415

Printed in the United States of America.

Library of Congress Cataloging-in-Publication Data

Aronson, Jonathan David.
  When countries talk.

  (American Enterprise Institute series on trade in services)
  Includes bibliographies and index.
  1. Telecommunication—International cooperation.
I. Cowhey, Peter F., 1948-   . II. Title.
III. Series.
HE7700.A76   1988   384   87-37415
ISBN 0-88730-284-X

When Countries Talk

International Trade in Telecommunications Services

Jonathan David Aronson

Peter F. Cowhey

An American Enterprise Institute/Ballinger Publication

Ballinger Publishing Company, Cambridge, Massachusetts
A Subsidiary of Harper & Row, Publishers, Inc.

International Standard Book Number: 0-88730-284-X

Library of Congress Catalog Card Number: 87-37415

Printed in the United States of America.

Library of Congress Cataloging-in-Publication Data

Aronson, Jonathan David.
  When countries talk.

  (American Enterprise Institute series on trade in services)
  Includes bibliographies and index.
  1. Telecommunication—International cooperation.
I. Cowhey, Peter F., 1948-   . II. Title.
III. Series.
HE7700.A76 1988 384 87-37415
ISBN 0-88730-284-X

CONTENTS

LIST OF TABLES

LIST OF ACRONYMS

ADAPSO	Association of Data Processing Service Organizations
AECO	aggregate equivalence of competitive opportunities
AIG	American International Group (insurance company)
ARABSAT	Arabian Satellite Communication Organization
ARINC	Aeronautical Radio Inc.
ASEAN	Association of South East Asian Nations
AT&T	American Telephone and Telegraph
CAD/CAM	computer-aided design and computer-aided manufacturing
CBEMA	Computer and Business Equipment Manufacturers Association
CCIR	International Consultative Committee for Radio (of ITU)
CCITT	International Consultative Committee for Telephones and Telegraph (of ITU)
CEI	comparably efficient interconnection
CEPT	Conference of European Postal and Telecommunications Administrations
Comsat	Communication Satellite Corporation
COS	Corporation for Open Systems
CNCP	Canadian National Canadian Pacific Telecommunications
CPE	customer premises equipment

CRTC	Canadian Radio-television and Telecommunications Commission
DEC	Digital Equipment Corporation
DGT	Direction Générale des Télécommunications, France's PTT
DOC	U.S. Department of Commerce
EC	European Community
ECS	European Communication System (Eutelsat)
EDS	Electronic Data Systems (General Motors subsidiary)
Esprit	European Strategic Programme for Research and Development in Information Technologies (of EC)
EUREKA	European Research Coordinating Agency
FCC	U.S. Federal Communications Commission
GAS	General Agreement on Services (proposed)
GATT	General Agreement on Tariffs and Trade
GE	General Electric
GNP	gross national product
GTE	General Telephone and Electric
IBI	Intergovernmental Bureau for Informatics
IBM	International Business Machines
ICAO	International Civil Aviation Organization
ICCP	Committee for Information, Computer and Communication Policy (of OECD)
IDC	International Digital Communications Planning Inc.
IMO	International Maritime Organization
Inmarsat	International Maritime Satellite Organization
Intelsat	International Satellite Communications Organization
INTUG	International Telecommunications Users Group
IPDC	International Program for Development of Communications
IRC	international record carrier
ISAC	Industrial Sectoral Advisory Committee (of USTR)

ISDN	integrated services digital network
ISO	International Standards Organization
ITU	International Telecommunication Union
KDD	Kokusai Denshin Denwa (Japan's international phone monopoly)
LAN	local area network
LATA	local access and transport area
MAP	Manufacturing Automation Protocol
MFJ	Modified Final Judgement
MFN	most-favored nation
MITI	Japanese Ministry of Trade and Industry
MOF	Japanese Ministry of Finance
MOFA	Japanese Ministry of Foreign Affairs
MPT	Japanese Ministry of Posts and Telecommunications
NICs	newly industrializing countries
NTIA	National Telecommunications and Information Administration (of DOC)
NTT	Nippon Telegraph and Telephone
OCC	other common carrier
OECD	Organization for Economic Cooperation and Development
ONA	Open Network Architecture
OSI	Open Systems Interconnection (developed by ISO)
OTA	Office of Technology Assessment (of U.S. Congress)
PABX	private automatic branch exchange
PBX	private branch exchange
PSTN	public switched telephone network
PTT	postal telegraph and telephone (authority)
RACE	Research and Development in Advanced Communications Technologies for Europe (of the EC)
R&D	research and development
RARC	Regional Administrative Radio Conference (sponsored by ITU)
RBOC	regional Bell operating company

RPOA	Recognized Private Operating Agencies
SIG	Senior Interagency Group
SITA	Société Internationale de Télécommunications Aéronautiques
SNA	Systems Network Architecture (developed by IBM)
SPAC	Services Policy Advisory Committee (of USTR)
SWIFT	Society for Worldwide Interbank Financial Telecommunications
TBDF	transborder data flows
UNCTAD	United Nations Conference for Trade and Development
UNCTC	United Nations Centre on Transnational Corporations
UNESCO	United Nations Educational, Scientific and Cultural Organization
USTR	Office of the United States Trade Representative
VAN	value-added network
WARC	World Administrative Radio Conference (sponsored by ITU)
WATTC	World Administrative Telegraph and Telephone Conference (sponsored by ITU)
WIPO	World Intellectual Property Organization

EDITOR'S FOREWORD

The American Enterprise Institute's *Trade in Services Series* represents an important step toward creating the policy alternatives necessary to enhance the international competitiveness of American services.

The series is part of a larger, continuing AEI project, *Competing in a Changing World Economy*. Launched in 1983, this project has produced a wealth of publications, seminars, and conferences, analyzing the most significant policy challenges confronting U.S. policymakers in the areas of international trade and finance, science and technology policy, and human capital development.

Early in the project, we concluded that the United States would be successful in its drive to initiate a new round of trade negotiations with the other major trading nations, under the auspices of the General Agreement on Tariffs and Trade (GATT). We also chose to concentrate our resources on the new issues that would be placed on the table in that round: trade in services, intellectual property, and trade-related investment. In September 1986, at Punta del Este, Uruguay, the United States and the other members of GATT did indeed reach an agreement to launch a new multilateral round of trade negotiations, the Uruguay Round. Trade in services, along with intellectual property and investment issues, was included on the agenda. Hence, over the next several years negotiators in Geneva and top policy officials in all the major trading nations will face the formidable task of forging trading rules for these new issues.

In the area of services, a number of countries, including the United States, have produced individual, national studies of service trade liberalization. Yet government and private-sector officials agree that these studies are only a first step, and that substantial research remains to be done in key service sectors before major policy questions can be answered regarding a new service trade regime.

Designed to fill this policy gap, *Trade in Services* brings together eleven outstanding writers who have committed their expertise to analyzing the seven key service sector industries:

- Aviation—Daniel M. Kasper, Harbridge House

- Banking—Ingo Walter, Graduate School of Business Administration, New York University

- Construction—James R. Lee, American University, and David Walters, Staff Economist, Office of the U.S. Trade Representative

- Professional services—Thierry J. Noyelle and Anna B. Dutka, Conservation of Human Resources, Columbia University

- Shipping—Lawrence J. White, Member, Federal Home Loan Bank Board, on leave from the Graduate School of Business Administration, New York University

- Telecommunications: Information and Data Processing— Jonathan David Aronson, School of International Relations, University of Southern California, and Peter F. Cowhey, Department of Political Science, University of California at San Diego

- Telecommunications: Motion Pictures, Television, and Prerecorded Entertainment—Steven S. Wildman and Stephen E. Siwek, Economists Incorporated

In addition, Geza Feketekuty, of the Office of the U.S. Trade Representative, has written an overview volume for the series.

All of the books in the series embody two main goals: first, to analyze the dynamics of international competition for each of the seven industries, identifying existing and potential barriers to trade; and second, to formulate and assess policy approaches for opening service markets through an umbrella service agreement and subsequent individual sector agreements in GATT.

A related goal is to disseminate the results of our research through conferences and seminars, televised forums, and a variety of publication formats. We aim to make our findings known to government officials, trade experts, the business and financial communities, and concerned members of the public. To that end, during 1987 we convened major conferences in London, Geneva, and Washington, and in early 1988 the team of authors traveled to Tokyo and Singapore. Thus, as with all AEI projects, we have sought to ensure that the studies not only make a significant contribution to scholarship but also become an important factor in the decision making and negotiating processes.

In addition to the authors, who have produced outstanding books, we would like to thank John H. Jackson, Hessel E. Yntema Professor of Law at the University of Michigan, and Gardner Patterson, who for many years served in the GATT Secretariat. Both of these men provided invaluable help and guidance as advisers to the project.

—Claude E. Barfield
Coordinator
Competing in a Changing World Economy

PREFACE

The telecommunications and information industries are reshaping technological capabilities, economic power, and international trade rules. But coherent analysis of how the politics, economics, and technology of these industries intermesh to transform international trade and investment is lacking. We try to fill some of the gaps with this book.

Concentrating on telecommunications and information services, we argue that decisions about the provision of services have important consequences for whether computers will come from IBM or Fujitsu and telephone switches from AT&T or Siemens. The services game is inexorably tied to the equipment game, and vice versa.

Our political focus is on the restructuring of the rules governing competition in the international markets for telecommunications and information services. We explore in depth whether the General Agreement on Tariffs and Trade (GATT), the international body that oversees the conduct of world trade in goods, can develop rules for services that would substantially transform world competition. This discussion leads us to examine why national frameworks for competition differ and what alternatives to the GATT exist for opening up international competition in service markets.

Our goal is to provide a framework for asking and answering questions about these markets that will help policymakers. Although we downplay explicit theorizing, we do present practitioners with a more detailed analysis of their strategic problems and choices than they normally find in their briefing books.

Although this book is best read in the old fashioned way (from start to finish), some alternative routes are possible. We urge readers who care more about the implicit theory underlying our analysis to examine first Chapters 2–4 and Chapter 8; Chapters 1 and 5–7 then provide selective case studies and Chapter 9 offers some policy suggestions. Readers seeking policy suggestions are urged to read Chapters 1 and 2, the beginning of Chapter 3, and Chapters 8 and 9. Chapters 3 and 4 provide detailed analysis of the market segments and of the potential for competition. The case studies in Chapters 5–7 can be sampled according to the reader's tastes and interests.

In trying to make this analysis relevant and interesting, we have benefited from the generous support of many institutions and the patient advice of numerous individuals. Both authors especially thank Claude Barfield and Sven Arndt of the Competing in a Changing World Economy Project of the American Enterprise Institute for commissioning this book and sponsoring many meetings among the authors working on the project. We also owe a great deal to the Council on Foreign Relations, which supported both of us as International Affairs Fellows in our research and encouraged us to organize a Study Group in 1985–1986 that proved important to this book. C. Michael Aho, Paul Kreisberg, and Kempton Dunn deserve special mention. We also thank Project Promethee in Paris for its hospitality to us individually and collectively. The Berkeley Roundtable on the International Economy also has helped us on more than one occasion.

Bits and pieces of a book always tumble out before the final product. We thank the following organizations for letting us present earlier versions of some of our ideas through their publications: *Trade in Services: A Case for Open Markets* (Washington, D.C.: American Enterprise Institute, 1984) (Chapter 1 in this book); "The Great Satellite Shootout," *Regulation* (May-June 1985) (Chapter 5); "Trade in Communication and Data Processing," in Robert Stern, ed., *Trade and Investment in Services: Canada/U.S. Perspectives* (Toronto: University of Toronto Press for the Ontario Economic Council, 1985) (Chapter 6); "Trade talks and the informatics sector." *International Journal*

(Winter 1986–1987), (Chapters 2 and 6); "Telecommunications Networks: Can They Save Europe's Computer and Microelectronics Industries?" in Alfred Phaller, ed., *Der Kampf um den Wohlstand von morgen — Internationaler Strukturwandel und neuer Merkantilismus* (Bonn: Friedrich Ebert Stiftung, 1986) (Chapter 7).

Peter Cowhey benefited from a generous sabbatical from the University of California, San Diego that allowed him to take full advantage of the generosity of the Rockefeller Foundation's international affairs fellowship for two years during this research. He also wishes to thank AT&T for letting him serve (under the sponsorship of the Council on Foreign Relations) as a market planner and consultant for various parts of the operations of AT&T International and AT&T Communications International. David Gompert arranged for this special opportunity, and Randy Lumb and Bobbie Boone cooperated generously in arranging for his rotating "apprenticeship." Naturally, AT&T bears no responsibility for anything in these pages, and many members of its exceptional staff will probably groan at some of the judgments offered here.

Jonathan Aronson thanks the School of International Relations and the Annenberg School of Communications at the University of Southern California. He is also grateful to the Office of the United States Trade Representative and particularly to Geza Feketekuty and Richard Self for introducing him to the intricacies of trade in telecommunications services while he worked there as a Council on Foreign Relations International Affairs Fellow in 1982–1983.

We thank the many corporate and government officials in the United States and abroad who consistently provided us with important information and insights. Those in the Office of the United States Trade Representative were always helpful, as were officials in the U.S. Departments of Commerce and State, and the Federal Communications Commission. Committee staff in both houses of Congress and officials of the Office of Technology Assessment all provided assistance. We were also warmly welcomed in Japan, the European Community, and Canada.

A very large number of people have contributed to this work by offering advice and reading drafts of various chapters. We have space here only to thank those who systematically aided, encouraged, and prodded us forward: Michael Borrus, Albert Bressand, Arthur Bushkin, Stephen Cohen, Greg Dahlin, William Davidson, Catherine Distler, Geza Feketekuty, John Jackson, Gary Jacobson, Daniel Kasper, Sy Lazarus, David Laitin, Pacy Markman, David Mowery, Eli Noam, Gardner Patterson, G. Russell Pipe, John Richardson, Peter Robinson, John Ruggie, Karl Sauvant, Richard Self, Christopher Wilkinson, Julia York, and John Zysman.

Finally, we thank Joan and Margaret for their patience, support, and comments. They were friends long before we entered their lives. We suspect that they exchanged many secret smiles while we tried to puzzle through the unfolding secrets of the information age. This book is for them.

WHEN COUNTRIES TALK

I

Dimensions of the
Telecommunications Sector

1

TELECOMMUNICATIONS AND THE STRUGGLE OVER THE SERVICE INDUSTRIES

The world economy evolves more rapidly than the institutions and rules that countries design to manage it. Eventually the rules become outdated. When the seriousness of the problem becomes evident, governments try to reengineer the rules. Sometimes they succeed. But when they fail, global economic growth suffers and the chance of a global economic crisis increases. Today the world economy is fragile and international interdependence guarantees that a systemic crisis would be transmitted to all corners of the globe. Even the political consequences of slower growth would be unpleasant. Therefore, some governments are urging the reform of rules and institutions that oversee the world economy before a crisis arises.[1]

The United States government has gambled that trade in services offers an attractive opening for shoring up the traditional coalition supporting free trade and investment. Although applying the regime of the General Agreement on Tariffs and Trade (GATT) to services involves significant intellectual and political challenges, Washington judged the economic returns to be lucrative enough to key states and industries to make services a symbol of progress for free traders. This book argues that Washington was right to tackle trade in telecommunications and information services. A general agreement is possible. As with many innovations of a fundamental nature, however, the government may at the same time be redefining what the world means by free trade and investment. In short, the U.S. initiative may inadvertently speak of a far broader set of changes in the rules governing world commerce than was ever contemplated. This book explains the economic stakes, the political interests, and the emerging bargain that will govern world commerce in telecommunications and information services.

WHY SERVICES ARE IMPORTANT

One key change in the world economy during the past four decades is the increased importance of services such as telecommunications, finance, travel and tourism, advertising, and accounting in global commerce. Table 1–1 indicates that the percentage of gross domestic product and employment accounted for by the service sector has increased dramatically in key

Table 1–1. Services as a Percentage of GDP and Employment in Selected Countries.

Country	Services as % of GDP		Services as % of Employment	
	1965	1984	1975	1984
Industrial				
Belgium	53	64	66	74[a]
Canada	61	72	72	75
Japan	48	56	61	66
Sweden	53	66	65	72
United Kingdom	56	62	65	72
United States	59	66	72	76
Developing				
Argentina	42	50	—	—
Brazil	48	52	47[b]	54[c]
India	31	38	—	—
Republic of Korea	37	47	35	48

Sources: GDP data from *World Development Report 1986* (New York: Oxford University Press, 1986); Employment data from *International Labor Organization, Yearbook of Labor Statistics 1985*. Data cited in James R. Basche, "Eliminating Barriers to International Trade and Investment in Services," Research Bulletin No. 200 (New York: The Conference Board, 1986).

a. 1983

b. 1976

c. 1982

industrial and developing countries. In many countries, increasing services employment has offset declining farm and production jobs. For example, the European Community (EC) estimates that during "the years between 1973 and 1981, the decrease in employment in the manufacturing sector of 4.1 million was largely compensated by an increase in 3.5 million employed in market services."[2] Similarly, the Institute of Manpower Studies estimates that services jobs in the United Kingdom will increase by about 540,000 by 1990, as compared with a fall of 665,000 jobs in the farming and production industries.

Unfortunately, the definition and measurement of services and trade in services have always been difficult.[3] For example, to sell services abroad traditionally required sending skilled people to the country wishing to buy the service or establishing a foreign subsidiary to provide the service. Therefore, the international sale of services was considered as an investment issue, not a trade issue. But the way the world economy works is changing. Today, the growing integration of the global telecommunications network is promoting international commerce by making many services more tradable. The line between trade and investment in services is being blurred.

The inability to precisely define or measure services is one reason that economists are trained to think in terms of goods, not services. This is particularly true in the area of trade. Naturally, most economic models are not designed to deal with the changes in economic behavior produced by a world economy united by inexpensive information flows. These information flows are services that are by their nature invisible. It is not surprising, therefore, that the contribution of services in national economies and in the world economy is little studied and poorly understood. Adam Smith, Karl Marx, and most of their economic heirs have maligned services as unproductive.[4]

Telecommunications services are at the heart of any modern service economy. Indeed, the merging of computer, communication, and broadcast technologies is creating a world information economy. Shortly we will be able to transmit voices, images, and data between any two points on the globe instantaneously. Borders are irrelevant to these technological advances.[5] And, in an integrated, international communication network, the cost of providing services is only marginally linked to the distance between the sender and receiver of information. The unit cost of providing telecommunications services will continue to fall. If policy permits, the price of telecommunications services should follow costs downward.

Similarly, trade in telecommunications services has both economic and political significance. On the economic side, this trade is important for three reasons. First, telecommunications revenues and trade in telecommunications services are growing rapidly. It seems plausible that in an information dominated society, expenditures on services will continue to rise relative to expenditures on goods. Freer trade in telecommunications services would likely allow telecommunications goods and services to grow as a percentage of total trade. In 1984 annual information technology revenues, narrowly defined, in the United States accounted for 3.5 percent of the gross national product. By 1994 the information industry's annual revenues could triple to equal 6 percent of the U.S. GNP.[6] Table 1–2 shows the size and breakdown of the world market for telecommunications and computer products and services in 1984 and estimates its growth to 1990.

An integrated, global telecommunications network allows for tremendous growth in the trade of nontelecommunications services, which until now could not easily be traded. Just as the transportation system provides the infrastructure that makes possible the trade of industrial products, a global telecommunications network could be the infrastructure necessary to build a world information economy. The location of a worker providing services makes less difference if all workers are connected through the communication network. Thus, many "internationally traded services such as advertising, accounting, financial services and insurance, have been made possible or substantially more efficient, practical and profitable by the worldwide communications network" without establishing an extensive foreign presence.[7] For example, American construction/engineering firms employ architectural drafters in the Philippines and India, much of the animation for television and movies is now drawn

Table 1–2. The World Market for Telecommunications and Computer Products and Services ($ billions).[a]

SIC Item[c]	1984		1990[b]		Annual Rate of Growth 1984–90E
	World	U.S.	World	U.S.	
Telecom equipment	60	(24)	95	(36)	8%
Computer equipment	80		195		16%
Telecom services	265	(103)	444	(165)	9%
Computer services	40		97		16%
Worldwide totals	445		831		11%

Source: *Issues in Domestic Telecommunications: Directions for National Policy*, NTIA Special Publication 85-16, (Washington, D.C.: U.S. Department of Commerce, July 1985), p. 160.

a. Estimates are not adjusted for inflation.

b. Estimated.

c. Telecom equipment includes SIC 3661 (Telephone and Telegraph Apparatus), 36621, and 36622.

Computer equipment covers SIC 3573 (Electronic Computing Equipment).

Telecom services include SIC 4811 and 4821 (Telephone and Telegraph Services).

Computer services cover SIC 737 (Computer services establishments including data processing, systems integration).

These estimates almost certainly underestimate the total. Videotext and electronic data base services have not been assigned a four-digit SIC number.

offshore, South Koreans contribute abstracts for legal data bases, data entry facilities for American Airlines and other U.S. firms are located in Barbados, and the booking and reservation system of the Polish national airline is installed in Atlanta.

Freer trade in communication services is important because the service component of manufactured products is rising. There were about 3.8 million new manufacturing jobs created in the United States between 1948 and 1978, but only about one-sixth were in production. Many of the rest were in service positions. Manufacturing still matters, but services are making manufacturers more productive. For example, when General Motors builds a new car, or Boeing a new airplane, they now rely more and more on computer-aided design and computer-aided manufacturing (CAD/CAM) to change designs and adjust machine tooling in plants around the world. Similarly, software programming services now account for approximately 80 percent of the development costs of a new computer and although digital telecommunications switches are less expensive to manufacture than their analog predecessors, 80 percent of the much higher development costs of a new digital telecommunications switch is accounted for by software.[8] A decade ago these figures were much lower. New, "just-in-time" manufacturing techniques, which reduce inventories, depend on sophisticated information systems to integrate the various stages of the production process. Thus, to the extent that information flows freely across national borders, the production and distribution of goods and services will be more efficient. (In the same vein, the international competitiveness of domestic manufacturing industries that are not linked into the global telecommunications network could decline.) Services are also a critical link in the delivery of the ultimate work that people want done by machinery such as computers. Manufacturers must become expert in delivering services if they are to sell hardware. Many U.S. producers are working hard to retain a comparative advantage through complex systems integration that has many service features.

At present, no set of coherent, internationally accepted rules and principles for managing trade and investment in services exists. The General Agreement on Tariffs and Trade, the key international organization concerned with trade and trade rules, was designed to deal with trade in goods. The trading system was not intended to cover services, much less telecommunications services. There was good reason for this. Most services were oriented to national markets. There was relatively little international sale of services (most of which were usually considered to require investment).[9]

International communications were treated somewhat differently but were still not considered to be trade. International communications by telephone, telegram, or telex were viewed as jointly provided services. Communication monopolies in each country struck deals with their counterparts for the exchange of international services. The receiving monopoly assumed responsibility for the message at the hypothetical midpoint between the sender and receiver. Each monopoly charged its own senders and the two monopolies settled among themselves to the extent that the traffic in both directions did not balance. Therefore, trade policymakers took little notice of telecommunications or other services.

Today, in contrast, the United States and other countries believe that extending the current trading rules and principles to cover services will benefit all countries by promoting growth and preempting vexing political disputes. For this reason, trade in services has emerged as a major item on the global trade agenda. Incorporating services into the GATT framework is a major goal of the new round multilateral negotiations launched in Uruguay in September 1986.[10] Can existing GATT trade rules and principles that cover goods be extended to services? Or, will new rules and principles need to be developed?

This book focuses on telecommunications, value-added, and information services (hereafter collectively designated as telecommunications services).[11] We also discuss the related markets for equipment. Because telecommunications services are linked to all services and are central to the operations of all multinational enterprises, any attempt to formulate a general framework to govern trade in services will need to cover the case of telecommunications. Indeed, the type of bargain struck on telecommunications will largely determine what kinds of agreements can be reached on other services. Similarly, the shape of any agreement on telecommunications services will fundamentally influence the opportunities for trade in computers, telecommunications equipment, and related high-technology products. This interplay between the general framework and the telecommunications sector forces us to adopt a broad scope.

THE BASIC ARGUMENT

One hundred years from now a historian will receive a grant from a foundation to review the diplomatic and economic history of the effort to rewrite the rules for competition in the global telecommunications and information industries in the late twentieth century. She will tell one of two tales, either of which

9

will be remarkable in itself. On the one hand, she might write that starting in the 1970s the world reversed its rigidly mercantilist controls over the telecommunications industry and opened up major new markets for global commerce even though global trade in other goods was subject to many new limitations. On the other hand, she might conclude that the telecommunications authorities of the world won a remarkable struggle to sustain their quasi-monopolistic control over the industry in the face of a major assault by their largest customers, much of the world services industry, and many of the important electronics firms. Which tale will she tell?

This book seeks to guide policymakers. It cannot hedge its bets without reducing its utility. So it argues that our future historian will tell the former story, not the latter. But it adds a significant twist to the plot of greater competition and regulatory innovation. It suggests that the effort to spur greater competition in telecommunications services will in itself reshape the definitions of free trade and foreign investment. In short, greater competition will prevail, but the principles governing trade and investment will have to be reframed to cope with the challenges of the politics, economics, and technology of the services industry. As is often the case in political history, the victors will discover that they have won something far different than they thought.

Today, the economics and technology of communications permit much greater competition than in the past, but it is the politics and specific economic benefits facing key actors that determine the extent and form of competition. Part I of this book lays out the dimensions of the telecommunications sector and explains why demands for reform in the regulation of the sector have become linked to the GATT negotiations concerning services. Part II examines the ways in which politics, economics, and technology intersect in three major dimensions of the market—transmission systems, value-added and long-distance services, and the computer equipment and information services markets—to goad the reformulation of the political bargain that long governed telecommunications. These chapters show that more competition is very likely but that a variety of alternatives exists for organizing the telecommunications sector in the future. The final two chapters, Part III, examine how to apply the GATT to telecommunications services and the alternatives to GATT for governing the telecommunications and information sector.

In addition to being a critical input to all services, telecommunications services are big business and they are critical sources of competitive advantage in even bigger businesses—the telecommunications and computer equipment markets—that are at the heart of the struggle for leadership in high technology. Many governments try to promote growth in such sectors, so there is little hope that the market will operate unimpeded. This is especially true for telecommunications services because they are traditionally heavily regulated and among the most mercantilist parts of the modern world economy. Moreover, every country eventually has to make massive investments in new switching and distribution systems for telecommunications services in order to accommodate new forms of information and video communications. The growth in the traditional monopoly market of voice telephone services may not be great enough to finance these investments. Countries must decide to what degree to maintain monopoly control over the faster growing data and video markets in order to assure rapidly growing revenues. Yet these are precisely the markets where the political and economic pressures to allow experimentation with competition are greatest. (For example, large users such as financial institutions seek to tie together world money markets as cheaply and efficiently as possible without regard to national borders or telecommunication administrations. Similarly, in the wake of the merging of computer and communication technologies, electronics and computer firms want to venture into markets formerly reserved for telecommunication equipment manufacturers.)

The three case studies in Part II illustrate the interplay of technology, economics, and politics in the telecommunications and information markets. They show that all domestic reforms will substantially redistribute economic rent generated by the telecommunications sector and, crucially, will force the reorganization of the international rules governing telecommunications services. Changes in the international rules will in turn lead to innovations in the domestic market. Variations in national industrial structure and political systems produce significantly different telecommunications policies. Nonetheless, the combination of transnational coalition of interests favoring competition and the declining credibility of the international cartel for telecommunications assure that the old monopoly model of telecommunications will fall in most industrial countries. The question is, What will replace it?

Part II uses three case studies to help understand how technological, economic and political forces are transforming the sector. It demonstrates that although Japan has introduced far-reaching competition, it continues to reconcile the role of the market and government very differently than the United States. Chapter 5 examines why the United States and Japan have decided that creating competition in transmission facilities (the hardware necessary to carry a message between two points, such as a telephone line) will promote general competition. Chapter 5 focuses on the domestic political considerations that led the United States to oppose the continuation of Intelsat's transoceanic satellite communication monopoly and on Japan's decision to permit international telecommunications competition.[12]

Chapter 6 examines how differences in Canadian industrial organization and politics (particularly the greater political importance of Canadian provinces) influence policy outcomes. The services debate is put into perspective by Canada's strength in telecommunications equipment and weakness in computer products. Chapter 6 reviews United States–Canada relations concerning telecommunications to show how international communications markets force the reorganization of domestic networks and how data communications alter the politics of the market for voice services.

Finally Chapter 7 explores the emerging relationship between the computer and communications markets by asking if Europe could unite behind a benign mercantilist strategy for telecommunications geared to take away many of IBM's competitive advantages in the computer market. It concludes that even a modified model would require a major departure from existing national monopoly practices and that the market bargains needed to refurbish the monopoly model are unlikely.

In short, we see a struggle of interests battling for the upper hand in the telecommunications arena. On the one hand, changing technology and shifting economic interests has led to an alteration of the positions of users, providers of data services and equipment, and, depending on national context, providers of basic voice services as well. While many of these entities are seeking more competition, powerful coalitions of small users and existing telephone monopolies, sometimes in cooperation with certain equipment suppliers, are arguing for and in some cases winning greater restrictions on competition. However, the advocates of greater competition are too influential not to win some big victories.

The problem for international policy is how to govern a world that is fundamentally divided between competitive and noncompetitive market segments. This is somewhat akin to Abraham Lincoln's dilemma of how can one nation survive, half slave and half free. These battles between pro- and anticompetitive forces in the telecommunications sector can be expected to become linked to broader choices about how public regulation will influence national competitive policies for the future computer and information markets.

Managing the world economy in a fast-changing, increasingly complicated world is one of the critical challenges facing governments. Finding a way to organize the emerging global service economy and particularly international telecommunications services is a big part of this task. What are the options for the future? Can the newly initiated multilateral trade talks lead to new and better ways of managing international telecommunications and trade in services? Part III examines what needs to be done to reform and extend the international economic regime and suggests what can be accomplished given existing rules and institutions.

Chapter 8 presents four contrasting models for managing telecommunications in the world economy. The first two models are the ones usually acknowledged. The monopoly/cartel model dominated international thought and practice for a century. The free trade/competitive model has often been applied to goods but is now being touted as applicable for the management of services as well. To oversimplify, most of the debate about trade in services concerns how far to move along the spectrum from monopoly control toward free trade. There is little awareness, however, that the issue can be cast in logic other than that of free trade versus protectionism. The stakes may be much higher.

The forces leading to the demand for greater competition will not disappear. But, if governments cannot reach agreement on free trade, firms still have to do business. The third and fourth models describe ways in which private and public firms might be transformed, ultimately making the debate over monopoly versus free trade less relevant. The direct foreign investment model suggests how something close to an international airline model might serve as a guide for organizing telecommunications. This would lead to new types of international telecommunications and information carriers. Finally, the international corporate alliances model indicates how major firms from different countries might join together in a series of arrangements to spread their risks and guarantee their access to all key markets. None of these four idealized models applies cleanly to the management of telecommunications in the world economy. But, with consideration of the problems and advantages associated with each of these models, a better understanding emerges of how telecommunications fits into the wider problem of managing the world economy.

Finally, Chapter 9 explores the possible benefits of GATT negotiations designed to yield freer trade in services. It explores whether and to what extent it is possible to extend trading rules that were designed for goods to services, and particularly telecommunications, under the auspices of a new round of multilateral trade negotiations. Although it is impossible to eliminate ill will or guarantee against perverse outcomes, GATT negotiations could allow governments to wrest the control of policy away from the narrowest of special interests and to seek more effective policies that can sustain growth with less overt conflict. As with other service sectors, such as shipping and airlines, telecommunications negotiations in the GATT will be as much a battle for control of domestic policy as a battle between nations. Trade talks, properly organized, will impel the telecommunications authorities of each nation to strike new bargains about the ways in which they exercise their authority. The GATT round could also prod the International Telecommunication Union (ITU), traditionally one of the world's largest legal cartels, to renovate its policies. After suggesting some ideas about how to achieve the strongest possible agreement within the GATT context, we explore alternative ways to manage telecommunications and information services in the fast changing global economy.

NOTES

1. Governments are usually better at defusing crises than at anticipating and avoiding them. Trade in services is an unusual case in which governments are attempting to act before a crisis arises. For an assessment of government responses to economic crises see Peter Gourevitch, *Politics in Hard Times: Comparative Responses to International Economic Crises* (Ithaca, N.Y.: Cornell University Press, 1986).
2. "Study on International Trade in Services" submitted by the European Communities to the GATT in 1984. The United Kingdom estimates come from the "The Report on UK Employment Trends" cited by the European Services Industries Forum.
3. The measurement of services is and always will be more difficult than the measurement of goods for several reasons. (1) Technological advances transform the service sector so rapidly that governments are unable to keep their monitoring systems current. (2) Many services are provided by multinational enterprises. The value added by services is diffused geographically and may be booked at a particular location for tax or regulatory reasons. This is also true for goods but may be even more important for services. (3) Manufacturing enterprises are increasingly providing services in conjunction with trade in goods and foreign investment. (4) The boundaries that separate particular types of services are blurring. Just as communication, computer, and broadcasting services are merging, so are banking, insurance, brokerage, and other financial services. (5) Many new kinds of services are being introduced on

which there is little or no data. (6) Many services are transacted in a nonmarket or black market environment. See Harald B. Malmgren, "Negotiating International Rules for Trade in Services," *The World Economy* 8, no. 1 (March 1985):12–13. Also see John B. Richardson, "A Subsectoral Approach to Services Trade Theory," in Orio Giarini, ed., *The Emerging Service Economy* (Elmsford, N.Y.: Pergamon, 1987).

4. Major exceptions to this generalization include Frank Knight, Kenneth Arrow, George Stigler, and Jagdish Bhagwati. See Robert M. Stern and Bernard M. Hoekman, "Conceptual Issues Related to Services in the International Economy," Research Seminar on International Economics, Department of Economics, the University of Michigan, Seminar Discussion Paper No. 188, Revised October 7, 1986; Stern and Hoekman, "GATT Negotiations on Services: Analytical Issues and Data Needs," Research Seminar on International Economics, Department of Economics, the University of Michigan, Seminar Discussion Paper No. 189, October 20, 1986. On the historical development of the role of information in the economy, see James E. Beniger, *The Control Revolution: Technological and Economic Origins of the Information Society* (Cambridge, Mass.: Harvard University Press, 1986). On current developments, see particularly Albert Bressand, "International Division of Labor in the Emerging Global Information Economy: The Need for a New Paradigm," Document Promethee No. 17 (Paris: Promethee, May 1986), mimeo. Journalists have the same difficulty dealing with services. As a consequence sophisticated publications such as *Business Week* decry the rise of the "Hollow Corporation," March 3, 1986. Similarly, the *Financial Times'* excellent country surveys almost always contain a single article on a country's banking sector but no mention of other service sectors.

5. On the emergence and nature of the information economy, see Marc U. Porat, *The Information Economy*, 9 vols. (Washington D.C.: U.S. Department of Commerce, 1977). Also see: Simon Nora and Alain Minc, *The Computerization of Society*, Report to the President of France (Cambridge, Mass.: MIT Press, 1980). An even broader concept of an information society (*johoka shakai*) was developed in Japan starting in the late 1960s. The possibilities and implications of a world information economy are only now being considered systematically.

6. *The Economist,* November 28, 1984; "The World on the Line," *The Economist,* November 23, 1985.
7. Geza Feketekuty and Kathryn Hauser with the assistance of Pippa Malmgren, "A Trade Perspective of International Telecommunications Issues," *Telematics and Informatics* 1, no. 4 (1984):361. There is no debate that services accounted for the bulk of new jobs in industrial countries during the past two decades. There is considerable debate as to the relative productivity of goods versus service jobs and about the desirability of moving toward a service economy. See "The False Paradise of a Service Economy," *Business Week,* March 3, 1986, pp. 78–81 and also Stephen S. Cohen and John Zysman, *Manufacturing Matters: The Myth of the Post-Industrial Economy* (New York: Basic Books, 1987) for criticism of this trend.
8. Jonathan D. Aronson and Peter F. Cowhey, *Trade in Services: The Case for Open Markets,* (Washington, D.C.: American Enterprise Institute, 1984), p. 41; "The World on the Line," *The Economist,* Telecommunications Survey, November 23, 1985, p. S1; "Only the Strong Will Survive in the Digital Switching Market," *Telephony,* December 29, 1986, p. 46. From the viewpoint of technological laggards, slowing the emergence of a world information economy may seem sensible as a way to protect their inefficient telecommunications sectors. This may be costly to their industries that need telecommunications inputs to be efficient.
9. Obviously, there were important exceptions. International shipping goes back to prehistory. Documentation on international banking goes back as far as the thirteenth century when the Bardi of Venice operated branches throughout Europe. The international banking activities of the Banco de Medici are explored in Raymond de Roover, *The Rise and Decline of the Medici Bank, 1397–1494* (Cambridge, Mass.: Harvard University Press, 1963). When Lloyds' of London was still a coffee house, international maritime insurance was written there.
10. Trade in services is the subject of Part II of the Ministerial Declaration that was issued at Punta del Este, Uruguay in September 1986. For political reasons, services will be negotiated under GATT auspices but separate from other negotiations during the Uruguay round.
11. Alternatively we could have used the term "information technologies," or IT. Some members of the value-added and informa-

tion services industries worry that telecommunications implies a "semantic imperialism" of the carriers. We disagree.

12. The United Kingdom's decision to allow Mercury, a subsidiary of Cable & Wireless, to compete with British Telecom is dealt with only in passing.

2

DEREGULATION AND INTERNATIONAL TELECOMMUNICATIONS

Services, including telephone and telegraph services, are usually more heavily regulated in industrial countries than manufacturing activities. Historically, control over roads and communications was the key to consolidating centralized authority over feudal societies. The industrial revolution never really undercut the state's control over many services. But, states developed a new, modern rationale. Regulators argued that the provision of basic telecommunications services required a natural monopoly that could take advantage of strong economies of scale. Moreover, they believed that governments had an obligation to foster economic growth and equity by providing basic telecommunications services to all citizens at affordable prices.

As a result, in most countries revenues from communications services subsidized postal services (especially for the influential publishing industry), long-distance services (and particularly international services) subsidized local services, business services subsidized personal services, and urban subscribers subsidized rural subscribers.[1] In essence, regulators redistributed benefits while trying to control abuses by monopoly providers of services. One consequence of this history was that basic communication services were everywhere tightly regulated. In contrast, information services, because they were considered a product of the private market in computer hardware, were generally less regulated.

The traditional bargain for telecommunications has begun to unravel. At a minimum, most countries will split apart their post and telecommunications authorities. Australia, the United Kingdom, and Japan have already done so. Under the prodding of the Commission of the European Community, it seems likely that most of Europe will do so in the future. This change reduces the propensity to use telecommunications as a form of cross-subsidy for the post by making such subsidies considerably more visible to the public eye and dividing up bureaucratic loyalties.

A more ambitious set of initiatives is emerging in many countries. These experiments take the form of considering privatization of some services and the introduction of more competition in selected segments of the market. At a minimum, this includes opening up competition in customer premises equipment. In most cases it also includes liberalizing some mix of broadcast and data communications services. For example, in June 1986, new legislation was introduced in the French Assembly to partially privatize the French broadcast system and to allow additional private firms to enter the market. France also decided to introduce more competition in data services. In 1987 Canada privatized Teleglobe Canada, its international service provider, and is likely to eventually license a second domestic long-distance company. And, countries as diverse as the Netherlands, Spain, Italy, Chile, Turkey, Australia, and Sri Lanka are exploring increased competition in at least some aspects of the telecommunications business.[2]

Most sweepingly, a troika of nations has permitted competition in the provision of basic services. In addition to the United States, the United Kingdom has granted Mercury, a subsidiary of Cable & Wireless, permission to compete with British Telecom at home and abroad. After 1989 other firms may also be allowed to compete. Similarly, the Japanese government has authorized five groups to compete in the domestic long-distance market with Nippon Telegraph and Telephone (NTT) and has sanctioned competition with Kokusai Denshin Denwa (KDD) in the provision of international telecommunications services.

There also are signs that governments are beginning intentionally and unintentionally to create competition in transmission facilities between countries. A spree of investment in fiber optic cables and satellites is opening the door for more aggressive bargaining by non-PTTs concerning their rights to own or lease capacity.

Understandably, entrenched postal, telegraph, and telephone (PTT) authorities, do not embrace the sweeping U.S. deregulatory vision. Therefore disagreements are proliferating. Debates rage over numerous questions: Should regulation be extended to new services or rolled back from basic services? How much regulation of value-added and information services is possible? How much competition is desirable in the provision of various services? Should services be provided by governments or by private firms? Should users be permitted to attach their own equipment to the network so long as it does not harm the network? Should it be possible to build new networks to provide services? Should users be able to bypass the PTT and the monopoly communication provider? Should leased lines be permitted? If so, should fixed or volume-sensitive pricing be practiced? Similarly, should resale and shared use of leased lines be permitted? The wide variety of existing practices is summarized in Table 2–1.

These questions are not easily answered in the abstract. Nor is there any reason to believe that a single right answer exists for any one of them. But a good place to begin understanding the question of how politics, economics, and technology can interact to reorder the regulatory structure for telecommunications is the United States. This chapter synthesizes the real message of the U.S. experience in order to serve as a baseline for examining other countries' choices. It then shows how the domestic bargain concerning telecommunications in the United States has influenced the agenda for international negotiations concerning international trade in telecommunications. An appendix to this chapter provides a brief summary of international institutions and their jurisdictions concerning telecommunications.

THE LESSONS FROM THE U.S.
EXPERIENCE WITH REGULATORY
REFORM

It is the liberal, pluralist bargaining system of U.S. politics that has produced a fundamental restructuring of the telecom-

Table 2–1. Present Telecommunications Market Structures in the European Communities.

	Belgium	Denmark	France	Germany	Greece
1. Relations with postal services	S (1)	PTT (5)	PTT	PTT	S
2. Basic service network					
a. Local	GM (PC)	OM (5)	GM	GM	GM (PC)
b. Long-distance	GM (PC)	OM	GM	GM	GM (PC)
c. International	GM (PC)	GM	GM	GM	GM (PC)
d. Mobile	GM (PC)	OM	GM (6)	GM	PL
3. Terminal equipment					
a. Supply					
Main telephone set	M	M	L	GM	M
PBX	PL	M	L	L	L
Telex	PL (2)	M	L	RC (LIM)	L
Modem	PL (3)	PL	L	L (20)	L
Data Terminal	L	L	L	L	L
Mobile	M	L	L	L	PL
b. Maintenance					
Main telephone set	M	M	L	M	M
PBX	PL	M	L	L	L
Telex	PL	M	L	M	M
Modem	PL	PL	L	L (20)	L
Data terminal	L	L	L	L	L
Mobile	M	L	L	L	L
4. Use of leased circuits					
a. Domestic					
Shared use/resale	N (4)	N	N (7)	Y (8a)	N
Interconnection with public network	N	N	N (7)	Y (8b)	N
b. International					
Shared use/resale	N (4)	N (4)	N (4)	Y (8a)	N (4)
Interconnection with public network	N (4)	N (4)	N (4)	Y (8c)	N (4)

munications industry. The United States has become the agenda setter for the rest of the world by virtue of the speed and breadth of the changes it made in its policy framework and because of the flexibility it showed in creating opportunities to exploit emerging technologies. To understand the nature of the agenda, it is necessary to examine not just the letter of the regulatory and

Ireland	Italy	Luxem-bourg	Netherlands	Portugal	Spain	United Kingdom
S	S/PTT (5)	PTT	PTT (10)	PTT (5)	S (16)	S
GM (PC)	GM (PC)	GM	GM (11)	GM (PC)	OM (16)	RC (LIM)
GM (PC)	GM (PC)	GM	GM (11)	GM (PC)	OM (16)	RC (LIM)
GM (PC)	GM (PC)	GM	GM (11)	GM (PC + OM) (5)	OM (16)	RC (LIM)
GM (PC)	GM (PC)	GM	GM (11)	-	OM (16)	RC (LIM)
M (21)	M	M	M (12)	M	M	L
L	L	L	M	L	RC (LIB) (19)	L
L	M (3)	L	M	M	L	L
L	M (3)	PL	L	PL	M	L
L	L	L	L	L	L	L
L	L	L	M (13)	-	L	L
M (21)	M	M	M	M	M	L
L	L	L	M	L	L	L
L	M	L	M	M	L	L
L	M	PL	L	PL	M	L
L	L	L	L	L	L	L
L	L	L	M (13)	-	L	L
N (4)	N (9)	N	N (14)	N (15)	N	Y (17)
N (4)	N (9)		N (14)	N (15)	N	Y (17)
N (4)	N	N (4)	N (4)	N (4)	N (4)	Y (18)
N (4)	N	N (4)	N (4)	N (4)	N (4)	Y (18)

trade laws, but also the ways that the competitive interests of the major players have been altered.

As the United States deregulated its internal telecommunications market, it altered the interests of four major sets of actors involved in the computer and communications industries: users of communications services, suppliers of telecommunications equipment, suppliers of computer equipment, and the

Table 2–1 continued.

	Australia	Canada	Finland	Japan
1. Relations with postal services	S	S	PTT (5)	S
2. Basic service network		RC (LIM)(LD)		RC(LIB)
a. Domestic	GM (PC)	OM (Local)	GM/OM (5)	RC(LIM)
b. International	GM (PC)	GM (PC)	GM/OM (5)	RC(LIM)
3. Terminal equipment				
a. Supply				
Main telephone set		L (23)	L (24)	L
PBX	PL	L (23)	L (24)	L
Telex	M	L (23)	L (24)	L
Modem	PL	L (23)	L (24)	L
4. Use of leased circuits				
a. Domestic				
Shared use/resale	N	N	Y	Y
Interconnection with public network	N	Y		Y

Sources: OECD, November 1985 as reported in *Transnational Data Report*, January 1986, pp. 8–9; EC Green Paper.

LEGEND

PTT	Posts and telecommunications services provided by the same organization
S	Separate organization
M	Monopoly
PL	Partly liberalized (some types liberalized, others not)
L	Liberalized
GM	Government monopoly (government agency)
GM (PC)	Government monopoly (public corporation)
OM	Monopoly of other types (private entity, etc.)
RC (LIM)	Regulated competition with limited entry
RC (LIB)	Regulated competition with liberalized entry
FC (LIB)	Free competition with liberalized entry
Y	Generally permitted
N	Generally prohibited

NOTES

(1)   RTT and Regie des Postes depend on the same PTT minister.
(2)   First telex terminal under monopoly, progressive liberalization announced.
(3)   On request by the CEC, progressive liberalization announced.
(4)   Subject to exceptions.
(5)   Telecommunications service providers exist in addition to PTT, on a monopolistic basis (concessionary basis, regional monopoly, etc.).

New Zealand	Norway	Sweden	Switzerland	Turkey	United States
PTT	S	S	PTT	PTT	S
GM	GM	GM	GM	GM	OM (Local)
GM	GM	GM	GM	GM	RC (LIM)
	M (22)	L	M		L
	M (22)	M			L
	M (22)	L	M		L
L	PL (22)	PL	PL		L
Y (25)	N	N	N	N	Y
		N	N	N	Y

(6)	Licensing of additional providers to be announced.
(7)	Steps regarding licensing of private providers of value-added services announced.
(8a)	Shared use permitted, resale prohibited.
(8b)	Voice-band circuits: as far as technically possible, but at one end only (TKO, July 1986).
(8c)	International fixed connections without restrictions; "flat-rate" circuits with restrictions.
(9)	New legislation on VANS is being discussed in Parliament.
(10)	A larger degree of separation between postal and telecommunication organizations within PTT has been announced for 1989.
(11)	PTT to be converted to limited liability company in 1989.
(12)	Government has decided to liberalize all terminal equipment as of January 1989.
(13)	Cordless telephone/car telephone/public pagers under monopoly; closed mobile systems, radio telephones on ships, etc. liberalized.
(14)	Usage for VANS to be liberalized.
(15)	Currently under consideration in commissions.
(16)	Telex, telegram, public facsimile (Burofax), etc. are provided by the PTT.
(17)	Pure resale prohibited until at least 1989.
(18)	As (17), subject to additional restrictions.

25

Table 2–1 continued.

NOTES continued.

(19)	Digital PBXs are supplied under monopoly.
(20)	Complete liberalization has now been implemented after agreement with the European Commission on July 30, 1986 and will take place after conversion of CCITT Recommendations into specifications and definition of testing procedures.
(21)	T.E. does not hold a monopoly, but is at present exclusively licensed by the Ministry.
(22)	To be liberalized in the near future.
(23)	In several jurisdictions monopoly is maintained.
(24)	Some local telephone companies maintain a monopoly to some extent.
(25)	Subject to special PTT condition.

major providers of public switched telecommunications networks. A brief examination of the regulatory bargain struck in the name of deregulation suggests how these interests were transformed. Once interests in the U.S. market were changed, interests of comparable groups in other countries also substantially changed in a similar manner. Transformation in the United States spilled over into other countries.

The Pre-1984 Regulatory Bargain

The interests and stakes involved in telecommunications and data processing are multidimensional. From the international perspective the question is not just how well a nation does in telecommunications, but which parts of the national economy benefit most from regulatory and trade arrangements.

Although there were some major differences, the traditional U.S. regulatory bargain resembled the bargains struck in other countries including Canada. The old regulatory bargain favored American Telephone and Telegraph (AT&T) in the United States (and other public switched telephone networks, PSTNs, elsewhere). The traditional system benefited households at the expense of large users by letting long-distance services subsidize local calls. It also helped preferred providers of transmission, switching, and terminal equipment for the PSTN through cross-subsidies that hit users of the telecommunications network. The U.S. system did differ from other systems in that AT&T was a private company that manufactured its own equipment instead of depending on a few favored outside suppliers.[3] AT&T's status spared it from having to cross-subsidize the post office and other government agencies and may partially account for the relatively high performance of the U.S. system in earlier years.

The traditional system disadvantaged some groups; over time their incentives to rebel grew stronger. The politics of telecommunications is significantly influenced by the fact that roughly 5 to 10 percent of all users generate half of the long-distance traffic in industrial countries and use of international long-distance services is even more concentrated. The result is that several hundred very large companies have an overwhelming economic interest in the rules of the telecommunications system.[4] These large users grew more determined to wield their influence as the telecommunications revolution became critical to their global plans and operations.

Suppliers of telecommunications equipment were another potential source of opposition to the established order. The cost of entry into their part of the market being relatively low, terminal equipment manufacturers were especially eager to push regulatory reform that allowed them to compete. In the United States many interim decisions pointing toward deregulation resulted from legal battles initiated by small companies that believed they could make large profits if allowed into the telephone business.

Equipment for the transmission of telecommunications services other than entertainment broadcast services is generally divided into three separate but not always distinct categories. *Transmission equipment* includes wire, coaxial, or fiber optic cable, microwave links, transponders, satellites, and earth stations. *Switching equipment* connects terminals and coordinates telecommunication networks from central offices (central office switching, message switching and communication processors). *Customer premises equipment* (CPE), also known as *terminal equipment* or *interconnect equipment*, is located on the user's premises and is used to transmit information through the network from one user to another (telephone subscriber sets, data communication terminals, modems, facsimile equipment, teletypewriters, multiplexers, private branch exchanges (PBXs and PABXs), teleconferencing equipment.[5] This book uses the term *network equipment* to cover the broader category of switching plus transmission equipment.

The old system also had mixed consequences for the computer industry. So long as AT&T retained its telephone monopoly, all U.S. computer companies feared AT&T's intrusion into their markets. They worried that AT&T might use its communications services to cross-subsidize its computer operations, especially in the vital research and development (R&D) area and that AT&T could discriminate in telecom services in favor of its own computers. Therefore, U.S. computer companies successfully worked to exclude AT&T from their industry under the pre-1984 regulatory bargain. But, to understand fully the ways in which telecommunications could be used to influence competitive advantages in the computer industry, it is helpful to distinguish between IBM and other computer firms.

IBM feared the continuation of a monopoly telecommunications system while the computer and communications networks were merging. Although it is overly simplistic, it clarifies matters to differentiate two general approaches for linking computers and communications systems. First, the communications link could be the world's best piece of string between two tin cans—in short, the communication system could provide a perfect conduit for linking computers but add no value to the system. All the intelligence in the system would reside in the computers that were being connected. Second, the communications link could be an intelligent mediator that translated among the different computer languages, added various data processing services to the mix, and significantly controlled the computers' activities in the informatics network. This second vision is generically called an *integrated services digital network*, or ISDN. There are, in fact, many varieties of ISDN. Here, we simplify by imagining a broadband ISDN in the spirit of the ideal system advocated by the German Bundespost.

The communications component of a true ISDN would dominate the definition of the system. Such an ISDN would also assure that all computers in the system could speak with one another by using a group of services defined by the PSTN. This approach would undermine IBM's market power by limiting the competitive advantage IBM could make of its position as the dominant global supplier of the mainframe computers used for data communications. In the absence of a PSTN-provided, universal ISDNs, IBM can capitalize on the fact that everyone must work out ways to communicate with an installed base of IBM computers. This guarantees, at least for the next several years, special market power to IBM's own system for communicating among its computers, Systems Network Architecture (SNA), now supplemented by Systems Application Architecture (SAA).[6]

Obviously, it is in IBM's interest to achieve greater telecommunications competition to foster the introduction of flexibility in new systems for data communications. Although conceding that the ISDN must be more than a "perfect piece of string," IBM wants it to be as small as possible. The rest of the computer industry has to some extent followed IBM. These companies favor developing the ISDN to facilitate a commonly defined system for computer communications as an alternative to SNA, but they oppose an extremely smart, centralized ISDN because they fear that PSTNs will constrain market growth by failing to provide the right mix of services at appropriate prices. Moreover, each company has specialized solutions for computer communications that could be excluded by a rigid ISDN. Control Data, a company with a major commitment to creating a global data processing network to provide remote computing services to major users, was a persistent and skillful critic of AT&T's monopoly. Similarly, firms like Digital Equipment Corporation (DEC) oppose strong ISDN systems as they pursue that next big sale by providing marginally better communications solutions.

In short, the old regulatory bargain benefited the PSTNs and their favored equipment suppliers (AT&T's Western Electric in the U.S. case). It also favored smaller users at the expense of larger users. But as communications became more vital to the global operations of large users, they started to rebel against subsidizing small users. Simultaneously, the computer industry, and especially IBM, grew restless with the old bargain.

The Regulatory Bargain Since 1984

The divestiture of the regional Bell operating companies (RBOCs) from AT&T in 1984 established a new, but frequently misunderstood, regulatory bargain. The contours of this bargain now effectively define the international telecommunications debate. When the new ground-rules are stated thematically, this is easy to see.

1. Large users of telecommunications services will be favored over smaller residential users by substantially cutting the cross-subsidies of the old system. Moreover, large users will be free to experiment with new ways of providing telecommunications services for their own use. However, in the short run small users will not suffer the full costs of efficient marginal cost pricing. A limited monopoly on local services will still provide them with a cross-subsidy. (The patchwork of cross-subsidies, plus the fact that economies of scope and scale have not been lost, has resulted in the costs for local phone service jumping only about $7 to $10 per month according to one estimate. And, the percentage of households with telephone service increased from 91.4 percent in November 1983 to 91.8 percent in July 1985.)[7]

2. New providers of services will have great freedom. Their actual market share is less important than their continuing credibility as a threat to take market share away from AT&T if AT&T is not more competitive in pricing and services. In practice, new entrants will probably win a small share of standard telephone traffic and a somewhat larger share of specialized services.

3. There will be a total freedom of competition in terminal (customer premises equipment)—a victory for new entrants, a loss for AT&T.

4. There will be *partial* competition in transmission and switching equipment. Formally, the complete liberalization of competition in these areas is mandated, but in practice the new regulatory bargain does not completely open these markets. Under divestiture AT&T was allowed to retain Western Electric (now AT&T Technologies). This means that AT&T can still support its equipment business from its lucrative long-distance service market. Moreover, AT&T's large base of installed equipment and its deep understanding of the regional Bell operating companies' systems gave it a continuing major advantage in the marketplace. Significantly, as foreign firms have started to make inroads in the U.S. market for network equipment, such proponents of competition as the Federal Communications Commission (FCC) and the National Telecommunications and Information Administration (NTIA) of the Department of Commerce have started to suggest potential safeguards to ensure "fair" international competition.[8]

5. The United States will not establish a strongly centralized ISDN. Although the precise shape of a future ISDN in the United States is unpredictable, it is plausible that several major networks will offer a weak ISDN. A weak ISDN would provide the "translation" services needed to permit intercommunication among computers and would contain some centralized services, but mostly it would serve as a base on which to develop specialized, "software-defined" networks for large customers. These software-defined networks would be jointly designed by the telecommunications network, the computer equipment suppliers, and the major users to serve specialized needs. In short, instead of one universally defined set of services for all computer communications, there would be many options for mixing and matching services with

some minimum degree of standardization.[9] This approach gives users greater bargaining power and balances the interests of the PSTN, IBM and the other computer makers.

The Redefinition of International Interests

As the process of deregulation proceeded in the United States, the competitive strategies and trade interests of U.S. firms were affected for two reasons. First, as telecommunications technology evolved, the major players discovered more about their competitive interests. Second, all U.S. competitors had to adjust to the unilateral U.S. decisions, which left the domestic market vulnerable to international competitors without guaranteeing reciprocity. (Other countries' companies gained access to the U.S. market, but U.S. firms did not win comparable access abroad. The U.S. trade balance in telecommunications equipment moved from a $1.5 billion surplus in 1983 to a $1.5 billion deficit in 1985.[10]) These two events created a new U.S. agenda for international telecommunications.

Competition changes the interests of players in important ways. The PSTNs find that they need to develop customized, value-added communications services, because changing technology permits enhanced services to encroach increasingly on the basic services. (For example, traditional phone calls can be "enhanced" through such services as voice message forwarding.) Once regulators allow the enhancement of voice services, providers of basic network services, are at risk unless they can respond by offering enhancement on competitive terms.

Moreover, PSTNs are now acutely aware that their biggest customers are global companies and that to be successful they must follow these customers. This reality is pushing U.S. public networks into offering new specialized services to their largest customers that bypass their own public networks. The new regulatory bargain also discourages networks from continuing to cross-subsidize smaller users or equipment companies.[11] For example, Daini-Den-Den and the other new Japanese long-distance competitors do not want to be tied only to the firms that NTT traditionally favored. The EC is trying to curb the traditional link between PTT and domestic suppliers. It now mandates that 10 percent of new network equipment purchases be open to international bids. The EC Commission hopes to increase that figure to 40 percent by 1992.

Large users understand that for them to reap the full benefits of U.S. deregulation, the advantages won in the United States must be duplicated abroad. They will therefore lobby for freer competition in telecommunications services, freedom to choose terminal equipment, and the end of cross-subsidies by PSTNs that cost them money. Computer and terminal equipment manufacturers, which are under international competitive pressure in the United States and want to follow their customers around the world, will back their demands.

Even the makers of transmission and switching equipment are redefining their interests. They now understand that to be world leaders they must increase their global market share by penetrating foreign markets and by preventing competitors from using their protected home markets to finance onslaughts abroad. Full liberalization of switching and transmission equipment markets is not in the cards but major suppliers from every country will exert fierce pressure to open a significant minority share in every other large country's national market to global competition. Northern Telecom's efforts to sell in the United States is a model of this strategy.

The United States is pursuing its position on trade in telecommunications by using bilateral negotiations to fight to resolve specific complaints of U.S. suppliers and users. The highest priority demands concern desired changes in the PTT and private PSTN procurement systems for telecommunications. These purchases are not covered under the GATT Government Procurement Code. One way to approach this problem is the model established in U.S.-Japanese negotiations on telecommunications equipment procurement.[12] These issues also will be raised in the Uruguay round of GATT negotiations, when telecommunications services will be a key indicator of the adequacy of any new framework.

Obviously, the U.S. position in international negotiations would be untenable if telecommunications policy elsewhere were static. Without outside allies, U.S. will and diplomatic might are insufficient to rewrite the global telecommunications regime. But, the interests of domestic groups in other countries were also altered when the United States moved toward telecommunications deregulation.[13] Differences in national politics and market structures cause variations from country to country, but these broad changes in interests in other countries are fairly clear:

1. Large users everywhere are starting to demand terms for service and terminal equipment equivalent to those available in the United States so that their competitive advantage does not suffer.

2. PSTNs are realizing that to hold onto their commanding domestic position requires that they coopt their large users. They are starting to reduce cross-subsidies to smaller users and equipment makers so that they can give better deals to large users. They are also experimenting more aggressively in organizing data services and acquiring equipment and technology for their networks. The barriers keeping out foreign switching and transmission equipment are weakening in many markets. The barriers keeping out terminal equipment are falling in virtually all markets.

3. The markets for computers and for terminal equipment are becoming irrevocably intertwined. This is forcing all players to redefine their own systems for data communications and to allow customers greater freedom to choose their own equipment.

4. Makers of switching and transmission equipment realize that in the future their national networks must be compatible with foreign networks. Otherwise, to compete internationally, switching and transmission equipment suppliers will have to design to meet two standards

of service. Moreover, these national suppliers now recognize that their PSTN may someday abandon them if they do not match world equipment standards. Yet liberalization in the United States and elsewhere has allowed a few companies to grow substantially and enlarge their market shares. Soon there will be a handful of huge companies that thrive by supplying large amounts to several national markets. Although every non-U.S. company would prefer the U.S. market to be open to competition and its own market to be closed, few firms can risk being shut out of other major industrial markets in order to keep their home markets closed. Therefore all of these players are susceptible to pressure to gain their support for limited liberalization of their home markets.

EMBEDDING TELECOMMUNICATIONS IN THE GATT ROUND

It does not follow automatically that changes in telecommunications rules should lead to a GATT negotiation concerning telecommunications services. But the political and policy agendas for telecommunications services are central to the broader commercial struggle concerning the future of the services sector. In order to project the future of international telecommunications regulation it is vital to understand the political intersection with services in the GATT.

There is no inherent economic reason why the GATT should govern telecommunications services. But it is, after all, political institutions, not equilibrium models of the world economy, that decide which priorities will dominate the agenda for liberalizing world trade. And, to understand the upcoming GATT negotiations on services, a brief review of the two rounds of political battles that set the agenda is needed. The first round made services a U.S. priority. The second put it on the GATT agenda.

From 1945 until recently a solid coalition of large exporters in farming and advanced manufacturing sectors in the United

States teamed with importers of consumer goods, such as department stores, in support of free trade. But, in the wake of U.S. trade deficits in excess of $123 billion in 1984 and in excess of $148 billion in 1985, many goods-producing sectors began to flirt with protectionism. When in 1986 the trade deficit jumped once more, Democrats promised to put trade at the top of the agenda for the One-hundredth Congress. (Provisions covering telecommunications in the 1987 trade bill are discussed in Chapter 9.) Not surprisingly, free trade advocates are seeking significant new political allies willing to pay the cost of lobbying for liberal policies and they need some examples of striking new gains to be made from free trade.[14] This is where services enter the scene.

The U.S. political system is often most innovative when it is possible to build a coalition of a few highly organized interests that, in pursuit of their own profits, are willing to provide support for advocates of the broader public interest. Some U.S. manufacturers, for example, championed public education in order to upgrade the workforce's skills. These alliances often promote less than the optimal policy because the public order must also meet the particular needs of its organized backers, but the alliances can often produce more good than ill. Recently, a potent new alliance coalesced in U.S. trade policy linking a handful of service companies and the free trade advocates in the U.S. government.

Until the passage of the Trade Act of 1974 "services" were not mentioned or covered by U.S. trade legislation. But afterward a few service companies championed their inclusion in U.S. trade legislation and called for services to be part of a new GATT round. These firms are the most internationally oriented of the firms in insurance (American International Group, or AIG), tourism and financial services (American Express, Citibank, Merrill Lynch), and shipping (Sea-Land). They received broad, if somewhat shallow, support from other firms in their own sectors and from those in fields such as data processing services (Control Data). All of these firms are involved in the international service economy as producers and consumers of services. As *producers* they want the right to compete and do business globally even though most national regulatory systems impose significant limitations on their right to do so. As *consumers* they need the input of certain key services—particularly telecommunications services—in order to produce their services internationally in a timely and cost effective manner. Yet the restrictive organization of the telecommunications services market often makes it impossible to get the desired inputs for production at acceptable terms. Finally, a handful of manufacturing firms in high-technology industries, especially IBM (see Chapter 7), recognized that the organization of the telecommunications and other service sectors vitally impedes their prospects for growth.

A small number of service and manufacturing companies helped assure that services were given equal billing in the Trade Agreements Act of 1979. They then provided a continual stream of congressional testimony, trade association publicity, and needed information to make sure that the Trade and Tariff Act of 1984 authorized the president to give high priority to the negotiation of multilateral and bilateral agreements governing services trade.[15]

Government trade officials had their own agenda. They were searching for prominent new supporters of free trade. They also were looking for economic returns from a new trade round that could convince Congress and informed public opinion that valuable gains could be made only through a daring new initiative in trade diplomacy. Finally, they believed large efficiency gains were available to the world economy that would generally improve the future of global economic relations.

The alliance of public officials and private interests has so far been a potent force. Although such coalitions of interests may advance broadly progressive changes, however, a danger exists that the specific priorities for change may be set less than optimally to satisfy the cravings of the small band of hardies. For example, from the viewpoint of promoting optimal global efficiency, should insurance be a high-priority sector?[16] The question is debatable, but the answer is clear to AIG and Lloyd's of London which wish to build their share of the global market. Or, should trade in computer services or telephone voice services receive higher priority during negotiations? The answer depends in part on the politics of the coalition that has championed the services initiative.

The machinations in the United States are additionally complicated by the reluctance of some service industries to be subject to any GATT discipline. The troubled U.S. construction industry, for example, wants subsidized export financing, not the right of Korean firms to bid for U.S. contracts on an equal footing. Manufacturing firms sometimes complain that services will divert attention from their priorities even though the very same manufacturers may not be willing to swear allegiance to free trade.

The outlines of these political tugs of war are already evident in the U.S. negotiating position. The United States bowed to pressure from other countries not to pursue services as part of the Tokyo round but promised interested U.S. firms that services would be dealt with the next time.[17] The Reagan administration followed through on this Carter administration commitment. The United States insisted that it would not participate in new GATT talks unless services were included. Still, services are not the top U.S. priority; agriculture, safeguards, and strengthening the rules governing nontariff barriers are at least as important. A general framework for services will be near the top of the negotiating agenda, but individual sectors will be addressed only when there is a sufficient consensus (thus allowing the United States to shelter some of its service sectors). Still, given the composition of the service coalition it is predictable that the United States will push hard on insurance, tourism, and telecommunications services. The insurance firms led the battle for services and are mired by restrictions that prevent them from doing business. By focusing on tourism, the interests of financial and data base industries as well as travel and hotel sectors can be satisfied. And, the insurance and financial service companies, along with IBM and some other manufacturers, insist that their needs as users make telecommunications services a priority.

Many countries hesitated to support services until they believed that the United States had a winning coalition at home for a services priority in trade negotiations. When victory for the coalition became likely, they had to decide whether to embrace, fight, or simply humor the American preference. At this point the second round of political battles preceding the new trade negotiations began.

Most major trading countries do not want to risk losing their continued access to the lucrative U.S. market under the terms provided by a general free trade format. Therefore, they will bend somewhat to accommodate the political realities necessary for Washington to stay on a free trade course. But can they afford to go along with the United States on services?

In the early 1980s, to launch services negotiations, the United States adopted a blunt tactic. Realizing that trade in services was ill-defined, U.S. negotiators claimed that their inability to identify specific negotiating goals was a strength, not a weakness, for three main reasons. First, if the United States knew what it wanted, others would suspect its motives. (On the other side, this lack of specificity caused great discomfort in Congress and the private sector, which believed that the United States never won negotiations.) Second, the United States saw the process of defining the agenda and goals as part of the negotiations, not as separate from them. By undertaking these clarifying discussions early in the negotiations it would help every country determine whether, to what extent, and in what areas rules governing trade in services would be in their interest. Third, the United States realized that the world economy was evolving faster than negotiators could reach agreements. Therefore, if explicit goals were set too firmly, too early, the negotiations would miss the mark.

But, when the Reagan administration sought new negotiations at the GATT ministerial meeting in November 1982, it was rebuffed. Other industrial countries gave lukewarm support, but the developing countries, led by India and Brazil, adamantly opposed any treatment of services within GATT for three main reasons. First, they contended that trade in services was beyond the competence of the GATT. They argued that rules and principles appropriate to deal with border tariffs on goods could not be applied adequately to services. Furthermore, they saw trade in services as an investment, not a trade issue. Second, they argued that services would overload the GATT and distract attention from unfinished work on tropical products, natural resources, textiles, quantitative restrictions, agriculture, and safeguards. Third, they worried that service negotiations would focus on high-technology services in which industrial countries enjoyed a clear comparative advantage and ignored labor-intensive services, whose provision requires moving cheap labor across borders. They saw no evidence that developed countries were prepared to "pay" for liberalization of trade in services by opening their borders to goods produced in developing countries.[18]

Ultimately, Brazil (which was preparing to receive President Reagan on a state visit and needed help to overcome its acute crisis) and India (always short of external development funds) relented just enough to permit acceptance of a weak resolution calling for national service studies. Even when national studies began to trickle in a year later, developing countries tried to block work on services within the GATT secretariat and to stifle official discussions on services.

Canada, the United Kingdom, Sweden, and Japan were the earliest supporters of the U.S. initiative on services. Each country has hesitations, but all accept the desirability of strengthening the trading system by extending it to cover services. Canada's economy is so closely tied to the United States' that support was probably inevitable. Although some Canadians remain cautious about service liberalization in the wake of disputes with the United States over border broadcasting, banking, and trucking, the overall mood is supportive.[19] Indeed, services received considerable attention during the U.S.-Canadian bilateral trade talks that concluded on October 4, 1987.[20] British financial and insurance services are likely winners from liberalization so the United Kingdom also was supportive. Sweden has long relied on open markets to sell its goods and services abroad and therefore was an ally of freer trade in services. Japan's motives were less straightforward. On the one hand, Japan hopes to become a significant service exporter, so strong rules will help Japanese industry over the long run. At the same time, by supporting the United States in an effort to seek multilateral negotiations the Japanese apparently hoped to dampen bilateral pressures building on it to open its domestic market for goods and services. If multilateral negotiations are extended, Japan might deflect some criticisms for a time and buy some breathing space.

Other industrial countries were slower to show their support. France and Italy were reluctant. Before negotiations began, France, which enjoys a large service surplus, wanted to know exactly what was to be accomplished. The French were uncomfortable with the American view that trade rules might be needed to deal with issues that had not yet arisen or even been anticipated. They were unhappy with the Americans' offhand confidence that problems would be solved as they arose. The United States replied, too often, with generalities and slogans.[21] Ultimately, however, France became services' strongest supporter in Europe. West Germany, generally a supporter of free trade, wondered what freer trade in services might mean for the Bundespost, the German monopoly responsible for postal and telecommunications services, and Germany's largest employer. Other industrial countries simply did not give services a very high priority. In Europe the difficulty of gaining support was compounded because the European Community speaks for its twelve members on trade matters (but it does not have responsibility for services). Building a united position was a slow process. Maintaining a united position could be even trickier because if some member countries want to slow negotiations, numerous legal loopholes are available.[22] However, solid EC support for the principle of negotiations on trade in services finally emerged in March 1985.

President Reagan hoped that the leaders of the key Western democracies would endorse a specific date for opening a new trade round at the Bonn Summit in May 1985, but President Mitterand balked. (Some saw this as the first French posturing of the new round.) Nonetheless, momentum was gaining. The United States turned up the pressure during the summer of 1985. In June ministers from twenty-two countries meeting in Stockholm agreed to submit papers describing their national goals and objectives for a new round to the GATT. When a few hard-core developing country opponents continued to balk, the industrial countries forced a vote of the GATT contracting parties that resulted in another meeting in September 1985 at which the developing countries gave further ground. This was followed by an important contracting parties' meeting in November 1985 at which the member countries agreed in principle to begin a new round of trade negotiations in which services might be included. A preparatory committee was set up under the chairmanship of GATT Director General Arthur Dunkel to develop a comprehensive plan for the new negotiations by mid-July 1986 for approval at the ministerial meeting in September.

To prepare for the final push for a new round, the industrial countries needed to divide the developing countries. First, Singapore, Hong Kong, the Philippines, and several other newly industrializing countries were persuaded that a new trade round and even freer trade in services might be in their interests. Then some important Latin American countries, particularly Colombia and Uruguay, and some key African countries were persuaded to reexamine their positions.[23] The European Community spearheaded a campaign to inform a large number of African and Latin American countries that Brazil and India, the two countries most vociferously opposed to trade in services, were also reaping large surpluses on trade in services with other developing countries. It was implied that perhaps their opposition to change had something to do with the monopolistic rents they were earning in restricted markets. By mid-1986 the number of countries against including services in the new trade round dwindled. Entering the September 1986 GATT ministerial meeting, the foes of services were reduced to a core Group of 10 led by India and Brazil and also including Argentina, Cuba, Egypt, Nicaragua, Nigeria, Peru, Tanzania, and Yugoslavia.

After a difficult week of negotiations at Punta del Este, Uruguay, the United States got what it wanted. Services were placed on the new round's agenda (along with intellectual property and investment issues). To appease the Group of 10, the decision to include services was separated from the rest of the ministerial declaration and attributed to the trade ministers and not to the contracting parties. In addition, the negotiators were explicitly charged to seek progressive liberalizations "as a means of promoting economic growth of all trading partners and the development of developing countries." But GATT procedures and rules will apply to negotiations involving services as well as goods. And the newly created Trade Negotiating Committee will oversee all of the negotiations, including those focused on services. The negotiations are supposed to take four years to complete their task. Then, the GATT ministers, acting in their capacity as GATT contracting parties, will decide if the results of these negotiations should be folded into GATT. Only at this last stage will outcomes of the goods and services negotiations be linked and concessions between the two negotiations be traded off.[24]

The world ultimately acquiesced to U.S. persistence and a skillful U.S. campaign to alter nations' perceptions of the stakes involved. This campaign had three parts. To begin, it stressed that services were not solely an issue working to the advantage of the United States. For years the U.S. position as the leading foreign investor confused calculations about comparative advantages in the services industries. It looked like the United States was overwhelming the world in earnings from services because the accounts on services payments included repatriated payments from overseas subsidiaries of U.S. multinational firms. In fáct, a closer examination eliminated the red herring of repatriated profits and showed a more widely distributed set of advantages in international commerce in services.[25]

The second part to the campaign was to convince developing countries that the United States was willing to "pay" for a new GATT round but would punish other countries if there were no round. The biggest carrots were the Baker Plan's willingness to reengineer debt arrangements for some countries and the decision to reduce U.S. interest rates and the foreign exchange value of the dollar. These policy shifts pleased a significant number of developing countries. At the same time, U.S. Trade Representative Clayton Yeutter showed the U.S. stick when he threatened to enter into bilateral or "plurilateral" negotiations with like-minded countries unless GATT took on services. Any benefits from these negotiations would be extended only to countries that cooperated. These were powerful admonitions, particularly for moderate developing countries that depended on trade with the

United States. The final task was to divide the developing countries on services.

In summary, other countries often accuse the United States of having imposed a major new challenge for international negotiations at the behest of a few of its companies. They are, to some extent, correct. But it is equally true that they miss the point. In the decentralized political process of the United States, the pursuit of the broader national and international interest often depends on the emergence of a coalition of private interests which has special selfish reasons to care about an issue. There is no reason that the public good should exclude private gain; in capitalist societies it should be the norm. Moreover, other countries will bend to keep their largest market committed to free trade only if they do not have to accept major burdens to do so. The U.S. diplomatic campaign succeeded because significant groups in other countries concluded that changes in trade rules might also be in their economic interests.[26]

Now countries with vastly differing interests must decide how to proceed. But most countries have just begun to develop national policies and priorities. The complexity of this task is daunting. Internal turf fights will have to be fought in every country at the national level and frequently between national and provincial governments as well. Will finance ministries allow trade ministries to negotiate about trade in financial services? Will defense ministries permit the free flow of transborder data that might benefit the Soviet Union? How will labor ministries respond when developing countries seek greater freedom of labor movement under the guise of freer trade in services? The Japanese Ministry of Trade and Industry (MITI), Ministry of Posts and Telecommunications (MPT), and the Ministries of Finance and Foreign Affairs will fight out a Japanese approach. The European PTTs will need to work out some compromise with their trade and economics ministries in their own countries. Will PTTs prevent their national governments from ceding negotiating authority to Brussels on issues that could affect their viability and operations? And, even if the European Community exerts its trade authority, setting a flexible EC policy that is not a lowest common denominator position will be complicated. The three cases in Part II clarify some of the key dynamics. Meanwhile, Chapters 3 and 4 present an analysis of the economic and policy issues that will confront the international trade negotiators. The appendix to this chapter provides a quick reference guide to who is who in the international negotiations.

APPENDIX

A USER'S GUIDE TO WHO'S WHO IN INTERNATIONAL TELECOMMUNICATIONS

Which institutions set the rules for managing international telecommunications? How is power distributed? Is their relative influence changing? If so, in which direction and for what reasons? Traditionally international telecommunications rule-making was primarily concerned with regulatory and standard-setting issues. Today, the International Telecommunication Union and to a lesser extent Intelsat dominate the scene. These institutions are insufficiently broad-ranging and flexible to meet the far-reaching demands for change now arising, but it may be politically impossible to create a new institution. Therefore, it is likely that politicians will shift the locus of major decisions involving international telecommunications to another existing institution. Although the GATT is not perfectly suited for such responsibilities, it comes closer than other existing bodies. Thus, the GATT will no doubt join (not replace!) the ITU at the center of the telecommunications stage.

Different bureaucracies have different priorities and positions on major issues. Turf fights occupy vast amounts of time and energy in any government.[27] Savvy politicians and national bureaucracies often try to increase their power by moving issues into forums where they control the agenda and the process. International organizations guard their turf just as jealously as national bureaucracies. One sure way to stir things up is for one bureaucracy to trespass onto another's turf. For example, the

GATT and the International Maritime Organization suddenly began to address developing countries' concerns in the mid-1960s when the United Nations Conference on Trade and Development (UNCTAD) tried to grab that turf. (Indeed, although we expect that the GATT will gain considerable prominence on telecommunications matters, we can expect that the ITU will be more active, not less, in the future.)

International telecommunications arrangements can be negotiated bilaterally or multilaterally. The point-to-point nature of international telecommunications traffic, particularly where there is heavy traffic flowing over cables, encourages governments toward bilateral coordination. But unless bilateral agreements are covered under a multilateral umbrella, they can easily become contradictory and can hamper instead of encourage the international flow of communications. Therefore, global coordination is simplified if rules and standards can be negotiated multilaterally. The main institutions and programs involved with international telecommunications are listed in Table 2–A1.

For our purposes, only a few of these organizations require description. Traditionally, the most important international communication organization was the *International Telecommunication Union*, which was created in 1932 by the merger of the International Telegraph Union (founded in 1865) and the signatories of the International Radio Telegraph Convention. Its two key bodies are the International Consultative Committee for Telephones and Telegraph (CCITT) and the International Consultative Committee for Radio (CCIR). The CCITT works to develop recommendations about telecommunication standards, to develop telecommunication facilities and networks, and to establish the lowest possible rates consistent with efficient service. The ITU also works to allocate the radio frequency spectrum, register radio frequency assignments (to avoid interference between radio stations), and help developing countries develop and improve their telecommunications equipment and networks. The most important forthcoming ITU events are the ITU Plenipotentiary Conference, which will consider and revise the basic charter of the ITU in early 1989 and the World Administrative Telegraph and Telephone Conference (WATTC),

Table 2–A1. Institutions Involved with International Telecommunications.

International organizations: general
General Agreement on Tariffs and Trade (GATT)
International Civil Aviation Organization (ICAO)
International Maritime Organization (IMO)
International Standards Organization (ISO)
Organization for Economic Cooperation and Development (OECD)
    Committee for Information, Computer and Communications Policy
    (ICCP)
    Trade Committee of the OECD
    Working Party on Transborder Data Flows of the ICCP
United Nations Centre on Transnational Corporations (UNCTC)
United Nations Development Program (UNDP)
United Nations Educational, Scientific and Cultural Organizations
    (UNESCO)
Universal Postal Union (UPU)
World Intellectual Property Organization (WIPO)

International organizations: communications
Intergovernmental Bureau of Informatics (IBI)
International Program for Development of Communication (IPDC)
International Telecommunications Union (ITU)
    International Consultative Committee for Radio (CCIR)
    International Consultative Committee for Telephones and Telegraph
    (CCITT)
United Nations Committee on Information

International organizations: satellite communications
International Maritime Satellite Organization (Inmarsat)
International Telecommunications Satellite Organization (Intelsat)
United Nations Committee on Peaceful Uses of Outer Space (UNCOPUOS)

Regional organizations
Conference of European Postal and Telecommunications Administrations
    (CEPT)
Conference of Inter-American Telecommunications (CITEL)
Council of Europe (CoE)
European Research Coordinating Agency (EUREKA)
European Satellite System (EUTELSAT)
European Strategic Programme for Research and Development in Information
    Technologies (Esprit) (Program of the EC)
Research and Development in Advanced Communications Technologies for
    Europe (RACE) (Program of the EC)

Source: Long-Range Goals in International Telecommunications and Information: An Outline for United States Policy, Report prepared for the U.S. Senate Committee on Commerce, Science, and Transportation by the NTIA (Washington, D.C.: U.S. Government Printing Office, March 11, 1983), p. 242. For brief descriptions of each organization: pp. 243–265.

which will convene in December 1988. WATTC will consider proposals for a regulatory framework for new telecommunications services that have resulted from technological advances.[28]

So far, the ITU sounds like a fairly anemic, technical, and dull organization. But under its auspices exists the CCITT, a virtual telephone cartel for PTTs. It is as if the Organization of Petroleum Exporting Countries had operated as a quiet subgroup of an international petroleum engineering society. For years, CCITT rules for international commerce in telecommunications services were almost absolute. ITU recommendations concerning telecommunications services used to function fairly smoothly for four reasons:

(1) The technology on which the services were based was changing relatively slowly; (2) the services were homogeneous, easily distinguished from each other and vertically integrated; (3) the same basic range of services was found in all countries; and, (4) the services [was] offered under more or less the same regulatory conditions in each country.[29]

The problem is that none of these "givens" still hold.

Another key international organization, the *International Satellite Communications Organization* (Intelsat), was formed in 1964.[30] The United States was the driving force in its founding and participates through the Communications Satellite Corporation (Comsat). Intelsat provides international satellite services and manages and coordinates international satellite communications among its member countries. Intelsat also must authorize the launch of commercial communication satellites. Its other activities involve leasing of its satellite capacity for domestic communications, earth station standards, regional satellite systems, allocation of satellite orbital slots, and provision of maritime services to the International Maritime Satellite Organization (Inmarsat). Intelsat resembles a PTT since it acts both as a carrier and a regulator. Over time its monopoly has been chipped away by regional satellite organizations. Intelsat strongly resisted the Reagan administration efforts to strip Intelsat of its monopoly position in the provision of international satellite services (see Chapter 5). Predictably, Intelsat's future form and activities will depend on the outcome of future negotiations on trade in telecommunications services.

On technical matters, the *International Standards Organization* (ISO) coordinates and promulgates international standards that cover all fields except electrical and engineering standards through its 163 technical committees. It is working on challenges posed by the GATT standards code. And, the *World Intellectual Property Organization* (WIPO) promotes the protection of intellectual property and administers the Paris Convention of Industrial Property of 1883 and the Berne Convention of 1886 for the Protection of Literary and Artistic Works.

Within Europe, several organizations also have played important roles on issues related to telecommunications. The *Conference of European Postal and Telecommunications Authorities* (CEPT) is the instrument of twenty-six European PTTs for coordinating their national policies, practices and standards in telecommunications and postal services. Another key European initiative was the 1984 *European Strategic Programme for Research and Development in Information Technologies* (Esprit), which was followed quickly by the announcement of the *Research and Development in Advanced Communications Technology for Europe* (RACE). Esprit is meant to contribute to a European industrial strategy aimed at strengthening the manufacture and use of information technology products in the EC.[31] RACE is intended to speed the development of a wide-band integrated services digital network and thus encourage international standards for information and compatibility among various types of telecommunications equipment. Both Esprit and RACE are meant to encourage cooperation within the European Community on research and development. Finally, in response to the U.S. Strategic Defense Initiative, eighteen European countries led by France created the *European Research Coordinating Agency* (EUREKA) in July 1985. EUREKA is designed to strengthen European productivity and competitiveness through cooperation of firms and research institutions in the area of high technology, including telecommunications.

Two other international organizations are becoming far more active on the international telecommunications front. First, the *Organization for Economic Cooperation and Development* (OECD), first through the work of its Committee on Information, Computer and Communication Policy (ICCP) on privacy and transborder data flows and subsequently through its Trade Committee's work on services has helped its twenty-four industrial country members to develop information and build consensus about issues related to telecommunications, information technology, and trade in services. The ICCP developed the 1981 OECD Guidelines Governing the Protection of Privacy and Transborder Flows of Personal Data.[32] The OECD also adopted a weak "data declaration" that put on record its member countries' intention to encourage the free flow of data. In addition, the Trade Committee undertook sectoral studies examining freer trade in services and has developed draft language for a possible "umbrella" agreement on trade in services.

Finally, there is the "new boy on the block." The *GATT* was launched in 1947 as a multilateral agreement designed to foster the liberalization of international trade in goods and to reduce international tensions and conflict. It had nothing to do with telecommunications services. As late as the end of 1986 the GATT had only two professionals assigned full-time to all service sectors.[33] Obviously, the GATT secretariat and the trade officials involved with the upcoming negotiations will need technical support from the ITU and communication ministries. A subtle challenge to GATT will concern the issues of overlapping jurisdictions and coordination.

As the GATT prepares for negotiations on telecommunications services, the industrial countries will turn to the OECD for assistance. Simultaneously, the developing countries will draw on the communications expertise of the United Nations Conference on Trade and Development (UNCTAD), the United Nations Centre on Transnational Corporations, the United Nations Educational, Scientific, and Cultural Organization (UNESCO), and the Intergovernmental Bureau for Informatics (IBI) during the coming GATT negotiations.[34]

It appears that the overall logic of trade talks in telecommunications will be different than the classic objective of removing barriers to exports and imports.[35] The United States is seeking a standard of effective market access that may be satisfied by a mixture of removing trade barriers or creating the right to establish a significant competitive presence by U.S. firms. It will also consider the terms of regulation of the domestic market of the country as another criterion of effective access.

The United States also has not decided how to approach talks about integrated services digital networks so as to assure that U.S. interests about equipment are protected fully (see Chapter 7). Difficult questions about how the design of an ISDN alters the balance of competitive advantages among different types of equipment suppliers (not just the relative strength of U.S. and foreign competitors) will have to be resolved.

Obviously, as GATT moves into the telecommunications arena, it will have to adapt its tranditional formulas for liberalizing trade. Negotiators will need to clarify which pieces of the telecommunications puzzle fit in the GATT. The three case studies that follow Chapter 4 show that many key issues will fall under the jurisdiction of other international bodies. Key questions facing services negotiators will include: To what extent should agreements concerning technical standards, pricing, and other issues made in the ITU/CCITT be subject to review and challenge under the GATT agreement? How will GATT have to change its scope and focus to manage the emerging services economy?

NOTES

1. It was argued that telecommunications was a "merit" service where positive externalities occurred for each user as the size of the population covered by the service increased. For an overview of changing regulatory thinking, see Roger G. Noll and Bruce M. Owen, *The Political Economy of Deregulation: Interest Groups in the Regulatory Process* (Washington, D.C.: American Enterprise Institute, 1983); a broad historical approach to regulation in the

United States is Thomas K. McCraw, ed., *Regulation in Perspective: Historical Essays* (Cambridge, Mass.: Harvard University Press, 1981); on regulating telecommunications see Eli M. Noam, ed., *Telecommunications Regulation Today and Tomorrow* (New York: Harcourt Brace Jovanovich, 1983).

2. For information on recent moves toward liberalization see Robert R. Bruce, Jeffrey P. Cunard, and Mark Director, *From Telecommunications to Electronic Services: A Global Spectrum of Definitions, Boundary Lines and Structures*, International Institute for Communications (London: Butterworth, 1986) and Marcellus S. Snow, ed., *Marketplace for Telecommunications: Regulation and Deregulation in Industrialized Democracies* (New York: Longman, 1986). A sector-by-sector assessment of the impact of greater telecommunications competition in the United States is U.S. Department of Commerce, National Telecommunications and Information Administration, *NTIA Competition Benefits Report*, Staff Papers Regarding the Benefits of Competition and Deregulation in Selected Lines of Communication Commerce (Washington, D.C.: NTIA, November 8, 1985), mimeo. On the United Kingdom case see Charles Jonscher, "Telecommunications Liberalization in the United Kingdom," in Marcellus S. Snow, ed., *Marketplace for Telecommunications*, pp. 153–72. On Japan see Ministry of Posts and Telecommunications, "Open Telecommunications Markets in Japan" (Tokyo: MPT, 1986) and Youichi Ito and Atsushi Iwata, "Deregulation and the Change of Telecommunications Market in Japan," paper prepared for the symposium Law and Economics of Transborder Telecommunications, March 2–6, 1986, Malente, West Germany, sponsored by the Max Planck Institute in Hamburg.

3. This arrangement more closely resembled the one in Canada. Bell Canada and British Columbia Telephone are privately owned, federally regulated carriers. But, Bell Canada is the major shareholder in Northern Telecom, Canada's dominant telecommunications equipment manufacturer.

4. The first viable alternative to the public switched telephone networks came when the television networks waged a regulatory battle for the right to build their own microwave transmission systems. The concentration of use did not lead large consumers to act strategically about the international communications market when cost was a minor factor in their calculations. For many years companies feared that service might be disrupted if

they complained too much about its price. By 1984, however, telecommunications expenses as a percentage of sales reached 6.02 percent in the computer service industry, 2.34 percent for nonbank financial firms, 1.86 percent for airlines, and 1.09 percent for banks. Figures are from the International Communications Association reported in H. P. Gassmann, "Telecommunications Market Structure Changes: Expectations and Experience," paper presented at the TIDE2000 Conference, Honolulu, Hawaii, May 12–14, 1986. Major lobbying groups include the International Telecommunications Users Group (INTUG), the Association of Data Processing Services Organizations (ADAPSO), the Business Roundtable, and the International Chamber of Commerce. See particularly the series Policy Statements on Telecommunications and Transborder Data Flows issued by the International Chamber of Commerce in Paris starting in 1982.

5. The U.S. International Trade Commission sometimes breaks out cable, wire, and lightguide as a separate category. Different groups categorize PBXs as switching or terminal equipment. And the Organization for Economic Cooperation and Development identifies categories that include mobile radios, private systems, and "other." In general these categories do not cover the computers, peripherals, and software that make up the data processing equipment industry. See, for example, "High Technology Industries: Profiles and Outlooks: The Telecommunications Industry" (Washington, D.C.: U.S. Department of Commerce, International Trade Administration, April 1983), pp. 14–15 and "Changes in the U.S. Telecommunications Industry and the Impact on U.S. Telecommunications Trade," Report to the Committee on Finance, U.S. Senate, on Investigation No. 332-172 Under Section 332 of the Tariff Act of 1930 (Washington, D.C.: U.S. International Trade Commission, June 1984), pp. 1–7.

6. The issue of technical standards is complicated. IBM is also part of a cooperative effort to create a common system to allow different types of computers to communicate with one another— Open Systems Interconnect. If successful, OSI presumably would make all computer systems fully interconnectable, thereby eliminating SNA's advantages. But the OSI project is more likely to produce a common minimum standard for all non-IBM makers and a series of "gateways" for crossing over to SNA rather than to eliminate SNA. This result would leave IBM with a real, but reduced, advantage. More details are provided in Chapter 7.

7. *Telephone Subscribership in the United States: A Post Divestiture Analysis*, Office of Policy Analysis and Development, National Telecommunications and Information Administration, U.S. Department of Commerce, Washington, D.C., December 10, 1985, p. 3. Worst hit by local services problems is the rural sector. Some analysts (such as Roger Noll) believe that the biggest problem in rural areas is their continuing reliance on copper or fiber optic cables instead of digital/cellular radio (or cable television) technologies.

8. Canada's Northern Telecom, which produces switching equipment compatible with the U.S. network, was initially the biggest winner from the regional Bell operating companies' desire to "leave home." On June 26, 1986, Ameritech became the first RBOC to receive authorization, subject to certain conditions, to engage in foreign manufacturing, international telecommunications, and foreign nontelecommunications businesses. The RBOCs still want a revision of the Modified Final Judgement that would permit them to enter the equipment manufacturing business in the United States. Even government supporters of their proposal suggested some scrutiny of joint ventures with foreign suppliers of network equipment. The U.S. government in 1987 discussed alternative regulatory restraints on Siemens' entry in light of U.S. problems with West Germany; see "Ameritech Takes the Lead in Foreign Manufacturing," *Telephony*, July 7, 1986, p. 18; "Huber Report Said to Endorse BOC Manufacturing Entry into Long-Distance Market," *Data Communications*, January 1987, p. 25.

9. A good analogy is "semi-bespoke tailoring," which allows tailors to use computerized cutting machines to customize standardized pieces of a garment partially to the unique fit of the customer. Since the breakup of the Bell System took effect on January 1, 1984, new competitive activity and innovation has exceeded most expectations. Moreover, continuing modification of the Modified Final Judgement (MFJ) through appeals processes has consistently leaned toward greater competition. Under the MFJ some restrictions were imposed to maintain regulatory safeguards. For example, AT&T was forced to keep certain business units separated—especially its computer and enhanced services. The RBOCs were not permitted to manufacture equipment or to provide nationwide long-distance telephone service. AT&T and the RBOCs were temporarily banned from entering the publishing business. How-

ever, since the breakup, the vast majority of service providers' appeals for revisions have been recommended by the FCC and approved by Judge Greene. AT&T is now being allowed to end the separation of its computer and enhanced services. In the wake of the Third Computer Inquiry further liberalization of domestic competition is likely.

10. *U.S. Industrial Outlook, 1984* (Washington, D.C.: U.S. Government Printing Office, 1984) and *U.S. Industrial Outlook, 1986* (Washington, D.C.: U.S. Government Printing Office, 1986).

11. Gerald Faulhaber suggests that flaws in the U.S. approach to regulating the local telecommunications network will promote inefficient investment in bypass technology in order to avoid costs imposed by inappropriate regulation. See "Deregulation and Innovation in Telecommunications," Discussion Paper 14, Fishman-Davidson Center for the Study of the Service Sector, The Wharton School, University of Pennsylvania, January 1986.

12. The GATT Government Procurement Code does not cover trade in services except to the extent that services are traded in association with goods. To be covered by the Code, government agencies must formally accede to it. Under great pressure from the United States and other countries, Nippon Telegraph and Telephone was the only telecommunications provider that signed on. Results have not measured up to U.S. expectations.

13. We would, however, demur from the NTIA's bold statement that "communication policymakers thus may not really enjoy a choice between sanctioning competition and prohibiting competition altogether. Competition, in short, may in fact prove inevitable and policymakers might instead more fruitfully focus on developing reasonable means of easing the necessary transition from monopoly toward more pluralistic and competitive marketplace conditions." See U.S. Department of Commerce, National Telecommunications and Information Administration, *NTIA Competition Benefits Report*, Staff Papers Regarding the Benefits of Competition and Deregulation in Selected Lines of Communication Commerce (Washington, D.C.: NTIA, November 8, 1985), mimeo, p. 3. Also see Evan Kwerel, "Promoting Competition Piecemeal in International Telecommunications," Working Paper 13 of the Office of Plans and Policy, FCC, December 1984, and Ronald Eward, *The Deregulation of International Telecommunications* (Dedham, Mass.: Artech House, 1985).

14.   I.M. Destler and John S. Odell, *Anti-Protection: Changing Forces in United States Trade Politics* (Washington, D.C.: Institute for International Economics, 1987). A more general model of the making of foreign economic policy is set forth in Peter F. Cowhey and Gary Jacobson, "The Political Organization of Domestic Markets and U.S. Foreign Economic Policy," paper presented to the September 1984 meeting of the American Political Science Association in Washington, D.C.

15.   A small "services mafia" in the private sector and in the Office of the U.S. Trade Representative were the first to take up services as an issue. The International Chamber of Commerce actively advocated freer trade in services during the 1970s. USTR established a Services Policy Advisory Committee (SPAC) for top corporate officials and Industrial Sector Advisory Committee 13 (ISAC-13) for lower level corporate officials. Other parts of the U.S. government became committed to services later. Finally, the service industries organized themselves as a lobby and created the Coalition of Service Industries in 1984.

16.   Insurance is a highly protected sector. There are more exceptions for insurance than for any other service sector under the Treaty of Rome. Only a few of the thousands of U.S. insurers, reinsurers and brokers have any interest in expanding overseas. Yet for AIG, Cigna, Marsh & McLennan, and a few others barriers to trade in insurance severely hamper their activities. They want progress. At the same time, U.S. policymakers see the results of insurance trade negotiations between the European Community and Switzerland as an object lesson. The treaty that was negotiated and signed in the early 1980s was so long and complicated that it foundered under its own weight. This failed model is one reason that U.S. trade policymakers seek agreement on broad principles and do not want to tackle every small issue.

17.   After the United States agreed to postpone consideration, services were dealt with only on the margins. The Government Procurement Code required signatories to consider developing rules for trade in services. Services are covered by the agreement when they are incidental to the supply of goods purchased by entities that subscribe to the code so long as the value of these incidental services does not exceed the value of the procured products. Service contracts per se are not covered. The Customs Valuation Agreement, which covers certain services associated with goods, could under some circumstances be extended to some aspects of

trade in services. The Standards Code, although not applicable to services in its present form, could be particularly relevant if extended to cover service transactions.

18. See Deepak Nayyar, "International Trade in Services: Implications for Developing Countries," Exim Bank Commencement Day Lecture: 1986 (Bombay: Export-Import Bank of India, 1986) and Jagdish Bhagwati, "Splintering and Disembodiment of Services and Developing Nations," *The World Economy* 7, no. 2 (June 1984): 133–44.

19. Rodney de C. Grey, "The Services Industries: A Note of Caution about the Proposal to Negotiate General Rules about Traded Services," in John Whalley, ed., *Canada and the Multilateral Trading System* (Ottawa: Ministry for Supply and Services, 1985), pp. 21–39.

20. For background see Robert Stern, ed., *Trade and Investment in Services: Canada/U.S. Perspectives* (Toronto: University of Toronto Press for the Ontario Economic Council, 1985) and Robert M. Stern, Philip H. Trezise, and John Whalley, eds., *Perspectives on a U.S.-Canadian Free Trade Agreement* (Washington, D.C.: Brookings Institution, 1987).

21. There is considerable justification for this fear. The early stages of the U.S.-Canadian bilateral free trade talks launched in the spring of 1986 saw the Canadians allocate more than seventy officials to the discussions at a time when there were only two U.S. negotiators working full-time on them. Although the United States increased its representation, the French and others might rightly wonder whether the United States can plan and man the new multilateral negotiations when other smaller negotiations are underway that are not being managed efficiently.

22. Finding ways to satisfy the southern tier of the EC (Italy, Spain, Portugal, and Greece) will pose problems similar to those facing industrial countries in addressing demands of developing countries concerning services.

23. Indeed, Felipe Jaramillo, the Colombian ambassador to GATT, was a leader in the efforts to develop consensus on including services in a new trade round. And, two of the reasons that Punta del Este was chosen to host the ministerial meeting in September 1986 was to allow Uruguay the honor of having the round bear its name and to send a message to Brazil across its border.

24. Ronald K. Shelp, "Trade in Services," *Foreign Policy* 65 (Winter 1986–87): 75–76.

25.   The U.S. case for freer trade in services is put forward in the *U.S. National Study on Trade in Services,* A Submission by the United States Government to the General Agreement on Tariffs and Trade, December 1983. Significantly, trade in services is not swamping trade in goods. Trade in services complements and facilitates trade in goods. Service exports are dominated by about twenty-five countries. The United States does not dominate. The United States is strong in higher technology and financial services, but data do not accurately reflect these advantages. The main alternative to telecommunications services as the linchpin of service negotiations is financial services, a favorite of the British government. Most doubted that finance ministries or central banks will allow trade ministers to usurp their banking turf so easily. But the European Community, to the surprise of everyone, was putting it high on the services agenda in the fall of 1986. See Jonathan David Aronson and Peter F. Cowhey, *Trade in Services: A Case for Open Markets* (Washington, D.C.: American Enterprise Institute, 1984). On the problems that plague the trading system, see Miriam Camps and William Diebold, Jr., *The New Multilateralism* (New York: Council on Foreign Relations, 1982) and Jan Tumlir, *Protectionism: Trade Policy in Democratic Societies* (Washington, D.C.: American Enterprise Institute, 1985).

26.   For a review of the issues, constraints, and prospects of the new trade round, see C. Michael Aho and Jonathan David Aronson, *Trade Talks: America Better Listen!* (New York: Council on Foreign Relations, 1985). A more macroeconomic approach to the same questions is Gary Clyde Hufbauer and Jeffrey J. Schott, *Trading for Growth: The Next Round of Trade Negotiations* (Washington, D.C.: Institute for International Economics, 1985). North-South trade issues are the focus of Ernest H. Preeg, ed., *Hard Bargaining Ahead: U.S. Trade Policy and Developing Countries* (New Brunswick, N.J.: Transaction Books, 1985).

27.   In the U.S. executive branch, for example, six separate bureaucracies, three of which have a telecommunications orientation and three of which have a trade perspective, struggle to set U.S. international telecommunications policy. The Federal Communications Commission, the National Telecommunications and Information Administration in the Department of Commerce, the Bureau of International Communication and Information Policy in the Department of State hold the technical expertise. USTR,

the International Trade Administration in the Department of Commerce and the Economic Bureau in the Department of State have the trade expertise. In Japan, the Ministry of International Trade and Industry, the Ministry of Posts and Telecommunications, and the Ministry of Finance are bitter rivals. See, for example, Youichi Ito, "Telecommunications and Industrial Policies in Japan: Recent Developments," in Marcellus S. Snow, ed., *Marketplace for Telecommunications*, pp. 201–30.

28. The standard source on the ITU is George Codding, Jr., and Anthony Rutkowski, *The International Telecommunication Union in a Changing World* (Dedham, Mass.: Artech House, 1982).

29. Ann Hutcheson Reid, "Trade in Telecommunications Services: The Current Institutional Framework and the Potential for Change," paper prepared for the Committee for Information, Computer and Communication Policy, Organization for Economic Cooperation and Development (ICCP(85)12) (Paris: OECD, September 9, 1985), pp. 16–25.

30. The Soviet Union and its allies operate their own international satellite communication system, Intersputnik. In addition Intelsat has authorized the operation of several regional satellite systems: Eutelsat, Arabsat, Palapa, and Cospas/Sarsat.

31. For more on Esprit, see M. English and A. Watson Brown, "National Policies in Information Technology: Challenges and Responses," *Oxford Surveys in Information Technology*, Vol. 1 (1984), pp. 117–26.

32. See *Transborder Data Flows: Proceedings of an OECD Conference* (Amsterdam: North Holland, 1985) and Karl P. Sauvant, *International Transactions in Services: The Politics of Transborder Data Flows* (Boulder Colo.: Westview, 1986), pp. 154–64.

33. Both wrote on trade in services. See Jacques Nusbaumer, *Les services: Nouvelle donne de l'economie* (Paris: Economica, 1984) (English version: *Services, the New Deal* (Boston: Kluwer-Nijhoff, 1987); Raymond J. Krommenacker, *World-Traded Services: The Challenge for the Eighties* (Dedham, Mass.: Artech House, 1984).

34. The developing countries would have preferred that services negotiations be held in UNCTAD, but the industrial countries refused to consider that possibility. See also UNCTAD, *Services and the Development Process* (Geneva: UNCTAD, 1984).

35. In the short run there will be a vigorous discussion about the priorities between services and equipment for telecommunica-

tions negotiations. The United States generally has stressed equipment issues somewhat more vigorously than services in its bilateral trade talks. Even if tough new legislation on telecommunications trade is not enacted, the United States will probably continue to press to open foreign markets to U.S. suppliers. The United States seems to be moving toward a new standard under which exports of U.S. firms and the sales of their overseas subsidiaries can both be used as evidence of satisfactory reciprocity.

3

REDEFINING THE INTERNATIONAL TELECOMMUNICATIONS MARKET

Trade negotiations will explore how governments could govern greater competition in telecommunications and information services. This is no easy task because these services have significant impact on who has what advantages in commercial rivalry for domination of the telecommunications and computer equipment markets. Moreover, there is vigorous debate but no consensus about which telecommunications services are or are not natural monopolies. Finally, information services are still such new products that there is virtually no framework governing their international commerce. (The vague Organization for Economic Cooperation and Development Declarations, discussed later, are a small effort in this direction.)

In the United States telecommunication services usually are classified as either basic or enhanced services. Enhanced services are broken down into value-added services and information services. Some schemes also try to bring software, broadcasting, and publishing services into the classification scheme. The present analysis explicitly excludes these last three categories and focuses on an often muddled component: infrastructure facilities (such as communications satellites) and infrastructure services (such as leased circuits).[1] This chapter focuses on these infrastructure facilities and services; the next chapter concentrates on a reformulated version of the more familiar troika of basic, value-added, and information services.

Infrastructure facilities have two components. Broadly speaking, infrastructure facilities are the physical plant needed to deliver communications services, and infrastructure services are the circuits or switching capacity that is leased from providers of infrastructure facilities to third parties. Traditionally it was generally accepted that, with a few exceptions, PTTs had a legitimate right to own or to exert regulatory authority over infrastructure facilities.[2] This near consensus has been called into question, and this is what much of the real telecommunications dispute is about. (At the same time there is increasing disagreement about whether and to what extent the PTTs have a legitimate right and obligation to regulate competition in the provision of infrastructure services.)

The distinction between infrastructure facilities and services is important because it helps clarify the international debate over the desirability of increased domestic and international telecommunications competition. The results of this debate, in turn, will have important consequences for forthcoming trade negotiations. Table 3–1 summarizes our views concerning the differences between infrastructure facilities and services. Table 3–2 lists the current differences about competition in infrastructure facilities.

Table 3–1. Infrastructure Capabilities.

Infrastructure Facilities	Infrastructure Services
Physical plant for transmission switching of large-scale, multiuser systems over multiple premises (but not LANs)	Circuits or switching capacity leased from providers of infrastructure facilities to third parties
Types of Facilities[a]	Regulatory choices influencing competitiveness
Local network facilities	Degree of competitiveness of infrastructure facilities
Long-distance network facilities	
Mobile service facilities	Shared use and resale or not
International facilities	Possibility of shared bypass networks
	Flat, volume-sensitive rate or nondiscriminatory prices
	Open or closed architecture
	Ease of becoming a RPOA

a. Includes specialized facilities for data services.

Table 3–2. How Competitive Are Facilities?[a]

Potential justifications for barriers to competition

Facilities for a network are a natural monopoly (economies of scale and/or scope).

Facilities are not a contestable market. (Investments for facilities serving a given market cannot be resold at a reasonable price or to another market.)

The size of the entry investment is prohibitively large in relation to the size of the potential market.

Predatory strategies by leading firms are credible (through pricing or by building surplus facilities capacity).

Transaction costs are high (the costs of information, bargaining, and specialized assets other than network facilities are high).

Current consensus about barriers to competition

Natural monopoly: perhaps true for local network.

Contestable: local is selectively contestable (downtown office district); long distance and international are imperfectly contestable at outset, but become more so over time.

Entry investment: very high for general coverage of any local market; high for general coverage of long-distance or international market; moderate for selective coverage of long distance or international.

Predatory practices: reasonably easy to impose at local level; possible at long-distance and international levels (especially if competitors control local facilities) but tends to decline over time.

Transaction costs: increases as the degree of government oversight over the market increases; higher for international facilities.

General observations about infrastructure facilities and competition

The monopoly for local network infrastructure poses the largest potential threat for competition in services (if the owner of the local infrastructure is able to compete in services and facilities markets other than for local infrastructure and local basic services).

New entrants prefer selective coverage of markets with large, affluent users to universal coverage of all users. But:

it is usually in the interest of those favoring selective coverage to support facilities for the rest of the market to assure their prime customers more universal service;

some facilities providers will profit by serving markets which are not most prized by most in the market.

Transaction costs related to the pursuit of large users in global markets may persuade some facilities providers to try to create a solely owned and controlled facilities network.

a. All statements in this table are subject to qualifications stated in the text of Chapter 3.

Much of the controversy about trade in telecommunications services is essentially a debate about how much competition should be allowed in the supply of the physical infrastructure for communications. Although it is resisted by most countries, competitive ownership of facilities is feasible and makes it much easier to assure competition in all forms of services. When governments refuse to permit competition in facilities, the users have to demand relatively inefficient (from an economic perspective) formulas to govern the use of the infrastructure because only inefficient formulas provide the users with sufficient protection against monopolists.

Chapter 4 examines the applications of telecommunications infrastructures. It distinguishes between two broad classes of telecommunications services—basic telecommunications services (voice, telex, telegraph) and enhanced services. The latter are divided into value-added and information services. The underlying economic conditions of the market suggest that competition should be feasible in all of these services with the possible exception of local telephone services. But monopoly ownership of facilities, cross-subsidies, and the potential for discriminatory technical standards pose real problems. Selective restrictions on the behavior of PTTs can overcome these difficulties, but they also restrict legitimate PTT actions to enhance public welfare and reduce the total benefits of competition. This dilemma suggests that the U.S. government should advance negotiating formulas that reduce the number of restraints on PTT behavior as the degree of competition in infrastructure increases.

HOW BIG IS THE MARKET?

Data on telecommunications services and particularly on trade in telecommunications services is very poor. Even existing data is suspect because it covers markets that are defined inconsistently. A sense of the total market is available, however.

The Office of Technology Assessment (OTA) of the U.S. Congress has provided one picture of the services component of the information industry (see Table 3–3). It estimates that total

Table 3–3. 1985 Telecommunications Services Revenues ($ billions).

Sector	United States	European Community	Japan	Total
Data processing	15.0	4.0	3.0	22.0
Database services	1.9	0.9?	0.6?	3.4?
Total information services	16.9	4.9?	3.6?	25.4?
Telecommunication services	110.0	42.0	22.0	174.0
Total	126.9	46.9	25.6	199.4

Sources: U.S. Industrial Outlook, 1986 (Washington, D.C.: U.S. Government Printing Office, 1986), p. 48-2; data from Arthur D. Little as compiled by the Office of Technology Assessment.

1985 global revenues in the United States, the European Community, and Japan reached about $200 billion, but about 85 percent of the total was in traditional telecommunications services (such as telex and telephone). Unfortunately, the OTA sheds little light on how much of the traditional telecommunications services included transmission capacity that was leased for data services. A quick glance at the totals for data communications services in Table 3–4 suggests that this is a significant number. (These estimates also do not include broadcasting, radio, and television, all of which may be vital at times for the information market.)[3]

Table 3–4 provides an estimate of the global market for data communications and equipment in 1987. Of the total $225 billion market, data communications services will reach almost $50 billion while data communications equipment (which covers significant amounts of both the communication and computer markets) will approach $175 billion.[4] Of these 1987 global totals the North American (largely U.S.) market for data communications service revenues should reach $24 billion with equipment accounting for an additional $81 billion. Total U.S. expenditures for data communications constitute about one-half of the world market, making any reorganization of the U.S. market pivotal to world leadership.

Table 3–4. Estimated 1987 World Data Communications Market ($ millions).

	Services[a]	Products[b]	Total
North America	24,710	86,780	111,500
Europe (not USSR)	11,370	39,900	51,290
Asia (with USSR)	12,360	43,390	55,750
Oceania	590	2,080	2,670
Latin America	1,380	4,860	6,240
Africa	490	1,740	2,230
Total	49,430	173,570	223,000

Sources: Estimates by Arthur D. Little, Computer and Business Equipment Manufacturers Association, Logica Consultancy, and Data Communications compiled in *Data Communications* (January 1987): 87.

a. Includes telephone, satellite, and specialized carriers services; communications expenditures for data base and time-sharing services, business time-sharing costs, and repair and maintenance services.

b. Includes digital switches; mainframe, micro and minicomputers; programmable terminals; front-end processors; diagnostic and test equipment (including network management equipment); local area networks; software (unbundled); nonprogrammable terminals; portable terminals; private fiber-optic links; modems and acoustic couplers; earth stations; teleprinters; computer printers; facsimile terminals; packet equipment and other concentrators; multiplexers; protocol converters; communicating word processors; and private microwave links.

Although this study does not report the data in detail, it is critical to recognize that the telecommunications network (switching plus transmission equipment) and customer premises equipment markets are smaller than the computer, integrated circuit, and software markets. The Department of Commerce estimated the U.S. market for network equipment in 1986 at $13.1 billion and the market for customer premises equipment at $5.1 billion. In contrast, it is estimated that the value of shipments of electronic computing equipment in the United States in 1986 was on the order of $50 billion and that the value of shipments of semiconductors and related devices was about $28 billion. The software industry is also growing rapidly. During 1986 revenues of U.S. suppliers of packaged and custom software climbed about 22 percent, reaching $22 billion. (The U.S. industry, with an estimated share of 70 percent, dominates the world market.) Yet a quick glance at the volume of data equipment sales reported in Table 3–4 suggests that much of the market for computers, semiconductors, and software is actually packaged into communication/information systems. Thus, telecommunications is crucial for success in the related computer, software, and chips markets.[5]

Three trends dominate recent developments in international telecommunications equipment sales. First, Hong Kong, South Korea, and Taiwan have become large exporters of customer premises equipment. Second, Japan is now a key exporter of telecommunications equipment to the world. (However, its prominence in the switching market, although growing, is smaller.) Third, in the wake of liberalization in the United States and to a lesser extent in the United Kingdom, both countries moved from net exporters to net importers of telecommunications equipment.

As Table 3–5 demonstrates, the United States is now a large net importer of telecommunications equipment. This imbalance is largely a result of trade in the low end of the customer premises equipment market, not the market for network equipment. Far Eastern nations other than Japan supply mostly telephone instruments and accounted for about half of U.S. telephone imports in 1986. Much of the U.S. deficit is caused by the willingness of the United States to import equipment. In 1985 the United States was the fourth largest exporter of telephone and telegraph equipment (behind Japan, Sweden, and West Germany), with 10.7 percent of the total.

Telecommunications equipment also is relevant because trade in telecommunications equipment is linked to the international provision of telecommunications services in several ways. First, unless telecommunications equipment is compatible, it may be impossible to exchange certain services internationally.[6] Second, some services will not work without specially designed, sophisticated equipment. If the PTT forbids attachment of the equipment to the network, the service cannot be delivered. Third, the ability to deliver services influences the sale of equipment. For example, the attractiveness of AT&T's most sophisticated digital switches partly depends on countries

Table 3–5. National Telephone and Telegraph Equipment Trade Balances ($ millions).

Principal Exporting Nations	1978	1979	1980	1983	1984	1985
Japan	408	448	562	1,250	1,638	2,004
Sweden	350	369	407	706	755	788
West Germany	455	405	534	577	532	685
France	88	72	121	381	347	394
Canada	8	71	114	303	435	394
Taiwan	–31	–15	–15	320	286	161
Belgium/Luxembourg	107	73	141	117	na	130
Hong Kong	na	49	–68	255	120	61
South Korea	–83	–20	–93	10	11	–8
Italy	29	11	13	4	–26	–26
The Netherlands	107	164	208	41	84	–29
United Kingdom	69	37	40	–66	–38	–110
United States	155	129	136	–418	–1,040	–1,196

Sources: Official trade publications of each nation reported in *Issues in Domestic Telecommunications: Directions for National Policy*, NTIA Special Publication 85–16 (Washington, D.C.: U.S. Department of Commerce, July 1985), p. 164, *U.S. Industrial Outlook, 1986* (Washington, D.C.: U.S. Government Printing Office, 1986), p. 30-4, and *U.S. Industrial Outlook, 1987* (Washington, D.C.: U.S. Government Printing Office, 1987), p. 30-6.

Note: 1978 and 1983 balances computed using 1983 exchange rates; 1979 and 1984 balances computed using 1984 exchange rates; 1980 and 1985 balances computed using 1985 exchange rates.

permitting the creation of "800 number services" similar to those available in the United States. (An "800" allows callers to call a company from anywhere in the United States at no cost to the caller.) Meanwhile, the regional Bell operating companies have contemplated the possibility that a new architecture for basic switching services would disadvantage the traditional manufacturers of switches and give them a chance for late entry into the manufacturing market. Fourth, the delivery of information services will strongly influence advantages in the computer market (see Chapter 6).

Industrial countries with large markets insist that telecommunications equipment for their network be produced domestically because it is such a big ticket item. Equipment manufacturers based in Belgium, Canada, France, Germany, Italy, Japan, the Netherlands, Sweden, the United Kingdom, and the United States dominate their domestic markets. Usually, however, second suppliers are chosen for 15–25 percent of domestic orders. However, foreign companies wishing to serve as the second provider to PTTs almost always must produce the equipment locally. Significantly, EC member countries almost never turned to companies headquartered in other EC members as second suppliers. (ITT or L. M. Ericsson usually wound up as number 2.) The stiffest competition for sales takes place in middle level and developing countries. Even then, those winning large contracts must usually establish manufacturing operations in the host country. A similar problem is that Japanese government entities (but not private Japanese companies) are prohibited from procuring foreign satellites.[7]

DEFINING TELECOMMUNICATIONS SERVICES

There are almost as many definitions of telecommunications services as there are telecommunications experts. In part this is because there are no clear lines separating communications, information services, computer and data processing services, broadcasting, and publishing. To illustrate, a "digitized telephone call travels as a string of data—is it thus data communications? A computer linked to the public switch telephone network via a modem is handled and charged for as if it were a telephone call—but is it one?"[8]

To avoid dwelling on definitional battles, this analysis distinguishes among telecommunications services in ways relevant to our interests in permitting more competition in international services. Definitions should be simple enough to guide negotiations, allow some sorting out of basic economic considerations, and be sensitive to the basic logic of the technologies involved. This book's approach, therefore, builds on existing regulatory practices by selectively reorganizing them so that they make more logical sense for our purposes.[9]

We propose to distinguish between *infrastructure* and *telecommunications service* capabilities. These categories subsume several components. Infrastructure capabilities include the physical infrastructure for communications (the transmission line and switching) and facilities services (transmission services rented from someone with physical infrastructure). Telecommunications service capabilities include basic services (the transmission of a message whose content and format remain essentially unaltered, as in a phone call), value-added services (which alters the format of a message in order to make it more efficient to user applications, as in converting computer protocols while sending messages between an IBM computer and an Apple computer), and information services (the processing of the content of a message, as in remote computing services). The laws of nature require the mixing of these components in order to deliver many products, and some capabilities easily fit more than one category.

This coding scheme clarifies some distinctions in regard to infrastructure capabilities and basic services that have proven confusing in the initial efforts to propose GATT negotiating guidelines. For example, it shows that it is competition in infrastructure that is crucial for much of the telecommunications services. Many of the accusations between U.S. data communications networks and foreign PTTs can best be understood by reviewing the economics of facilities services.

INFRASTRUCTURE CAPABILITIES

Infrastructure capabilities refer to physical infrastructure and facilities services. Physical infrastructure investment in transmission and switching allows communications between two or more parties in geographically diverse premises.[10] Facilities services allow a third party to use the capabilities of the physical plant to send messages (much as one might rent an airplane to travel rather than buy a ticket on a commercial carrier). The most common form of facilities service is the renting of leased lines (or circuits) by a large user for its internal communications needs. But the meaning and role of facilities services are in a state of flux.

Physical Infrastructure

Most PTTs obstruct competition in services by insisting on monopoly control over transmission and switching facilities. National security and sovereignty are important rationales for this policy. The national security argument is not very convincing on technical grounds even in the United States which needs to maintain a very complicated nuclear command and control system. But there is no doubt that most countries, including the United States, will insist on some degree of national control over some share of their communications infrastructure. The question is, How much?

PTTs also argue that it makes no sense to permit competition in facilities if the basic network is a monopoly. Most countries assumed that a natural monopoly existed for the telecommunications infrastructure as a result of economies of scale (larger output of a single product reduces costs) and scope (reduced costs because of complementarities between two or more products, such as technologies that are synergistic).

The attack on monopoly in the United States reflected the conclusion of many analysts that technological innovation has eliminated the condition of natural monopoly (if it ever existed) for long distance and probably for the local market as well. To the extent that economies of scope and scale do exist, there is no longer a need to have a single monopoly to reap them. Ordinary commercial contracts among multiple providers (such as local phone services and long-distance phone services) would suffice.[11] (Some special issues about large users and the mix of services and equipment are reviewed later.)

Lessons from the United States. The United States has the most experience with the economics of competition, so it is useful to start an analysis of a world market by a quick recap of the U.S. findings. The United States decided to permit competition in the provision of facilities for selective uses (for example, the creation of "private line" microwave facilities linking the internal operations of a single customer over several premises) earlier than other countries. Nonetheless, it broke up AT&T largely on the theory that monopoly control over a bottleneck facility (the local telephone exchange) allowed AT&T to compete unfairly in long-distance services (where competitive ownership of facilities was legal).

Companies may use bottlenecks aggressively to block competition (even if it is not optimal to do so in an economic sense) in order to build a reputation as a tough competitor and thereby to deter prospective new entrants.[12] Now that AT&T's competitors have more fiber optic transmission capacity than AT&T, AT&T cannot as easily act as a predator. But elsewhere, where the PTT may hold much greater monopoly control over segments of the market, the ability and incentive for predatory actions is real. (Thus, because PTTs know that large users will press their bargaining leverage to get favorable terms, PTTs may try to "stimulate" the market for residences and smaller businesses. To the extent that they can write off their investments in these markets as part of their regulated rate of return, PTTs may overinvest in providing ever more elaborate international services for the segment of the market with the least strategic bargaining power. Chapter 7 discusses one version of this option.)

Even if there is no natural monopoly, some markets yield little competition because of major barriers to new entrants, particularly large fixed investment costs. There is a continuing controversy over the degree to which telecommunications infrastructure facilities are a contestable market. (Economists consider a market contestable if it is possible to take an investment for "market A" and substantially salvage its value by rededicating it to use in "market B.")

Some argue that transmission for the local market is characterized by relatively few customers for lots of expensive physical plant (and demand elasticity is fairly low, so aggregate demand will not respond to price cutting). Therefore, except for selected downtown business areas, the local loop may not be easily contestable (some believe that this too is changing), and the local loop remains by far the most expensive part of any long-distance call in the United States. It is certainly true that some combination of more efficient technology and pricing incentives created by regulation (making the costs of local switched connections to long-distance carriers high in order to subsidize purely local service) have driven about 14 percent of the total local traffic being connected to long-distance services to use private leased lines or their own local transmission facilities.[13]

There is also some argument about the degree of contestability in the long distance transmissions market. Typically, this argument points to pricing distortions created by regulation as the original incentive for new entrants (which usually won exemptions from some of the distortions). If regulators had chosen a rational policy for pricing, there would have been no reason for competition, according to this logic. This argument overlooks the fact that there were clear technological capabilities for at least limited competition since 1946, if not before.[14] But the main flaw with this reasoning is that regulation never exists independent of the political bargains that authorize regulation. The reversal of the original political bargain that produced irrational pricing depends on the political forces mobilized by new entrants. (For a quick analogy consider that a Platonic wise dictator should never need political competition to continue being efficient. However, we value competition politically precisely because dictators too frequently have little incentive to reverse mistakes.)

Moreover, there has now been so much investment in fiber optic, microwave, and private satellite systems that future contestability seems assured. (If nothing else, once a fiber optic cable is laid, someone can buy it even if the original builder goes bankrupt. The "fire sale" lowers entry costs for the next generation.) That large users are finding it economic to purchase private switching facilities is equally striking.

International Practice and Issues. The U.S. experiment with competition in infrastructure facilities has influenced global policy. The three countries most committed to the competitive model for telecommunications (which account for over 60 percent of the world market) have all concluded that competition in facilities is the prerequisite for competition in services. (And Canada is moving in this direction as well.) Japan even made the right of a service provider to own facilities or not the primary regulatory distinction for telecommunications services. And in contrast to the United States, both the United Kingdom and Japan have decided that competition in the provision of local service facilities (at least for the larger markets) is important. Unlike the United States, they have formal (United Kingdom) or informal (Japan) controls over the total number of facilities providers in the long-distance market on the implicit theory that fewer total providers will allow for the continuation of cross-subsidies. In addition, both countries believe that this is a market with imperfections that make it prone to socially wasteful surplus capacity in facilities.

The introduction of competition in facilities may surface in the creation of competition in the facilities *between* countries. At the international level facilities have been traditionally provided by the joint investment of two or more countries using the facility. (The facilities in question are transmission; switching remained in national hands at either end of the transmission line.) The transoceanic cable systems have consortium ownership that traditionally reflected the degree of individual national use of the cable. The international satellite transmission facilities were collectively owned and operated by the world's governments through an international organization, Intelsat (see Chapter 5). Ownership shares in Intelsat depended on national use of the system. A series of intergovernmental agreements effectively divided up transmission between satellites and cables, and only systems sanctioned by the major PTTs were built.

The introduction of satellites as a rival to cables produced some tension in the international facilities market because national regulatory arrangements sometimes made the major carrier prefer one or the other. For example, changes in the self-imposed U.S. policy on proportional loading of international facilities would affect competitive options significantly. Proportional loading requires major carriers (AT&T) to distribute their transoceanic transmissions equally between marine cables and international satellites. The obligation arose from the fear that AT&T would favor cables, in which it has an equity interest, over Intelsat facilities, in which it has no ownership. The FCC now questions this policy.[15]

Moreover, carriers of different nations might differ in their preferences concerning the pace of expansion of international facilities. Such tensions in the most important international market, the Atlantic, led to the creation of facilities planning exercises between North American and European authorities. It largely resulted from fears of overbuilding cable capacity because some carriers had incentives to discriminate against satellites.

Deregulation in some major markets has changed the dynamics of the international facilities market. Both established PTTs and various newcomers want to enhance their range of options in serving the global market. In May 1985 the FCC even authorized the construction of a private, undersea fiber optic communications link between the United States and the United Kingdom. Users of these facilities can engineer them to meet their specific needs and have no obligation to offer service to the public.

Firms interested in launching their own transmission facilities and services are focusing on selective service niches where PTTs have arguably under invested. For example, a private group wishing to provide direct broadcasting of television by satellite in Europe argued that it could promptly launch its service with a proven technology while PTTs decided what to do next. However, another more ambitious approach might be to allow service providers to own facilities (both transmission and switching equipment) and provide services on a global basis.

Our interviewing leaves little doubt that most major service providers prefer to own their own international transmission capacity. This rush to launch new projects will strike many as odd because the total projected capacity far exceeds most demand projections. Indeed, many large users are banking on overbuilding to produce attractive rental terms. A mixture of motives is at work in these projects.

Monopoly PTTs, on the one hand, can cross-subsidize projects to blunt entry. It is plausible that they are promoting excess capacity today to reduce the chance of future entrants into the international facilities market. However, this strategy could produce so much installed capacity that each PTT will have an incentive to bend the rules restricting competition in order to find customers or co-investors. This could open the back door for international competition in facilities or facilities services.

On the other hand, firms in countries that have or expect domestic communications competition believe that significant cost and quality advantages will come from controlling their own facilities to significant global markets. Early leadership will let them survive a later shakeout.

The firms based in competitive markets are also exploring a more profound possibility. Earlier, we suggested that there is no particular reason why facilities must have a single owner in order to reap economies of scale or scope. A standard contract would suffice. (This may be less true in the emerging global market.)

The emerging global services market has a mixture of competitive imperfections (and new openings for competition), specialized investment requirements to serve major customers, and difficulties of providing customers with integrated global services of rapidly growing complexity. These circumstances increase transaction costs for all market participants (the costs of information, bargaining, and risks assigned to specialized investments that are not easily recoverable if a contract goes wrong), including customers. One consequence of these costs is to make it worth the large users' time and effort to manage more of their own global network and use outside providers on a more flexible basis. At the same time, to the extent that large users rely on telecommunications service firms, these high transaction costs may give a significant advantage to firms that find a successful way of providing flexible mixes of integrated services on a global level. (By way of analogy large companies now have much larger in-house legal staffs and also prefer outside law firms with sophisticated capabilities in more than one city.) This advantage may drive firms to seek to become global multinational telecommunications services (and equipment) firms, much closer to the traditional model of manufacturing multinationals. Great Britain's Cable & Wireless appears to be betting precisely on this logic, and it is one reason why they have tried to force Japan to accept a new transpacific cable that they are sponsoring (see Chapters 5 and 8).

In summary, infrastructure is the dimension that too often drops out of discussion of the organization of trade in services. Yet it is crucial to competition in services, if the experience of the three major countries committed to competition is any guide. The method of organizing the supply of infrastructure facilities between countries may also be changing. Although many warn that there may be a wasteful overbuilding of international facilities, this phenomenon may be a symptom of a deeper reorganization of the information market. If facilities are not subject to competition, however, there is an alternative, strict rules governing facilities services. This involves some trade-offs requiring clearer scrutiny than much of the trade debate has provided so far.

Facilities Services

Facilities services involve the capacity of a third party to use the physical infrastructure facilities for its own transmission or switching purposes. The most common form of facilities services are leased lines. (The renter may want to use the circuit to run its own remote computing service, for example.) But options are ever more ingenious. The FCC has allowed users to purchase "indefeasible rights of use" in international cables, which would give the users all but voting rights in the cable. (Carriers like AT&T are under no obligation to sell such rights, however.)[16]

Much of the structure of the international business in computer communications services had its origins because in the 1960s PTTs could not meet users' data communication demands, so they began to lease communication circuits to private users with massive data transmission needs. Carriers provided these leased circuits for a flat monthly fee on the understanding that they would not be used in ways that would undermine the overall financial or technical soundness of the network. Users were only authorized to exchange communications directly related to their business, but they were able to make significant cost savings and technical efficiency gains. In effect, corporate users of leased lines could maximize their efficiency and stop subsidizing smaller users. A leased circuit used to maximum efficiency can transmit about twice as much data as would be possible by paying the equivalent fee for using the public network. Most users estimate their costs would rise by much more if they lost flat-rate, leased circuits.

The PTTs are sensitive to the fact that use of leased circuits is exploding because of the needs of large users and because they are the building blocks of new competitors offering global value-added and information services. In addition, many users wish to share or resell part of the capacity of the lines they lease because the lines they rent have more capacity then they need. At present this is possible only in a few countries, notably the United States, the United Kingdom, Japan, and Finland; the Netherlands is exploring the prospect as well. Other PTTs remain adamantly opposed to such liberalization.[17] Many telecommunications administrations outside the United States want to end the practice of flat rates for leased lines and replace them with volume-sensitive tariffs.

The PTTs know that an important impetus for competition in the United States was the ability of new entrants (resellers) to engage in price arbitrage between the cost of circuits that they leased from AT&T and the prices the resellers charged to small users. (Regulators hindered AT&T from matching these rates.) The PTTs wish to avoid a similar political dynamic. Technically, they argue that volume-sensitive tariffs would guarantee them a fair return for all traffic on the network, take advantage of digital technology to promote efficient marginal-cost pricing (which would be a rare novelty for most PTTs), and therefore would remove any reason to restrict the resale of leased circuit capacity.[18] Moreover, the PTTs are concerned that the migration of traffic to leased circuits, which would grow more acute if users can share or resell leased line capacity, will limit their ability to cross-subsidize local services. Limiting cross-subsidization, respond the large users, is the goal.

Thus, there is an impasse. PTTs are correct that flat rates are often inefficient. Users are correct that the general rate structure is inefficient, and any major departure from the prevailing simple formulas (like leased circuits) leaves them open to the PTTs introducing bewildering and possibly capricious rate schedules that would take trade negotiators years to sort out. A simple formula is easier for the users to protect in regulatory battles.

The controversy over leased lines is primarily a surrogate for the fundamental impasse over competition in facilities. As noted in the U.S. case, when there is no competition in switching or transmission facilities, it is much more difficult to assure efficient competition in enhanced services. If foreign countries forbid competition in facilities, then leased lines are a second-best solution to protect would-be service competitors. In short, the PTTs may be right that flat rates are not an optimal system for leased lines, but flat rates are a political function of the failure to permit competition in facilities.

Trade negotiators will seek compromises on leased-line issues. One option may focus less on arguments over flat rates versus usage-sensitive rates than on whether rates permit effective competition by foreign firms. Negotiators will need to agree on principles for rate design that preclude discriminatory pricing (whereby the public value-added networks and foreign private systems are charged the same rate for the use of basic telecommunications transport services, for example). And they must decide how PTTs should factor in the relatively lower cost of serving large users when setting prices.[19]

Another way to sort out the controversy over leased circuits is to encourage *shared bypass networks*. PTTs recognize shared bypass systems as groups of users that may need the same function supported by many users.[20] For example, the airlines established the Société Internationale de Télécommunications Aéronautique (SITA) for airline reservation and other services and the banks maintain the Society for Worldwide Interbank Financial Telecommunications (SWIFT) to assist them with interbank transactions. The procedures and criteria for establishing such systems are quite restrictive. One alternative on the international agenda could be to liberalize these conditions.

(However, there is some question as to whether most sectors would want a common users' service.) A slight variant is being explored by the United States and Japan. They are liberalizing the definition of who can be a recognized private operating agency (RPOA) for enhanced services providers because it is much easier for a RPOA to use and resell capacity in foreign nations.

Even if there is some easy way to sort out the question of pricing, technology has posed another challenge to the proponents of competition. The new digital switches make it logical to offer many value-added services through the central network for some users. The traditional U.S. effort to restrict the entry of the major common carriers into enhanced services is not sustainable at the global level (and is being abandoned in the United States). Therefore, the effort of the United States to define a new architecture for facilities services and packet switching or protocol conversion is important as a precedent for the rest of the ·world.

As initiated by the FCC, the regional Bell operating companies are drawing up plans for comparably efficient interconnection (CEI) and open network architecture (ONA) intended to break these services into such fundamental building blocks (called "primitives" by some RBOCs) that any value-added network could mix or match the elements freely. The value-added networks could buy the building blocks at the same price charged to the RBOC (or AT&T) and own entry into the enhanced market. As a result, in theory the PTT could not require its competitors in enhanced services to take any technical capability that was undesired. Although U.S. users are far from convinced, the development of open network architecture is an important precedent for competition in global services.[21]

NOTES

1. Robert Bruce, Jeffrey P. Cunard, and Mark D. Director (*From Telecommunications to Electronic Services: A Global Spectrum of Definitions, Boundary Lines, and Structures*, Report of the Study of Telecommunications Structures, International Institute

of Communications [London: Butterworths, 1986]) share our concern about facilities, although their classification is built on a legal rather than a trade basis that leads to certain differences. They argue that regulators always have to decide if the provider of facilities must make it available for all services. Accordingly, in some senses, a facilities owner is a regulated provider of services. We believe that all trade negotiators should heed this point.

2. PTTs should not have regulatory authority over communications cable or microwave facilities that tie together closely spaced buildings of the same organization. In working out legalities of regulations this distinction is important. We do not believe that PTTs should be able to regulate such local area networks (LANs).

3. The most comprehensive treatment of this prospect is from the European Community, *Television Without Frontiers*, the Green Paper on the establishment of the common market for broadcasting, especially by satellite and cable, doc. COM(84)300 Final of 14.6.1984.

4. An alternative method for estimating the market is to look at the total revenues of firms primarily in the market. According to Booz-Allen & Hamilton, annual revenues of the 300 largest firms involved in the information industry (broadly defined to include equipment and services in the communications, computer, and entertainment sectors) reached $500 billion by mid-1985. This estimate does not include revenues of government-owned or controlled monopolies. "Booz-Allen's Top-300 Information Industry Firms, As of June 1985," Booz-Allen & Hamilton, 1985.

5. Data from *U.S. Industrial Outlook, 1987* (Washington, D.C.: U.S. Government Printing Office, 1987), chapters 28, 30, and 32.

6. For example, modems legally available through the Belgian and Italian phone monopolies are just slightly different, making it impossible for companies to set up an internal phone link between offices in Italy and Belgium. See "Can Europe Untangle Its Telecommunications Mess?" *Business Week*, March 31, 1986, p. 68.

7. ITT's telecommunications equipment activities were based in Belgium even when ITT was a U.S. firm. Other pairings are Canada: Northern Telecom; France: CIT-Alcatel-Thomson; Germany: Siemens; Italy: Italtel; Japan: NEC and Fujitsu; the Netherlands: Philips; Sweden: L.M. Ericsson; U.K.: Plessey; U.S.: AT&T and GTE (but GTE recently joined forces with Siemens).

It is unclear whether ITT, which through its SEL subsidiary is Germany's traditional second supplier, will be able to hold its share now that ITT's telecommunications business is under French ownership. For a list of barriers to trade in telecommunications see Office of the United States Trade Representative, *Annual Report on National Trade Estimates: 1985*, as required by Section 303 of the Trade and Tariff Act of 1984.

8. Ann Hutcheson Reid, "Trade in Telecommunications Services: The Current Institutional Framework and the Potential for Change," paper prepared for the Committee for Information, Computer and Communication Policy, Organization for Economic Cooperation and Development (ICCP(85)12) (Paris: OECD, September 9, 1985), p. 22.

9. Bruce, Cunard, and Director, *From Telecommunications to Electronic Services*. This important comparative study of telecommunications structures in industrial countries emphasizes distinctions between basic and enhanced services, between basic and informational services, between the provision of facilities and services, and between telecommunications and cable television services.

10. A modern private branch exchange (PBX) has considerable switching capacity, but it does not follow automatically that a country permitting private PBXs will allow someone to purchase and operate a large telephone switch (as is the case in the United States). We do not mean this to suggest that PTTs should regulate local area networks (LANs) or wide-area LANs.

11. This is the fundamental point of the rather dramatic engineering metaphor developed in the January 1987 advisory report to the U.S. Justice Department concerning telecommunications (the Huber Report). It argued that the price of switching and transmission is dropping rapidly when measured in costs for a given amount of capacity. This is fundamentally a function of extraordinary increases in the productivity of microelectronics underlying modern switching and multiplexing and fiber optics. Thus, the overall network is being reorganized from a pyramid (where there was a strict hierarchy in routing from local to long distance because large central switches were very expensive) to a geodesic (three-dimensional, fully flexible routing) structure because switching and transmission are cheap, and even sophisticated users can organize the market. Although Huber may be overenthusiastic about the degree to which complete competition is

inevitable in a geodesic system, his basic point about the importance of abundant and inexpensive facilities is accurate. See U.S. Department of Justice (Antitrust Division), *The Geodesic Network—1987 Report on Competition in the Telephone Industry* (cited hereafter as Huber Report).

12. Strictly speaking, the predator has to have some profitable monopoly segments to tap for this purpose. AT&T's monopoly segments of the market are those that are least profitable to serve. We thank Leonard Waverman and Robert Crandall for allowing us to read unpublished work that helped us immensely in our thinking. See David M. Kreps and Robert Wilson, "Reputation and Imperfect Information," *Journal of Economic Theory* 27 (August 1982):253–79; Oliver Williamson, *The Economic Institutions of Capitalism* (New York: Free Press, 1986); John T. Wenders, *The Economics of Telecommunications* (Cambridge, Mass.: Ballinger, 1987); William Baumol, John Panzer, and Robert Willig, *Contestable Markets* (New York: Harcourt Brace Jovanovich, 1982).

13. See Table IX.4 in Huber Report. Most of the bypassing is done on facilities services (leased lines) rented from the Bell operating company. Individual customers may further ease problems caused by local "bottlenecks" by purchasing their own equipment. The Huber Report estimates that private buyers in the United States account for 40 percent of the market for switching equipment, including PBXs, p.1.11.

14. G.R. Faulhaber, *Telecommunications in Turmoil: Technology and Public Policy* (Cambridge, Mass.: Ballinger, 1987). There is a variety of other potential barriers to entry, including superior reputation (based on a long history of service by the telephone companies) and customer contacts. In addition, no newcomer can match the coverage that AT&T or the regional Bell operating companies can provide in their respective markets. These barriers seem more telling in regard to smaller residences than to large sophisticated users.

15. The FCC staff wants gradually to phase out the policy while slowly reducing regulation of AT&T: Evan R. Kwerel and James E. McNally, Jr., *Promoting Competition Between International Telecommunication Cables and Satellites*. OPP Working Paper Series #19, FCC, January 1986. U.S. policy about the allocation of the spectrum and geosynchronous orbital slots, although not discussed here, could also influence trade competitiveness.

16. *Communications Week*, May 5, 1986. At the same time, the FCC is toying with the possibility that it may let AT&T charge what the traffic will bear in the future for leased circuits. There is no consensus about this idea. *International Communications Week*, March 6, 1987, p. 1.

17. "Long-Range Goals in International Telecommunications and Information: An Outline for United States Policy," report prepared for the U.S. Senate Committee on Commerce, Science, and Transportation by the National Telecommunications and Information Administration (Washington, D.C.: U.S. Government Printing Office, March 11, 1983), pp. 136–43.

18. A similar issue is whether a caller who makes a one minute local call should be charged the same rate as a caller who talks for an hour. Or, should the caller who ties his home computer to a mainframe with a local telephone call and occupies the line for hours on end be charged more than someone who makes a short call?

19. Shared end-user (bypass) systems are recognized by Recommendation D-6 of the International Telegraph and Telephone Consultative Committee (CCITT) of the International Telecommunication Union (ITU).

20. The twelve members of the EC currently agree on the necessity of securing the financial viability of their Administrations, either by excluding pure resale of voice on leased lines or by tariff schemes which make pure resale of voice to third parties unattractive, such as usage-based tariffs. Both methods will have to be accommodated in the Community. However, both methods must be limited to a legitimate level of protection of financial viability and must not represent the misuse of a dominant position. Commission of the European Communities, *Toward a Dynamic European Economy*, COM(87) 290 final, Green Paper on the Development of the Common Market for Telecommunications Services and Equipment (Brussels: Commission of the European Communities, June 30, 1987), p. 96.

21. AT&T and the RBOCs would offer protocol processing as an enhanced service in order to keep these services out of the rate base. Huber Report, pp. 6-23–26. "FCC generally affirms major findings of initial computer inquiry II decision," *Telecommunications Reports*, March 30, 1987, pp. 1–4.

4

REDEFINING THE INTERNATIONAL TELECOMMUNICATIONS MARKET (II)
Telecommunications Services

BASIC TELECOMMUNICATIONS SERVICES

Basic telecommunications services are the plain old telephone, telex, and telegraph services. Services that are in essence based on new communications technologies are called *value-added services*. The term *value-added networks*, or VANs, often is used interchangeably with the term *value-added services*. Database, data processing, on-line services, and other new services that are essentially computer services that can be transmitted over telecommunications networks are called *information services*. This distinction is important because telecommunications services in most countries traditionally were highly regulated while computer services generally were less regulated or even unregulated.[1]

Table 4–1 is a roadmap through Chapter 4 designed to help the reader place the gamut of telecommunications services in the context of three broad categories: basic transport services, value-added services, or information services. Where disputes about classification persist, they are noted.

Trade negotiators quickly become confused by the differences in the types of providers of basic services. The classic monopoly company controlled all the communications infrastructure, offered few facilities services, provided all basic services and also had a public obligation to serve all customers. (These were called *common carriers*.)[2] But it is also possible for basic

85

Table 4–1. Classification of Telecommunications Services.[a]

Basic	Value-added[b]	Information
Telephone	Videotex	Data-base services
Telex/Teletext (without store and forward)	Telex/Teletext (with store and forward)	On-line computer services
Telegraph	Electronic mail	Electronic mail[c]
Facsimile	Voice mail	Voice mail[c]
Centrex	Centrex[d]	Information brokers
	Protocol conversion	
	Packet switching	
	Video conferencing	

a. Does not include infrastructure capabilities.

b. Value-added services require basic services to function. Information services require basic and value-added services to operate.

c. Classification in dispute. Some also try to argue that these are basic services. This view is unlikely to prevail.

d. Centrex is in dispute.

voice, telex and telegraph services to be delivered on private networks that simply lease infrastructure facilities services and have no public service obligation.

Basic communications services are voice and nonvoice services consisting of the transmission of information between points specified by a user in which the information delivered by the telecommunications agency to the recipient is identical in form and content to the information received by the telecommunications agency from the user. In practice telephone, telegram, and facsimile services are usually basic communications services. Telex and teletext services also qualify as basic communications services so long as messages are not stored and forwarded as part of the services (in which case they are value-added services).[3]

It is difficult to estimate the size of the market for basic telecommunications services. Because prices are subject to extraordinary manipulation through regulation and practices of cross-subsidization, the dollar totals often do not reflect volumes in predictable ways, especially when comparing across countries.

Yet the dollar figures are vital because they are the best clue about what PTTs consider politically and economically feasible to charge for various classes of services. Another difficulty is that the definition of what constitutes a local or a long-distance call differs from country to country.

If we use the basic concept of the Intra-LATA (local access and transport area) call to define local calling, then the U.S. market for local telecommunications services was about $55 billion in 1984 while the market in the rest of the world was about $59 billion. (However, local calls are often delivered for nominal fees outside the United States.) Domestic long-distance services amounted to about $45 billion in the United States and about $76 billion in the rest of the world. (But U.S. long-distance rates are often much lower than elsewhere.) U.S. revenues from international traffic involving the United States were $4.5 billion (about 75 percent of this total was telephone services) while they were about $34 billion for the rest of the world. The highest growth rates for all of these services were in international services, which have grown at over 12 percent per annum during the 1980s. To put this in perspective, telecommunications equipment exports of the thirteen largest exporting countries (SIC3661 only) in 1985 totaled approximately $7.75 billion as compared to $3.48 billion in 1980.[4]

U.S. telecommunications deregulation raised new, complicated international economic issues that could not be handled under the old system. Most postal, telegraph, and telephone authorities were furious when the United States upset the status quo. Part of their anger arose from the peculiar fiscal legacy that constrains most PTTs. PTTs usually make substantial direct contributions to their national treasuries. Those PTTs that also subsidize their postal services are even more committed to maintaining their monopolies over basic telephone services. Moreover, most PTTs want to avoid significant rationalization of labor practices of the kind forced by policy changes in the United States. (PTT unions outside the United States are typically more powerful than their counterparts in the United States.) In addition, PTTs engage in elaborate cross-subsidies for local voice services; they constantly remind their politicians that the anger of many U.S. voters over rising local service costs more than offsets any happiness about lower long-distance rates.

Beyond the issue of cross-subsidies and labor practices is the problem of financing modernization. As noted earlier, investments in modernization will have to be extremely large in the next fifteen years. Yet the overwhelming share of demand is for basic voice services (over 90 percent in most countries), and the largest amount is for local calls that have the lowest rate of demand growth and (usually) the lowest profit rates. Thus, the PTTs are very sensitive to any erosion of their share of the market for the much more profitable long-distance market (especially the extremely profitable market for international long distance) and the much more rapidly growing markets for value-added and information services.[5]

Until recently there was no need for trade rules for telecommunications services. Monopoly service providers managed their own ends of international transactions. Technical recommendations negotiated within the ITU's International Consultative Committee for Telephone and Telegraph (CCITT) assured technical compatibility and provided guidelines for settling accounts when the flow of traffic between any two parties was not in balance. Indeed, because each monopolist controlled half the circuit connecting two countries (and the national network inside each nation), PTTs argue that international phone calls are a product of joint investment (hence, the term *jointly provided service*), not an item of international trade. This was, and is, a fundamental intellectual mistake.

The decision to provide basic services through joint investment is an arbitrary way of organizing the market. It is roughly the equivalent of having international airlines agree to jointly own the world's airports and split all revenues up equally. If they then declared that international air transport was an investment arrangement, not trade, they would have achieved what the PTTs do routinely. Neither the hypothetical or actual case constitutes a plausible case for saying that the industry is not engaged in trade.[6]

Many countries resist increased competition in basic local and long-distance services. Although these same countries may permit some of the U.S. other common carriers (OCCs) such as MCI and US Sprint to deliver international long-distance traffic to their market, they will not permit competition in international long distance originating in their countries. At present, Canada, Australia, Japan, and the United Kingdom all allow the OCCs to service them directly and route calls in transit on to other destinations, mainly in smaller markets.[7] At the end of October 1987, Mexico was the only key country that had not signed an agreement with the OCCs, but it is expected to do so shortly. Only the United Kingdom and Japan have joined the United States in sanctioning competition in the provision of international services.

PTTs also favor retaining the CCITT rules governing the prices of international basic services.[8] Those recommendations boil down to three essentials.

First, phone rates for international calls are set bilaterally between the carriers of the country of ultimate origin and ultimate destination. When all countries had a monopoly telephone system, this meant that the two national monopoly carriers established a single "accounting rate" for calls between their countries and then split the revenues "fifty-fifty" (with a fee for any third countries through which the call passed). The accounting rate usually closely reflected the price to the actual user.

Second, no matter which route a call actually follows between the carriers of two countries, the accounting rate will remain the same. Thus, unlike an airline traveler, a telecommunications carrier cannot take a cheap route from New York to Brussels and then take a more expensive short hop to Frankfurt in order to save money over the expensive direct route from New York to Frankfurt. In short, the CCITT rules governing pricing constitute a perfect cartel arrangement.[9]

Third, PTTs are obligated to keep prices as low as possible and to relate them to costs. Nonetheless, PTTs may cross-subsidize some services for social purposes, and they are obligated to avoid "harmful" competition among services. PTTs often cite this latter obligation to justify refusing special pricing arrangements requested by large users.[10]

The licensing of multiple carriers by the United States complicated matters for the PTTs in several ways. Although the United States has declined to challenge the second CCITT principle, it has worried that AT&T and MCI (for example) could each agree to different accounting rates with a foreign PTT. The firm with the lower accounting rate would win a competitive advantage. Since 1986 the FCC has required all common carriers to have the same settlements policy with a foreign PTT to prevent "whipsawing." AT&T has opposed this policy because it would deny AT&T the competitive advantages of bargaining rooted in superior knowledge and contacts in the market.[11] Moreover, some other common carriers wonder if a whipsaw rule would delay their entry into the world market by barring them from offering incentives to foreign PTTs to compensate for the inconvenience created by their entry.

(There are precedents for the FCC policy which show some of the weaknesses of the approach. U.S. international record carriers (IRCs) had telex revenues of about $380 million in 1984. The profits on this service are extremely large. The U.S. government has tried to protect U.S. IRCs from being played off against one another by foreign PTTs. For example, in the Nordtel case in 1982–1983 the United States insisted that all IRCs must have an equal opportunity to serve a country and must concur in any change in the rates negotiated with a foreign PTT.[12] The problem with this system is that the IRCs can prevent price competition by means of the veto system.)

In addition, a monopoly PTT can distribute return traffic to the U.S. carriers as it chooses. Although the FCC may enforce the "whipsaw prohibition" to voice services, this threat or incentive may give a foreign PTT added bargaining leverage when it is dealing with several carriers at once.[13]

A final important complication from U.S. competition is that the difference between accounting rates and the price to U.S. and non-U.S. users is greater now than in the past. Foreign PTTs often charge higher prices to users than U.S. carriers. This may ultimately generate enormous pressure in other countries for loopholes in international rate structures for larger users or changes in the rules governing international basic services.

In short, the decline of the consensus concerning natural monopoly is also distressing because it may force a fundamental reconceptualization of the basis for doing international business among PTTs. It is as if the PTTs were switching from a barter economy to a monetary economy. Because basic telecommunications and infrastructure services remain at the heart of the international services market, the stakes are very large for all involved.

The U.S. position to date has been to leave basic services largely within the framework of ITU rules, but it has nudged the issue onto the trade agenda occasionally in order to gain service rights for other common carriers seeking to meet the needs of their U.S. customers. Because value-added and information services involve smaller sums of service revenues and are tied most directly to priorities for the computer industry, they have taken pride of place in preparing for the GATT round. (They are also the fastest growing parts of the services market.) But there is no inherent reason why basic services cannot be treated as trade issues. Because international basic services are less visible to the general public and highly important to big users, we expect that the organization of the international market (as opposed to domestic long-distance services) will change. The question is whether it will occur by creating quiet loopholes in the rate structure for large users or by allowing some limited form of competition in international basic services.

ENHANCED SERVICES: VALUE-ADDED AND INFORMATION SERVICES

Value-added and information services are a product of the linkage of computers into the communication network. Many users could share access to the same computer, and data and computers in different locations could be linked, allowing firms to integrate their overall data processing resources and make computer resources available to clients. This new remote computer service industry required much cheaper telecommunications costs to be economic and much lower error rates than voice communication networks generally supplied because a few bits of incorrectly transmitted data could garble the meaning of a message.[14]

Moreover, the marriage of computing and communications has cast doubt on the core technology of the telecommunications system and fragmented the old commodity market for telecommunications services. The core technology is in question because no clearly superior solution for engineering a system handling communications and computation has emerged. Thus, there are many opportunities for technological innovators. Fragmentation occurs because the market has so far responded to technological and economic uncertainty by producing many specialized suppliers rather than universal suppliers for each type of enhanced service.[15] PTTs hope to overcome fragmentation by creation of an integrated services digital network that will create two voice channels and one data channel plus a "signaling" channel on a single telephone line.

Common sense suggests that the difference between plain old telephone services and a computer transmission should be easy to observe. Unfortunately, this is not the only necessary distinction. *Enhanced services* are defined to be more than basic when the information provided by the sender is changed, stored, manipulated, or otherwise acted upon in the network before the recipient receives it. Value-added and information services are all enhanced services.[16] But the United States' own history until recently has been plagued by the effort to limit AT&T and the regional Bell operating companies to basic telecommunications and infrastructure services, while limiting their ability to offer enhanced services.

The line between value-added and information services is murky. The difference arises from their origins and the way in which they are regulated. Value-added services, to the extent that they were available, were deregulated in the early 1980s in the United States. Information services that arose from the computer sectors were never regulated. The push for deregulation of value-added services in the United States came because it often became impossible to distinguish between the two types of services.[17] Much of the debate in the world telecommunications arena arises for two reasons. First, some PTT authorities want to extend their control and regulation over data processing services instead of yielding their influence over enhanced telecommunications services. At the same time, they hope to strengthen national equipment manufacturers. Second, the PTTs have a legitimate case that many smaller and dispersed users of enhanced services would benefit from a public network capable of delivering them. Therefore, a simple ban on PTTs as sources of these services makes little sense, as the U.S. frustration with excluding the RBOCs from the market shows.

Value-Added Services

Value-added services can be very simple or incredibly complicated. They may include the design of a common entry format for sales transactions done between two computers in a single industry. Or if basic telecommunication services such as telex or teletext are stored and forwarded in the network (for example, a single message sent to multiple addresses and not transmitted until the lowest rates are available), then they become value-added services. There is considerable argument about whether to classify electronic and voice mail and storage as basic, value-added, or information services. To us they look like value-added or information services, but PTTs are wary of losing anything that comes so close to their bread and butter of voice traffic in basic services. Indeed, voice mail and other enhancements pose a serious threat to the old regulatory bargain for core services.

The U.S. Experience. A large portion of value-added services involve packet switching and protocol conversion, which are essential to many forms of data transmission that require high speed but intermittent connections between computers using different protocols.[18] The packet switching and protocol conversion can be done either on public packet networks or on private bypass networks. The assembly of packets can also be done by either the central network or by the sophisticated customer

93

premises equipment of large users; and large users can use either computers or private branch exchanges (PBXs) if they assemble packets. These potential options mean that there are significant incentives for participants in the information market to manipulate the design of the network to favor their services or equipment (see Chapter 7).

In Europe and Asia PTTs operate most of the public packet networks. These networks dominate data transmission in these regions. In the United States, however, the majority of data transmission is performed either without the use of packet switching or over private bypass networks. Public packet networks in the United States are provided by a variety of companies, but Tymnet, Telenet, and Uninet (none of which are owned by AT&T or the regional Bell operating companies) dominate the business. So far, private networks have proven cheaper and more sophisticated than most PTT efforts.

Three trends dominate the packet switching business. First, a larger percentage of data transmission is being switched to public packet networks in the United States; revenues have grown at 35 percent annually since 1983.[19] Second, nobody makes significant profits in the public packet network business. Therefore, this business is being increasingly subsumed by information service providers that offer packet switching as an auxiliary to their main business. Third, large users of data communications in Europe and Asia are rebelling against the terms for the use of the public packet networks. These users want some combination of more competition and the right to lease facilities for private bypass networks.

Determining the size of the data communication market is extremely difficult because public packet networks do not carry all data communications. The most recent estimate in the United States suggests that in 1985 public packet networks carried only 6 percent of all data transmissions by corporations (the dominant users in the market).[20] Although there is considerable uncertainty about the revenues of public packet networks in the United States, a rough estimate of $400-$700 million suggests that the total U.S. corporate market for data transmission was on the order of $7 billion in 1985. This figure does not include information services, which are discussed shortly.

It is even more difficult to figure out the precise totals for international data transmission. One indication is that the international record carriers received revenues of about $150 million (after settlements with their foreign partners) from leasing private international circuits involving a U.S. connection. But these numbers do not fully reflect the complexity and size of the developing international market for enhanced services. For example, some of the private leased circuits are used by noncarriers providing public packet switched networks. An important question for organization of the international market will be how to classify such services as international "800" and "900" numbers that allow customers to either call a company toll-free or to use a service for a fee billed directly and automatically to their phone ("Dial A Joke," for example). The total growth rate for all enhanced services internationally is, at minimum, over 18 percent annually until the early 1990s.

International Issues. Among those countries favoring new trade negotiations, there are two main perspectives about whether foreign entities should have a right to compete in value-added and information services. One side insists on *national treatment.* They argue that foreign suppliers should have exactly the same rights and duties as local suppliers. If there is little competition within a country, then foreign suppliers would be similarly constrained. Others insist that foreigners should be given the *right to establish a competitive presence.* This position goes beyond national treatment and argues that countries have a positive obligation to permit competition, even if they continue to restrict direct foreign investment.[21] This latter approach is more practical if trade in services is organized through a series of bilateral agreements or if countries may voluntarily accede to a GATT code. Proposed U.S. legislation requiring reciprocity in the trade of telecommunications goods and services follows the latter approach when dealing with countries whose firms establish competitive ventures in the United States.

Both approaches would make it possible for the right to compete to be subject to reasonable constraints for reasons such as national security so long as such obstacles were clearly identified and made *transparent*. (There would also have to be an obligation to let foreign competitors have a right to consultation in the national administrative procedures.) In the early stages of the trade talks it might also be possible to negotiate a moratorium on the erection of new barriers to the provision of both enhanced and basic services.

Formulating a position on the right to enter will be complicated because large users and private value-added networks have bargaining power independent of governments. In particular, there are some conspicuous cases of "grandfathering" of the largest users into sweetheart deals with the PTTs. This occurs because some of the private packet switching and information services already have spent years building privileged relationships with the PTTs to obtain comparatively more favorable rates and greater freedom to engineer their private systems. It is, for example, commonplace for industry representatives to spend years building personal ties with local PTT officials in order to get permission to act in ways that make sense for their private network. Acting individually and collectively, the largest users may obtain relatively favorable terms for themselves while the needs of medium-sized firms and residences are neglected. A recent example was the protest by the value-added networks in the United States against the FCC's extension of its "whipsaw" rules to settlements between U.S. value-added networks and foreign governments. The value-added networks argued that they did not need this protection and the rule would sanction foreign PTTs treating enhanced services as regulated services, something that U.S. value-added networks have consistently fought (see Chapter 6).[22]

A final problem about the right to compete concerns the design of the network. Trade negotiations have so far concentrated on technical standards for customer premises equipment by pushing for global adoption the U.S. standard of "no harm to the network." But the technical design of the network of the future may also impede the ability of foreign firms to compete.

For example, the design of European networks may move in divergent directions if current efforts to improve compatibility do not improve. And, the signaling system planned for Japan's future network differs significantly from the standards of other countries. Current practices do not make clear under what circumstances such differences constitute a trade barrier.[23] And, the discussion about the design of network standards may be a surrogate for concerns of enhanced service providers that they can use their own customized networks internationally.

One way to ease such problems might be to negotiate explicit guarantees of the right of enhanced service providers to design and use their own customized architecture. For example, a GATT agreement might allow a user to file a trade grievance if a country introduced national standards that required any user to extensively modify a systems architecture that is consistent with existing international standards. Such an arrangement was recently reached in principle among IBM, Tymnet, and Pacific Bell for their U.S. operations.

Information Services

Information services are those that permit end users to manipulate and access data before or after transmission over the network. Information providers add value to raw data by organizing, processing, manipulating, and distributing information as a service. *Because information services in most countries are more liberally regulated than are value-added services, there is an incentive to classify most services as information services.*

The information services industry consists of database producers, on-line vendors, and information brokers.[24] It also includes data processing services which use telecommunications services to deliver processing services, or companies that provide integrated turnkey operations for managing software and computing operations and necessary communications to support these services.

The heart of the economics of this industry is driven by the relative costs of data communications and computing. The

Huber Report estimated that the former has declined by a factor of 10 since 1982 while the latter has gone down by a factor of 100 to 10,000.[25] This means that it is almost impossible for any network to keep up with the range of information service options. Larger networks are emphasizing their roles as gateways that make it convenient to use many information services. Just as critically, communications costs and capabilities are a relatively more important inhibition to the growth of information services than any limits in computing technology or software. Therefore, even if a PTT sees itself as an information gateway, information services provide strong incentives to search out novel ways to lower communications costs and increase technical flexibility. This is producing such experiments as using the "empty space" on a FM radio station transmission to send stock quotations to special receivers, and many experiments with the use of cable television systems.

The Department of Commerce estimates that expenditures on data processing in the United States grew 12.7 percent in 1986 to reach $19.5 billion and estimates that revenues could climb to $22 billion in 1987. By contrast, Japan, the second largest consumer of data processing services had revenues amounting to $3.5 billion in 1986. France ($1.5 billion), West Germany ($985 million), and the United Kingdom ($881 million) were the next three largest users. Significantly, about 10 percent of U.S. firms' revenues were obtained from foreign sources. A similar pattern is evident in the much smaller market for electronic database services. U.S. revenues in 1986 were estimated at $2.3 billion and are forecast to reach $2.7 billion in 1987. The U.S. share of database producers is just under 30 percent and its share of on-line vendors is about 60 percent. By comparison, the videotext services industry is minuscule and trailing the rest of the world.[26]

Many PTTs want to provide both information and value-added services over the public network. Although there are always problems of abuse of monopoly power in basic services and the potential for cross-subsidies, the involvement of the PTTs in providing these services is not a problem so long as it is not done in a way that precludes alternative provision of these services. (Indeed, Japan has kept a strong commitment to public programs working through its public networks to stimulate new information services.) The problems will occur if the PTTs, for example, design their networks to make it difficult for noncarrier service providers to provide their own versions of these functions.[27] In short, negotiators must recognize that many sophisticated enhanced services cut across value-added and information processing services. Therefore, it is not enough to make a deal to exempt information services from telecommunications regulations.

Indeed, Judge Harold Greene decided in September 1987 to allow a limited entry of regional Bell operating companies into the value-added network market. Judge Greene evidently modeled his decision on the successful French minitel videotex system, but the RBOCs complain that he did not go far enough and that the French model he emulated was already out of date. In effect, Judge Greene gave the RBOCs the opportunity to be "supermarkets" for all VANs and information services by allowing them to offer a single directory and interconnect point for users through the public switched network. He may believe that there are some economies of scope in value-added services, although the decree will not reduce competition by other providers. The new situation is as if a supermarket could not offer its own generic brands for sale.[28]

Transborder Data Flows

There is a special set of problems that relate to information services that are frequently summarized as barriers to transborder data flows. Governments also erect barriers that hamper transborder data flows. These obstacles are variously justified on the basis of privacy protection, cultural preservation, sovereignty, national security, as well as economic motivations.

For example, since the early 1970s Sweden, Austria, Canada, Denmark, France, Germany, Hungary, Iceland, Israel, Luxembourg, New Zealand, Norway, and the United Kingdom have adopted data-protection laws to safeguard the privacy of their citizens. The laws of the first four of these also protect the privacy of corporations and associations as well.[29] Other countries, such as Canada and Switzerland, strive to protect sensitive data, such as banking records, from foreign scrutiny. The stated goal of such measures is to assure that in an age of global information networks unauthorized access to private and proprietary data is restricted.

Peter Robinson, the Chairman of the Committee for Information, Computer and Communications Policy (ICCP) Working Party on Transborder Data Flows within the OECD, has identified several trade-related issues associated with transborder data flows.[30] The prominent ones are regulations that influence the location of data processing activities. Countries such as Canada and West Germany require that certain data must be stored or processed domestically. For example, the Canadian Banking Act of 1980 required that data on Canadian banking transactions must be stored in Canada. They want national data always to be under national control. And West Germany insists that there be some measure of local data processing as a precondition to interconnection to its carrier. Supporters of this position felt vindicated when in 1982 the Reagan administration forbid Dresser Industries from providing data to its French subsidiary in an effort to stall the building of a natural gas pipeline between Western Europe and the Soviet Union. There remain, however, stark differences in opinion about whether such restrictions are justifiable on sovereignty and security grounds even if they distort economic activities.

One potential trade-related problem is the prospect that some governments might impose import taxes on data and data services obtained from abroad. A worry for multinational enterprises is that governments in order to meet their own domestic welfare objectives might impose new restrictions on intrafirm data flows.[31] Some firms may not use the full capabilities of existing telecommunications technologies because they fear future reprisals if they behave on the basis of a global strategy.

The absence of domestic intellectual property laws to protect software, firmware, and the contents of databases also may constitute a barrier to the free flow of information. Complaints about the absence of intellectual property rules (involving copyright, trademarks, trade secrets, unfair competition, and counterfeiting) are common. (Allegedly, some countries require the registration of imported software and databases, but fail to provide protection for them. Without such protection, those with proprietary information may not transfer it abroad.) And, direct broadcasting by satellite raises concerns both for senders and receivers. Broadcasters worry that their signals may be picked up and rebroadcast without proper royalties being paid. Recipients worry about cultural domination from abroad.[32]

National security considerations are another legitimate reason that some countries restrict information flows. But distinguishing what information, if made generally available, would constitute a threat to national security is difficult. For example, the United States restricts the export of secret and technical information to the Soviet Union under the Export Administration Act of 1979.[33] But when the Young Commission suggested in January 1987 that overzealous restrictions were harming U.S. competitiveness abroad, the Defense Department immediately disagreed.

Developing countries have their own special fears that have led them to voice complaints about transborder data flows. Brazil contends that remote-sensing by satellites might place developing countries at a potentially serious disadvantage in negotiations on contracts for oil and mineral concessions, in the management of mineral resources, and in developing strategies for intervention in agricultural commodity markets. To diminish this risk, Brazil requires that a copy of all databases be kept in Brazil. Ecuador sometimes has taken a different approach, asserting its ownership of the geosynchronous arc 22,300 miles above the equator.[34] More ambitious still was the attempt by some, mostly developing, countries to restrict the flow of news, through adoption of a new world information order within UNESCO.

Finally, countries often restrict transborder data flows in order to promote or protect their own industries. Sometimes the reasons for these restrictions are transparent. At other times economic objectives are justified in terms of privacy, culture, sovereignty, or national security. Those favoring freer flows of data across borders, do not dispute the legitimate rights of countries to restrain data flows in the national interest. The goal for liberalizers is that barriers that are economically motivated should be notified and subject to negotiations with regard to their liberalization.[35]

SUMMARY

Predictions are that trade in enhanced services, with the exception of standard data processing will increase rapidly, but from a low base. Trade in basic telecommunications services should increase at a slower rate, but from a much larger base. Over the long run, three developments seem inevitable with regard to growth. First, the variety of services available will increase rapidly, forcing regulators to scramble to remain relevant. Second, the share of the United States in total trade in value-added and information services will decline. Third, the share of telecommunications revenues accounted for by value-added and information services relative to trade in equipment and basic services will rise.

NOTES

1. These distinctions, it should be noted, differ from breakdowns made by the U.S. government. The Department of Commerce, for example, divides what we call information services into two categories—data processing services and information services—in its separate competitive assessments of the U.S. information services, data processing services, and software services industries. The FCC stressed the basic-versus-enhanced distinction in its Computer Inquiry II announced in 1980. It contended that basic services should be regulated and that enhanced services should be unregulated. In its Computer Inquiry III announced in May 1986 the FCC acknowledges, however, that the line between basic and enhanced services is eroding. USTR used the distinction between "telecommunications, data processing and information services" in its U.S. National Study submitted to the GATT in

December 1983. The most elaborate efforts to map the information industry were undertaken at the Harvard Center for Information Policy Research Program on Information Resources Policy.

2. A *carrier* is usually defined as an entity that provides infrastructure facilities and basic services with a public service obligation.

3. There is a dispute whether centrex service (voice message forwarding done at the central switch of the network) is a basic communications or value-added service.

4. Our data are drawn from interviews with major providers of telecommunications services. They are consistent with published data of the U.S. Department of Commerce. Over $650 million of 1984 revenues (after splitting with foreign carriers) were generated by the five U.S. International Record Carriers (ITT Worldcom, RCA Globecom, TRT Telecommunications Corporation, Western Union International, and FTC Communications). About $380 million of this total was for telex. Comsat's international satellite revenues in 1985 was $238 million while total Intelsat revenues climbed to $457 million in 1985. IRC and satellite revenues include, it should be noted, revenues for leasing circuits for data transmission. *U.S. Industrial Outlook, 1985, 1986* and *1987* (Washington, D.C.: U.S. Government Printing Office, 1985, 1986, 1987), chapters 30 and 31.

5. Rudolf Trachsel, the director general of the Swiss PTT, has stated that in 1985 his organization derived 70 percent of its profits from international telephone services (speech at a conference on International Implications of United States Competitive Policies and the AT&T Divestiture sponsored by the Washington Program of The Annenberg School of Communications, Lucerne, Switzerland, June 1–3, 1986). In contrast it was reported to one of the authors that in 1985 British Telecom earned about a third of their profits from international telephone services. This figure has been falling and is expected to continue to decline. Data on AT&T's profits from international telephone traffic are not available, but it is presumed to be very profitable.

6. Some analysts also conclude that joint investment implies a bilateral monopoly should exist for international basic services. This thesis has two flaws. It confuses the fact that it may (no one has proved it) be cheaper to have two countries cooperate in investing in an international transmission facility with the conclusion that the services over the facilities should be monop-

olies. (In any event as ownership of facilities is diversified, the right to provide basic services internationally ought to increase.) Moreover, it errs in arguing that only the service providers that can provide local national switching should be entitled to send or receive international traffic. This is the same fallacy as saying that only local phone companies in the United States ought to have the right to provide long-distance services.

7. The structure of international phone arrangements makes sure that the PTT will receive at least the same, if not more, revenue from an MCI call as an AT&T call. On incoming calls the PTT will balance the additional expense and bother of dealing with more than one U.S. carrier against the possibility that added carriers, which will lower customer costs by advertising and cutting margins on their end of the call, will stimulate demand significantly. They will also examine the potential for making money as a transit point for the OCC to other countries. For example, Australia profits from letting MCI and US Sprint route calls through its network from the United States to the lucrative Taiwan market. Mexico, on the other hand, receives 70 percent of the split in its dealings with AT&T and has resisted the entreaties of other carriers to do business.

8. Usually the domestic monopoly phone company also controlled the international franchise. In a few cases (in Australia, Canada, Italy, and Japan) separate monopolies handled international services. In the United States before 1982 AT&T Long Lines was the monopoly provider of international telephone services but was barred from providing telegram and telex services and from providing enhanced services. Although AT&T lost its monopoly on international telephone services under the Modified Final Judgement in 1982, it won the right to enter the information and enhanced services areas in the United States and abroad from which it had been banned under the 1956 Consent Decree. Western Union had a legal monopoly for domestic telegraph and telex services and a handful of international record carriers provided these services internationally. In addition, after the signing of the Intelsat Agreement in 1962, Comsat became the exclusive U.S. provider of international satellite communications services.

9. Each country is obligated to charge an identical rate for transit services to all other countries.

10. See Ann Hutcheson Reid, "Trade in Telecommunications Services: The Current Institutional Framework and the Potential for Change," paper prepared for the Committee for Information, Computer and Communications Policy (ICCP(85)12) (Paris: OECD, September 1985).

11. Evan Kwerel, "Promoting Competition Piecemeal in International Telecommunications," Working Paper 13 of the Federal Communications Commission Office of Plans and Policy (December 1984). The FCC defines whipsawing as "the ability of the foreign correspondent to utilize its monopoly power to play one carrier against others to gain concessions and benefits from the U.S. international carriers." Fears that the IRCs might be "whipsawed" by PTTs in the absence of FCC intervention increased after the deregulation of enhanced services in 1982. See Richard J. O'Rorke, Jr., and Jack E. Cole, "The Implications of Foreign Entry into U.S. International Telecommunications Service Markets," Office of International Affairs, NTIA, U.S. Department of Commerce, March 1982, mimeo.

12. Before the Modified Final Judgement, AT&T was not allowed to provide telex and telegram services internationally. Several IRCs competed for this business. Foreign PTTs dealt with several private service providers simultaneously. The FCC tried to assure that foreign PTTs contracts with IRCs did not favor one over another, so that IRCs could not be played off against each other. In 1982 the PTTs of the Nordic and Benelux countries asked U.S. IRCs to bid for the right to provide new value-added services to their countries. They indicated that they would select one or several bidders. Fearing that they might be whipsawed, U.S. IRCs sought help from the U.S. government. Ultimately the European PTTs backed down. For a description of these events see Geza Feketekuty and Jonathan D. Aronson, "Restrictions on Trade in Communications and Information Services," in *Regulation .of Transnational Communications*, Michigan Yearbook of International Legal Studies (1984), pp. 145–61.

13. Before deregulation the FCC policed settlement agreements between IRCs and foreign PTTs to prevent whipsawing. Return traffic was generally distributed to the IRCs in the same percentage that they sent traffic to a PTT. All settlement prices between U.S. IRCs and a given PTT were the same. U.S. officials, however, worried that a foreign monopoly might set up a carrier in the United States to which it would send a disproportionate amount

of its traffic. However, now that the communications resale field has been deregulated, no "U.S. laws restrict foreign telecommunications authorities from acquiring other resale or enhanced service providers. Nor are there any restrictions on the construction of facilities that do not use the radio spectrum." Indeed, Cable & Wireless does own TDX, a U.S. resale carrier. See *Issues in Domestic Telecommunications: Directions for National Policy*, NTIA Special Publication 85-16, (Washington, D.C.: U.S. Department of Commerce, July 1985), p. 162. Since January 1986 the FCC has experimented with applying the whipsaw rule to international voice services ("FCC's International Settlements Policy Challenged in Court," *International Communications Week*, May 1, 1987, p. 9).

14. A telephone line will work acceptably with an error rate of 5 percent. This same error rate would be unacceptable for an airline reservation system and disastrous for the electronic transfer of funds among banks.

15. Data processing has encouraged independent firms such as Automatic Data Processing and Computer Science Corporation and helped launch fast-growing subsidiaries of General Motors (EDS), General Electric (GEISCO), McDonnell Douglas, Boeing, and Martin Marietta. The number of software and information services providers also has expanded rapidly. Significantly, important private firms providing software, value-added, and information services have appeared outside the United States, most notably in Japan, France, Britain and Canada. (For example as of September 1986, almost 3,000 separate information services, mostly provided by private firms, were available to individuals linked to Minitel, the French PTT's videotex service.) U.S. data processing firms are the largest in the world, but Japan boasts seven firms and France six firms with 1984 revenues over $50 million. In addition, Scicon International, a subsidiary of British Petroleum, had 1984 revenues of $142 million in 1984. See Jeffrey Hart, "Data Processing, Information Services, Software and Telecommunications Services in the International Economy," draft chapter prepared for the Office of Technology Assessment, April 1986, mimeo, p. 37.; "The Minitel Revolution," *Newsweek*, March 24, 1986, p. 43 and "Videotex—In France It's the Rage," *Los Angeles Times*, September 12, 1986, p. 1.

16. Experts debate the significance of open systems interconnection (OSI) standards for the ability of trade negotiators to distinguish

among telecommunications services. OSI distinguishes between "bearer services" (OSI levels 1–3), which define the interface between users and the network and "teleservices," which define the overall services and the customer premises equipment functions necessary to communicate between users. Robert Bruce, Jeffrey P. Cunard, and Mark D. Director (*From Telecommunications to Electronic Services: A Global Spectrum of Definitions, Boundary Lines, and Structures*, Report of the Study of Telecommunications Structures, International Institute of Communications [London: Butterworths, 1986]) suggest that the problem is manageable.

17. The U.S. experience demonstrates how hard it can be to establish precise groundrules, but it is actually encouraging if one only wants a sensible framework. The complexity of the U.S. experiment in distinguishing services arose from the desire to prevent any possibility of cross-subsidized, unfair competitive practices by AT&T. Therefore, the United States sought a definition that would serve as a basis for structural separation of a subsidiary for information services to be offered by AT&T. A GATT negotiation would not need such safeguards because structural separation is not the issue.

18. Packet switching stores data into 100 character "packets" for transmission. The packet assemblers and disassemblers are an adjunct of a digital switch; protocols specify how to construct the packet. Continuous connections taking whole circuits (for large data flows) are called circuit switching. The introduction of new technologies did not always reflect levels of national development. For example, Spain introduced packet switching in 1978, but Italy only began testing its public packet switching network in 1986. Similarly, Canada moved quickly to cable television, while Germany lagged. And Indonesia, pushed by its island geography, became a leader in satellite communications.

19. Huber Report, p. 5.1. There is some evidence that large users now prefer to lease the packet switching and protocol conversion capacity of other users in the same industry rather than to rely on either a PTT or a conventional VAN. Elisabeth Horwitt, "VAN Clan Starts Corporate, Vertical Market Move," *Computerworld*, August 31, 1987, pp. 41, 44.

20. "Corporate uses of public data networks are on the rise," *Data Communications*, July 1986, pp. 85–86. It is estimated that this figure could rise to 11 percent in 1987. Huber Report, Chapter 5,

pp. 4 and 10, provides a variety of estimates closer to the upper boundary of the estimate.

21. Before the Uruguay round, the GATT was never allowed to deal directly with investment issues. This formulation would permit a country to insist on the use of a distributor.

22. "FCC's International Settlements Policy Challenged in Court," *International Communications Weekly,* May 1, 1987, pp. 9–10.

23. An analogous issue involves the Soviet Intersputnik system, which is only partially tied to the Intelsat system. The Soviet Union (and the Defense Department) prefer only marginal inter-connectedness. The situation resembles the situation during the nineteenth century when countries laid different gauge track for their railroad systems. Invasion was more difficult if foreign trains could not operate on domestic tracks.

24. Recommendation D-6 of the International Telegraph and Tele-phone Consultative Committee (CCITT) of the International Telecommunications Union recognizes this distinction. The Department of Commerce considers the information services industry to include (1) bibliographic and source databases in either electronic form or hard copy; (2) on-line computer services for the storage of databases, retrieval of bibliographic citations, abstracts, or text; retrieval, manipulation, and analysis or numeric data, and the production of customized or standard reports; (3) document supply services, and (4) customized search and abstracting serv-ices. See U.S. Department of Commerce, International Trade Administration, "A Competitive Assessment of the U.S. Infor-mation Services Industry (Washington, D.C.: DOC, May 1984), pp. 1, 5.

25. Huber Report.

26. Between 1981 and 1986 the number of electronic databases available increased by about 35 percent each year. The United States has about 900 on-line database producers and about 300 on-line vendors. Foreign buyers seeking information on U.S. markets and technology (particularly from Canada, the United Kingdom, France, West Germany, and Japan) provide significant revenues to U.S. firms. Total videotext revenues in the United States were about $75 million in 1985 and are projected to reach about $170 million in 1990. However, it should be noted that videotext services are developing faster in such countries as France (Minitel), Japan (CAPTAIN), West Germany (Bildschirm-text), and the United Kingdom (Prestel) than in the United States.

U.S. Industrial Outlook, 1987 (Washington, D.C.: U.S. Government Printing Office, 1987), chapter 47. Information of databases is from the July 1986 edition of the Cuadra/Elsevier *Directory on Online Databases.*

27. In general, we concentrate more on conduit and standards that allow for the international provision of telecommunications services than on the content that is transmitted across national boundaries. There is a rich and growing literature on transborder data flow issues, and the policy disputes in this realm are often intense. We deal with these issues only when they overlap with our main concerns. See for example, "International Information Flow: A Plan for Action," a Statement by the Business Roundtable (New York: Business Roundtable, January 1985) and G. Russell Pipe, "International Information Policy: Evolution of Transborder Data Flow Issues," *Telematics and Informatics* 1, no. 4 (1984): 408–18.

28. "Bell Firms Get Mixed Ruling on Expansion," *Wall Street Journal*, September 11, 1987, p. 3.

29. *Transnational Data and Communication Report*, January 1987, p. 23; Pipe, "International Information Policy."

30. Peter Robinson, "Transborder Data Flows: An Overview of Issues," in OECD, *Transborder Data Flows: Proceedings of an OECD Conference* (Amsterdam: North-Holland, 1985), pp. 19–29.

31. See Karl P. Sauvant, *International Transactions in Services: The Politics of Transborder Data Flows* (Boulder, Colo.: Westview, 1986), pp. 79–119.

32. Restrictions on information flows based on cultural and social objectives are complicated to deal with in the context of this study. Such restrictions may limit the distribution of foreign cultural information from movies, television broadcasts, magazines, or newspapers. Screen quotas are one such restriction. Another example is Canadian tax provisions that discourage imports of news magazines produced abroad and make it less desirable for broadcasters in the northern portions of the United States to aim their signals at Canadian audiences.

33. The extraterritorial application of U.S. laws in the Dresser case was undertaken for national security reasons. The damage to the image that U.S. firms were dependable suppliers, however, was devastating. And Republican business leaders almost universally

condemned the pipeline decision and the actions that accompanied it.

34. United Nations Centre on Transnational Corporations, *Transborder Data Flows and Brazil: Brazilian Case Study*, prepared by the Special Secretariat of Informatics of the National Security Council of the Presidency of the Republic of Brazil in cooperation with the Ministry of Communications of Brazil (New York: United Nations, 1983); United Nations Centre on Transnational Corporations, *Transborder Data Flows: Access to the International On-Line Database Market: A Technical Paper* (New York: United Nations, 1983); *The Missing Link*, report of the Independent Commission for World-wide Telecommunications Development (Chaired by Sir Donald Maitland) (Geneva: International Telecommunication Union, December 1984). Karl P. Sauvant, "Transborder Data Flows and the Developing Countries," *International Organization* 37, no. 2 (Spring 1983):359–71.

35. The goals of private business are clearly stated in The Business Roundtable, "International Information Flow: A Plan for Action."

II
Case Studies

5

DOES DOMESTIC DEREGULATION LEAD TO INTERNATIONAL COMPETITION?
Facilities and Services in the United States and Japan

Three factors are critical in shaping international tele-communications services: the degree of competition allowed in the provision of facilities for transmitting and switching services, the interdependence between equipment and services, and the interrelationship among the different types of services. In the United States economists successfully argued that monopoly control over switching and transmission facilities creates a critical bottleneck for competition in services. They concluded that competition in equipment is prerequisite for efficient competition in services.

The current policy discussion surrounding trade in telecommunications services usually begins with the opposite premise. It is assumed that there will be only slight competition in the international ownership of facilities, but that clever negotiators might limit the ability of owners of facilities to distort egregiously the competition in services. This chapter reexamines this premise. It asks whether there is any opportunity for significant competition in international transmission facilities.

The complexity of international ownership arrangements makes it hard to define significant competition. Indeed, this case study of policymaking in the United States and Japan shows that there are two sets of international transmission facilities that represent the two major technological options—satellites and cables (especially undersea cables). These ventures are all jointly owned by multiple telephone companies. Most international satellites are owned by a single international consortium, Intelsat, which is jointly owned by all the major telecommunication authorities in the world.[1] Cables are usually a joint investment of the major telecommunications authorities that intend to use the cable. There may be more than one cable—with differing ownership mixes—serving the same route, and cables compete with satellites (although the same set of owners are often involved in both).

There are four obvious opportunities for possible competition. First, one or more companies could set up their own transmission facilities in competition with existing ventures. Until recently, separate independent satellite transmission facilities were not allowed to operate. In theory it is possible to install an independent cable, but cables are licensed by government authorities that traditionally took a dim view of wholesale entry into this business.

Second, companies could buy and sell shares in existing or planned facilities freely. Only government-designated shareholders can be members of Intelsat. And until recently, when the United Kingdom designated Mercury as a second participant, no country had authorized more than one member (always an official national monopoly). The ownership of transoceanic cables was always somewhat more widely spread, because the international record carriers (IRCs) could own shares. Today, the other common carriers (OCCs) of the United Kingdom and the United States, in particular, are expanding the pool of cable ownership. Some financial institutions and U.S. regional Bell operating companies are also starting to get involved. But the pool remains relatively small and is largely dominated by existing postal, telegraph, and telecommunications authorities (PTTs).

Third, different transmission facilities could compete against each other freely. Satellites and cables could compete for traffic. But traditionally most countries had either a single telecommunications authority that treated the choice as a monopoly profit maximization game, while in the United States the Federal Communications Commission (FCC) insisted that AT&T divide the outgoing traffic through a system of balanced loading between the two facilities.[2]

Fourth, companies could purchase or rent the use of segments of joint facilities, and also might be allowed the same rights in delivering services as the established PTTs that also own the facilities. Traditionally, non-PTTs have not had the same rights to rent or own shares of these facilities. Usually, the range of services they could offer over these facilities was sharply restricted.

Our analysis suggests the prospects for these types of competition. The argument is fairly straightforward. The experience of both the United States and Japan show that domestic deregulation quickly induces action to introduce more competition and diversity of supply in the provision of international transmission facilities. Significant players want to rebalance their competitive strategies by expanding gains at home (or offsetting losses) through new international initiatives.

Everyone realizes that competition in international services and facilities carries special risks. Governments almost certainly will continue to play a role in monitoring entry. As a result, early participants may enjoy special advantages as governments grow warier of new entrants later on. In addition, customers that use these facilities experience high information costs. Suppliers believe that (given reasonable prices) early good performance will lock in key customers for substantial periods of time. Therefore, it is commonly believed that when entry becomes possible there will be a rush to enter and establish early leadership. Subsequently, there will be a shakeout. In the medium term there probably will be more investment in transmission facilities than the market can support. Those facilities (and the service networks that feature them) that rapidly attract traffic will survive the shakeout and their specific technologies (such as fiber optics versus satellites) will have an advantage in subsequent rounds of investment.[3]

The shakeout scenario has two important implications. First, it means that even if unilateral national initiatives to remove all the significant barriers to competition do not succeed, the construction of excess capacity and the frantic search for customers can modify the terms for price and service in the world market. Therefore, a government strategy to raise the credibility of new entrants may yield large benefits even if new entrants remain small in number. Second, this scenario also implies that equipment makers have an important interest in market developments. Coalitions of facilities suppliers and their champions in the scientific community predictably push for rules governing competition in services that most favors early breakthroughs for their technologies. In short, this battle involves participants other than providers and purchasers of services.

By examining policymaking in the United States and Japan, this chapter shows how politics and economics are producing changes in the international market for telecommunications facilities. The U.S. debate about international satellite communications demonstrates the links between domestic and international reforms and the limits on unilateral national initiatives. The Japanese case confirms that these dynamics are not idiosyncratic to the United States.

THE RISE OF INTELSAT AND COMSAT: A U.S. LEGACY[4]

The International Telecommunications Satellite Organization (Intelsat), and Communications Satellite Corporation (Comsat), its U.S. affiliate, ruled international satellite communications for two decades. Beginning in March 1983, however, they came under attack from a pack of aspiring competitors led by a small company called Orion that had no satellites and no known customers. In July 1985, the FCC agreed that private firms should be licensed to compete with Comsat and Intelsat for international satellite communication services even though they rejected Orion's bid. The new U.S. policy undercut Comsat's position and will likely end Intelsat's monopoly.

The FCC decision marked a sharp reversal in U.S. diplomacy. Intelsat is a child of U.S. diplomacy. In the early phases of space exploration American policymakers urged the creation of a single international satellite communication consortium, jointly owned and managed by all governments. The new enterprise was meant to demonstrate America's commitment to the shared peaceful use of outer space, guarantee adequate transmission facilities to meet rapidly growing demand, provide lower costs by permitting large economies of scale, prevent wasteful duplication of ground facilities or poor utilization of the frequency spectrum, and provide universal service. At the same time it would help developing countries by equalizing rates on each individual service for users with high and low volumes of traffic.

As a preparatory move, in 1962, Congress created Comsat, a privately owned corporation. The only direct control retained by the U.S. government was the right to appoint three of its fifteen directors. Comsat was created as a "carrier's carrier," the sole link between U.S. carriers and international satellite traffic. However, the enabling legislation left open the possibility that the president and the FCC could authorize other new systems if they were in the national interest. Because of the company's monopoly position, the FCC instructed Comsat to make its circuits available to all American carriers, and until 1982, forbade it from providing direct domestic service. The legislation also directed Comsat to negotiate with other governments to set up the single global system that became Intelsat.

Intelsat was established in 1964 by an interim agreement of eleven members; until 1979 it was managed by Comsat. Its growth over the years has been impressive. Technological innovation made it possible for circuit capacity for the Atlantic region to rise an average of 35 percent a year from 1965 to 1982, even as rates were reduced a dozen times in twenty years. As of mid-1987 the consortium had 109 members, served by sixteen satellites in geosynchronous orbit above the Atlantic, Pacific, and Indian Ocean regions. Most of the traffic it carries is international, but about 20 percent consists of domestic service within twenty-six countries.

The enterprise is owned and funded by its members in proportion to their share of total Intelsat traffic; Comsat's current share is 23 percent. The United States is even stronger than this because it is the major provider and recipient of Intelsat services. Roughly half of all Intelsat traffic originates or terminates in the United States. Only the U.S. traffic is dense enough to attract significant investment and expansion by a competitor, and only U.S. routes provide major opportunities for driving down unit costs per message through economies of scale.

Intelsat remains overwhelmingly dependent on phone traffic and on the transatlantic market for its prosperity. As Table 5–1 shows, about two-thirds of its circuits serve the Atlantic region. In 1983 about 82 percent of the half-circuits that Comsat rented from Intelsat served the Atlantic region. Any policy change that undercut the Comsat-Intelsat monopoly for service between the United States and Europe will significantly alter the market as a whole.

Cracks in the Dike

Despite Intelsat's rapid growth, it ran into a number of problems. Intelsat I had 240 circuits and one TV channel while Intelsat V has 12,000 circuits and two channels. Intelsat VI "satellites will be able to send simultaneously at least 120,000 telephone calls, or, in an all video mode, over 200 television

Table 5–1. Comparison of Submarine Cable and Intelsat Capacity, 1965–1982 (number of circuits).

Year	Cable[a]	Intelsat[b]	Total	% of All Intelsat[c]
1965	2,006	240	2,246	100.0
1968	3,454	1,513	4,967	62.5
1971	9,499	6,277	15,776	59.9
1972	10,579	10,133	20,712	63.3
1976	24,389	13,054	37,443	65.3
1979	38,089	16,442	54,531	64.5
1982	44,509	42,253	86,762	66.0

Source: Dale N. Hatfield Associates, *Issues in International Telecommunications Pricing and Demand*, report prepared for the Orion Satellite Corporation, November 27, 1984, p. 23.

a. Systems of at least 500 miles in length.

b. Estimated.

c. Percentage of all Intelsat circuits.

channels, or 3 billion bits of information per second."[5] However, the capacity of undersea cable also grew rapidly. Together, the growth of satellite and cable made surplus capacity one of Intelsat's chief economic problems. Even though the consortium carries approximately two-thirds of all transoceanic telecommunications traffic, its circuit utilization rate averaged only 49.7 percent for 1981–1983 after a new transatlantic telephone cable began operation and world recession slowed demand growth.

Critics attribute this surplus capacity in part to Intelsat's technological preferences. The consortium preferred to launch the high-capacity satellites permitted by new technology, even if the added capacity overshoots the level of current demand. Moreover, Intelsat used low-powered satellites, which required large, expensive earth stations and local phone connections, which (according to both Intelsat and Orion) account for 90 percent of the cost of transatlantic calls. Intelsat's design, in other words, hindered direct service to customer premises, a major new market. (Intelsat plans to alter its design somewhat in the future.)

A second Intelsat problem involves the incentives to users to bypass it. Until the mid-1980s Intelsat charged users the same amount for each voice channel. If a user engineered a line to provide several channels, then the user paid for each one. Thus users had no incentive to use lines provided by Intelsat efficiently. In addition, the consortium "rate averages" a given series across high- and low-volume users, holding down rates for low-volume developing countries by making major industrial countries pay more. Some critics have questioned the value of the subsidy to the beneficiaries. Many of the low-traffic countries that are subsidized are not poor. Moreover, critics say, the major factor that causes costs to vary among users is the cost of on-the-ground equipment. Intelsat's reliance on large earth stations (and its pricing of services to low-capacity stations) makes it uneconomic for the consortium to serve many small users in developing countries, one of the system's original intended markets.

In any event, the subsidy gives many of Intelsat's larger user-members a financial incentive to bypass the global system and operate their own alternative facilities. This incentive was

119

strongest for services connecting high-volume users, where Intelsat's charges were higher than its true costs. A further incentive for bypass, according to critics, was that Intelsat did not offer "customized" services, such as high-speed data transmission and sophisticated video transmission such as teleconferencing, that primarily serve the internal needs of large organizations. These customers could profit from the efficiencies of a network that serves specific sites instead of linking all conceivable locations.

To fend off bypass efforts by member countries or others, Article XIV(d) of the Intelsat agreement permits member countries to operate other satellites for "international public telecommunications services" only if they are technically compatible with Intelsat and do it no "significant economic harm." Through 1984 the Intelsat Board of Governors had approved only five satellite systems outside of Intelsat. They are the Arabian Satellite Communications Organization (Arabsat), the European Communications System (ECS), the Palapa system (which serves Indonesia and some of its neighbors), the hookup of the Soviet Intersputnik system with Algeria, and transmission from U.S. domestic satellites to Canada and Bermuda.

Intelsat's own consultants concede that the criteria used to assess "significant economic harm" is muddled. For example, the decision approving the European Communications System (also known as Eutelsat) apparently held that the system would not harm Intelsat because Europe's PTT administrations declared that they would not use satellites at all if they could not put up their own system! But Intelsat officials argue that the European case involves relatively small flows of traffic. To try to discourage bypass requests, Intelsat started to favor a stricter assessment of significant harm based on the cumulative impact of applications. Intelsat successfully discouraged, for example, Indonesia's plan to use its Palapa-B satellite to form a regional satellite news system.

The incentives to bypass have multiplied. Many countries are interested in launching alternative satellite systems. France's Telecom system is positioned to serve France and the French Caribbean and could be modified to link the United States and eastern Canada (including Quebec). Iberoamerican proposes to link Spain with Latin America. In addition, Luxembourg and Ireland have discussed an Atlantic system and Sweden, a Scandinavian system. More recently the EC has decided to allow new satellite competitors on a case-by-case basis. Finally, Japanese companies are studying a Pacific Basin configuration.

Until 1983 Intelsat strategy was to accommodate regional satellite systems that did not impinge on the U.S. market. Everything else was secondary. Regulating the U.S. market set the terms for competing around the world. If Intelsat could limit entry to the United States, its future was reasonably secure.

Orion Rising

On March 11, 1983, a new firm, Orion Satellite Corporation, petitioned the FCC for permission to launch a transatlantic satellite service. The FCC took the highly unusual step of using ITU channels to advance publish the request of Orion for an orbital slot well situated to serve the East Coast of the United States and Western Europe.[6] Orion proposed to establish a service aimed at a particular market niche: providing "customized" services to private customers that had enormous flows of communications within their own organizations. Individual users would buy or lease transponders from Orion and then route traffic over Orion's satellites to their own receiving facilities. The new enterprise would be a global communications condominium. It would not offer public switched service, which would permit subscribers to call other unrelated subscribers. (The telephone system is the model of such switched service.) Applications from four other companies quickly followed Orion's.

Orion was a small company. Its co-founders were veterans of U.S. executive branch and congressional policymaking on telecommunications. No one knew whether it had the financial resources to launch a satellite. It had no research laboratories or major customers that an outsider could easily identify. But the United States was accustomed to small entrepreneurs in big

121

technological markets, so many in Washington gave Orion the benefit of the doubt.

In any event, Orion's strategy for achieving liberalization of competition in international markets was a textbook example of three cardinal principles of the regulatory game in the United States. First, a push for international deregulation acquires maximum political impetus if it immediately follows the deregulation of a domestic market. Second, legislators would rather signal their intent and leave the initiation of new policies to the executive branch than make the hard regulatory choices themselves. Third, legislators prefer incremental deregulation to abrupt change. Usually, congressional intervention works to limit the scope of the immediate decisions, tailor reform to attack scapegoats, and leave ambiguous the ultimate changes spawned by the immediate choice.

Assaults on regulation in the international market are generally precipitated by deregulation in domestic markets. After all, if competition is beneficial at home, why should global monopoly be encouraged? Major customers hope to extend the efficiencies gained at home to their international operations, and domestic producers often are eager to extend the gains or mitigate the losses from new competition at home by seeking opportunities abroad. With the deregulation of domestic telecommunications underway, it was therefore not surprising that a number of bills to deregulate the international telecommunications markets were introduced in Congress in 1983. The time was right for "international reform."

But, favorable sentiment does not produce legislative action, and the second element of Orion's strategy took advantage of this fact. Congress hates being blamed for foreign policy failures, in part because they produce devastating press. So on regulatory issues that have big international implications, lawmakers prefer to retire prudently from the battlefront. Members of key subcommittees will introduce legislation with no intention of pushing it to passage, their purpose being to signal their preferences to regulators and to win political support from interested parties. The burden for concrete action, however, is on the executive branch. (When it passes any legislation, Congress prefers to do it as a response to executive branch initiatives. Congress can then cast itself in the role of tempering or moderating the White House's proposals.)

Regulatory reform is thus most likely when the White House favors it and regulatory agencies have the power to initiate it on their own. Again, Orion correctly recognized that these factors favored its chances. Its sole miscalculation concerned the degree to which Congress would act to temper the scope of deregulation.

The third element of the strategy—be incremental—was reflected in Orion's determination to keep the decision narrowly focused. Implicitly, Orion characterized its challenge as applying competitive discipline to an outdated, inept middleman, Comsat, while simultaneously stimulating selective housecleaning at Intelsat. Orion argued that it would serve a vigorous but narrow market that stood largely untapped by the Intelsat system and that its application conformed perfectly to the Intelsat agreement.

Orion's original application tiptoed around Article XIV(d)'s requirement that new satellite systems be coordinated with Intelsat by claiming that Orion intended to offer not "public" but rather "specialized" communications as defined under Article XIV(e). In other words, Orion's clients would not link their internal communications systems to public phone facilities. Orion would therefore be serving a market not covered under Article XIV(d). Accordingly, though requiring it to engage in technical coordination with Intelsat would be acceptable, it should not have to meet the noninjury test.

For good measure, however, in an argument reminiscent of the original MCI attack on AT&T's long-distance monopoly, Orion also argued that it would create a new market, not divert traffic from the old one. Orion's individual users could configure their circuits to their special needs without using local phone networks. Because Orion would be tapping a market not available to Intelsat, it would not cause "significant harm." Orion carefully disassociated itself from the request of a subsequent applicant, International Satellites, Inc., for permission to enter the market for switched international calls from AT&T.

Orion had every reason to be optimistic. Congress and the executive branch were sending all the right signals. The FCC deregulated the domestic satellite market in 1970. In 1981 it allowed U.S. domestic satellites to serve Canada and Bermuda under special circumstances. That same year Congress made the FCC responsible for promoting competition in the international record carrier (telex and telegram) business. In 1982 the FCC ruled that AT&T and the traditional international record carriers could compete in each others' markets. Then, in 1983, the House and Senate Commerce committees both reported favorably on bills for more sweeping deregulation of international satellite communications.

These bills spurred on reformers in the executive branch. In 1984 the FCC revoked a longstanding rule guaranteeing 50 percent ownership of all U.S. ground stations. And congressional leaders began criticizing the FCC's "proportional loading rule," which forces common carriers to balance their use of international cable and satellite facilities. If, as seems likely, the rule is phased out, the opening of three new transatlantic fiber optic cables between 1988 and the early 1990s will add enormous transmission capacity for both voice and data and will ensure a competitive scramble between satellites and cable systems. Amid this groundswell, the petition of Orion and those that followed it merely seemed to ask the FCC to go one tiny step further.

Comsat and Intelsat Respond

Comsat and Intelsat counterattacked in a big way; Intelsat alone spent $2 million on lobbying in 1984. Their case against Orion rested on four main grounds. It has since become the standard brief against new competition.

First, Intelsat and Comsat questioned the credibility of the potential competitors. They speculated that most would-be entrants would never manage to launch a satellite even if they won government approval. Most have neither the $250 million needed to launch a system, nor the technical expertise to attract the money.[7]

Second, Intelsat insisted that the new system would constitute public telecommunications, not a private system as Orion contended, and would therefore require coordination to avoid economic damage to Intelsat. Orion's distinction between private and public services may conform to U.S. domestic law, but in the international arena *any* sale of commercial services is considered public. Moreover, modern technology further blurs any practical distinction between public and private communications. Large corporations use private branch exchanges (PBXs) as switchboards. A PBX in Citibank's New York offices could, for example, take an incoming call from one of the bank's European branches over a leased Orion satellite circuit and switch it onto the local phone system in order to terminate the call at a customer's factory in Buffalo. Regulators may try to forbid such "leaking" from private circuits to the public system, but PBX technology makes evasion easy. Orion's presence in the market would inevitably tempt major users to try it.

Third, Intelsat contended that it would suffer significant economic injury from Orion and its colleagues. The demand for customized satellite communications is smaller than Orion suggests, and adequate facilities are already available. Data traffic and teleconferencing would not be enough to sustain new entrants, which would siphon off phone and video business from Intelsat. Even the loss of corporations' internal phone calls would be costly, considering that Intelsat's unused capacity averaged 30 to 50 percent in 1981–83 (depending on when and how it is measured). Intelsat's consultants concluded that if the consortium lost its monopoly, the costs for using satellites would rise by 15–36 percent.

Finally, and most decisively, Intelsat and Comsat claimed that, as offspring of U.S. diplomacy, they deserved diplomatic support. The Intelsat agreement calls for a single commercial system. Orion's entry would change the rules of the game unilaterally. It would render untenable the service-by-service average rates that benefit (by Intelsat's calculations) some sixty other countries and it would threaten enormous markups that most PTTs, especially those in developing countries, now charge for use of Intelsat's services. Indeed, Intelsat's management rallied a unanimous vote opposing the Orion initiative at the October 1983 meeting of the Assembly of Parties in Washington, triggering concern within the U.S. foreign policy establishment.

On top of all this, Intelsat's defenders said, foreign PTTs would refuse to accept service from Orion and the others, so that the new entrants would call on the State Department for help. This would draw the United States into contentious and ultimately fruitless international economic negotiations. When several U.S. carriers negotiate with a single foreign national phone monopoly, the monopoly would have the better bargaining position. It could play the U.S. carriers off against one another to extract maximum benefits for itself. In the end, deregulation would simply reshuffle benefits within the satellite communications business without aiding the consumer.

Yet Orion's case with the U.S. government remained politically strong. The U.S. government need go no further in helping the new entrants than the usual representations it makes for U.S. businesses operating abroad. Also, Intelsat convinced no one that a decision to license Orion would in itself destroy the existing system. Even Comsat admitted that at most one or two new transatlantic satellite systems are ever likely to be launched. If any party suffered serious losses from that, it would be Comsat; and Comsat is a U.S. problem, not an international one.

Interestingly, many of the parties that might be expected to speak out about the situation remained mostly in the background. AT&T only offered the opinion that the new satellite systems were acceptable as long as they did not lead to new requirements for carriers concerning proportional loading on satellites. Actually, AT&T was far more interested in eroding the Comsat monopoly but let others carry the initiative. Meanwhile, the satellite makers had to be very careful because of their sales to Intelsat and some of the foreign governments supporting Intelsat. Hughes offered public statements of support for Intelsat but it was not a prominent actor. RCA, a firm with little Intelsat business and a design for high-power satellites for a time proposed its own satellite system. It quietly supported the new entrants.

126

But the real lesson here was that the major players were content to let the immediate protagonists struggle. Their lassitude indicated to regulators that they had the freedom to play out the logic of the case.

By early 1985 Intelsat conceded political defeat on the separate satellite issue. It turned its attention to minimizing the damage by several means.

First, it wanted the United States to sponsor an amendment to the Intelsat agreement that would give the consortium the discretion to charge different prices for the same service instead of rate averaging. Intelsat argued that only the thorough rate reorganization that such an amendment would permit, would allow it to compete effectively. In the meantime, the consortium began marketing its Intelsat Business Service, which catered to the market targeted by Orion. (Ironically, the commercial success of this venture was limited by the refusal of some European PTTs to accept the idea of a private communications service for large users, especially one that required them to invest in new types of earth stations.)[8]

Second, Intelsat emphasized that Orion would have the technical ability to carry public switched calls as well as private traffic. The consortium's objective in raising this issue was to stiffen political and regulatory resolve against letting Orion carry switched service at a later date.

Third, Intelsat quietly distanced itself from Comsat. It supported the FCC decision to strip Comsat of its guaranteed equity in earth stations. It also hinted that it favored authorizing direct access to its system by other carriers that wish to bypass Comsat. After all, the United Kingdom already allowed two companies direct access to Intelsat: British Telecom and its officially designated competitor, Mercury.

Comsat, for its part, had a dramatic response in reserve. On September 29, 1986, it announced that it would merge with Contel, a large holding company for domestic telecommunications carriers and equipment lines in the United States. Contel's subsidiary, American Satellites, was already in the domestic satellite communications business.[9] Although the merger was ultimately called off, it raised the possibility that Comsat or another new venture might eventually seek authorization to launch its own satellites to compete against Intelsat (if Comsat is stripped of its present monopoly on direct access, a prospect made more likely by the proposed merger). Already, Comsat International, which was created during the turmoil over Orion, plans to lease satellite *and* cable circuits in the Atlantic and Pacific to deliver communications services for its clients.

Despite the growing rift between Comsat and Intelsat — a rift that played right into Orion's hands — the joint lobbying effort to defend the current system continues. Comsat and Intelsat have tried two tactics in this lobbying war: exploiting turf fights within the executive branch and appealing to sympathetic congressional committees.

Who's in Charge?

Official Washington grappled with the Orion application for more than two years. As often happens in Washington, agencies that have traditionally battled for control over major parts of telecommunications policy (in this case from the commerce and state departments) managed to find particular items to dispute. But all sides favored freer entry into the market. The major issue was whether Intelsat should be allowed to use aggressive commercial countermeasures to retaliate against new entrants, and specifically whether Intelsat's charter should be amended to allow it more flexibility in cutting prices to meet the competitive challenge. The Commerce Department's National Telecommunications and Information Administration (NTIA) opposed restraining Intelsat's fair competitive response. Citing lessons learned in the deregulation of the domestic U.S. telephone market, it argued that the success of competitors was less important than the efficiency of pricing and service.

The State Department maintained that Intelsat's current operating authority already gives it enough pricing flexibility. For example, State argued, when Intelsat leases circuits to new U.S. customers it routinely defines the new service in such a way that no developing country can qualify, thus eliminating the need for a subsidy. In fact, State contended, the consortium could repackage its older services in a similar manner to end subsidies if it wanted. State feared that what Intelsat really wanted to do with new pricing flexibility was to funnel cross-subsidies to those services that compete with Orion.

The State Department has worried that for the United States to sponsor flexible pricing might rally foreign opinion against Orion, since the effect of such flexibility would be to end subsidies currently paid by U.S. consumers. The weighted voting system used by Intelsat's Board of Governors gives the United States a good opportunity to block an adverse finding by the board regarding the Article XIV(d) consultations concerning Orion. But sponsorship of a pricing amendment (even though Intelsat's management pledged to cooperate with such an initiative) might provoke the often somnolent Assembly of Parties, which allots one vote to each member, to take adverse action on the Orion consultation decision.

On November 28, 1984, President Reagan determined "that separate international communication systems are required in the national interest," but promised that the United States would "consult [that is, coordinate] with Intelsat regarding such separate systems as are authorized by the Federal Communications Commission." On January 4, 1985, the FCC began to evaluate the new applicants.

Secretary of State George Shultz and the late Secretary of Commerce Malcolm Baldrige carefully highlighted their points of agreement, while downplaying contentious issues, in a letter to FCC Chairman Mark Fowler sent at the time of Reagan's decision, and then in a "white paper" of February 1985. First, they said, the FCC should authorize new international satellite facilities only for "customized" services, not for services involving the public switched network. The white paper acknowledged that some illegal "leaking" from private to switched service might occur but argued that a volume sufficient to harm Intelsat would be detectable and subject to correction. Second, permission to enter should be contingent on the entrant's first gaining authorization for service in at least one foreign country and the subsequent completion of the Intelsat consultation process under

Article XIV(d). (However, the Intelsat decision on coordination would *not* bind the United States.) Third, the FCC should consider allowing U.S. commercial users and carriers to bypass Comsat on customized services and have direct cost-based access to Intelsat. Finally, the United States reaffirmed its commitment to Intelsat.

The political process handled these issues in ways closely conforming to the strategic principles that Orion recognized when it started the ball rolling. In particular, Congress underscored its support for executive branch's push for "incremental" and "evolutionary" change, but now that serious choices are at hand, it is retreating to its oversight role.[10] Intelsat's congressional champion, Representative Don Bonker (D., Washington), introduced a rider to the State Department's budget in the spring of 1985 providing, *inter alia*, that Intelsat's decisions on coordination be binding on the United States and that State be required to sponsor an amendment to the Intelsat agreement to authorize route-by-route pricing. After intense bargaining Congress ultimately endorsed increased competition, deleted the binding character of Intelsat's decision on coordination, and left State with latitude concerning its sponsorship of an Intelsat amendment on pricing. However, it also required that any other country authorizing a new satellite system to the United States had to honor the restrictions set in the white paper discussed above. It also gave Congress a last chance to act by requiring State to respond to any negative Intelsat vote by informing Congress on how it planned to limit the diplomatic damage at least sixty days before sending its final approval to the FCC.

The FCC's final decision appeared to rest on the idea that protecting the core of the Intelsat market was a U.S. commitment, and as a result of this commitment plus the growing commercial appeal of fiber optic cables, the number of new satellite entrants would be small. Therefore, it allowed for great leniency in what the satellite firms could offer to customers. Although customers had to take out one year leases at a minimum, they could rent or lease only part of a circuit; moreover, shared use among unrelated users was approved and the satellite firms could offer virtually any type of service (including occasional television broadcasting) that did not connect to a public switched network.

Ironically, the FCC temporarily withheld approval of the Orion application (because it wanted more financial data) while granting those for three other firms. Orion was subsequently given its preliminary approval.

After the first flurry, the greatest action was in areas where Intelsat's service is weakest. Amstar (a domestic U.S. satellite corporation) and Jamaica proposed Teleport International (backed by Nippon Telegraph and Telephone of Japan) for a private line business service between the United States and Montego Bay, Jamaica. Western Union nominated its domestic Westar satellite to provide service among Caribbean countries. Meanwhile, the Swedish government proposed a project for a private satellite communications system to link Sweden with the subsidiaries of Swedish corporations throughout the developing world. (The satellites would not be in geosynchronous orbit so a continuous communications link would not be possible.) And, several satellite ventures (such as TRT's proposed PacStar system which was based and co-owned by the Government of Papua New Guinea) were stirring in Asia.[11]

Yet, as of October 1987, only two systems, the Jamaican Teleport project (involving the United States) and PanAmSat, have won the approval of a foreign government (Peru) to launch operations to the United States. The more significant project was PanAmSat. PanAmSat's chief U.S. client appeared to be the Hispanic Television Network, a commercial Spanish language programming group operating out of Florida, which has a huge comparative advantage in such areas as MTV-style productions for the Spanish-speaking population of the world.

PanAmSat's experience with coordination with Intelsat raised many questions about U.S. strategy that the earlier policy pronouncements ducked. The diplomatic bargaining about coordination was fierce. Each side accused the other of dirty tricks. The United States supported PanAmSat in arguing that the company only had to coordinate with Intelsat concerning the five transponders dedicated to Latin America (nineteen other transponders were for domestic Latin American service and six for

131

European service that is not yet scheduled for commissioning). Intelsat successfully argued that it could not coordinate until plans for the transponders potentially earmarked for Europe were clearer.[12] Moreover, Intelsat suspected that the FCC and some others in the U.S. government were interested in pulling the United States out of Intelsat.

Meanwhile, Congress, able to play its favorite role of concerned oversight, held hearings to criticize U.S. diplomats for a failure to handle the case better. At the same time, Intelsat uncovered a scandal involving its director general, Richard Colino, that led to his firing. This switch may have refocused the U.S. government on its broader interests on providing leadership in Intelsat, and Intelsat's need for the cooperation of the United States in handling the Colino scandal. Certainly there were rumors that the United States promised many governments to be more understanding of Intelsat if (as happened) an American who was more sympathetic to some competition was chosen as the new director general. But the compromise reached by the Intelsat Board meeting of December 1986 was broadly consistent with many insiders' expectations prior to the scandal. It authorized PanAmSat to use five transponders to Peru for five years with a possible five to ten-year extension. The Assembly ratified the agreement in 1987. At the same time, Intelsat authorized the Jamaican Teleport project.[13]

Winners and Losers

In the end, the balancing of political interest in Washington led to a surprising outcome. Both Intelsat and Orion won, while Comsat lost. The United States technically upheld the Intelsat agreement. It barred new entrants from providing international switched service and thereby protected most of Intelsat's market. It will also support the flexibility Intelsat needs in order to become a more effective competitor. So Intelsat should not fare too badly in practice. (Indeed, PanAmSat was complaining that Intelsat was preempting competition by predatory pricing.)

More important, the United States recommitted itself in principle to the welfare of Intelsat during the 1980s. In many ways Intelsat successfully positioned itself as the international counterpart to the Bell operating companies under domestic regulation. When faced with the threat of bypass, the operating companies successfully focused local politicians' attention on the danger that bypass would lead to higher rates for ordinary local households. They managed to persuade those lawmakers that bolstering local telephone company revenues was the best way to reduce price hikes for the households. Intelsat likewise made itself into the ostensible champion of the many countries of the third world and thus forced Orion's advocates to condition their victory on Intelsat's protection during the remainder of the 1980s. If Intelsat runs into trouble in the next few years, it will have substantial political leverage with which to coax regulators into making quiet adjustments to ease its pains. It also received a ready made rationale for revising its tariffed offerings so as to woo large users with discounted digital circuits and other innovative offerings.[14]

Comsat's fate is not so well assured. If Intelsat gradually withdraws its close support, Comsat will have no major constituency left. Comsat's leadership has great hopes for its new commercial ventures in the U.S. domestic market. But its dramatic plans for a merger with Contel, a major independent phone company in the United States, died when Contel withdrew. Contel reportedly was in part discouraged because the executive branch and Congress were expressing doubts about letting Comsat retain even its reduced role with Intelsat if the merger progressed. As a result, Comsat will surely have to consider a more aggressive strategy for competing (however subtly) against Intelsat. For example, it recently announced plans to buy an ownership share of TAT-8, a new international cable facility.[15]

The U.S. commitment to alternative satellite systems without harming Intelsat has important implications for other facilities systems. For one, it will encourage proposals for the thinner, lower traffic routes and ones that are immediately in the U.S. neighborhood. (For example, in 1987 AT&T proposed private line satellite services to the Caribbean using its domestic Telstar system.) For another, the emphasis on new services will put a premium on finding ways to package basic services in ways that fit the bill of new offerings. A very attractive option is to formulate large users into special groups that request a comprehensive package of services. This is precisely what happened when TRT's PacStar project and Aeronautical Radio Inc. (ARINC), a consortium of fourteen major airlines, proposed the AVSAT system of four to six satellites with earth stations in the United States and Asia (and Europe later). It would deliver dedicated or leased space segment capacity for digital voice and data for everything from aircraft communications to reservation systems to phone services for in-flight passengers.[16]

New competitors in satellites are likely to get into the major U.S. routes to Europe and Asia only at a later date, after establishing supporters among governments on their "thin routes." The delay will leave a window open where only fiber optic cables are viable competitors for Intelsat on the heavy traffic routes. Given their cost advantages and attractions to major carriers (AT&T supplied half of Comsat's revenues in 1983 yet owns a large share of the future TAT 8 and TAT 9 cables) fiber optics will surely dominate the major international routes. But providing enough traffic to make these large capacity systems viable will be difficult.

There is likely to be a faster development of surplus capacity in transmission facilities if fiber optics dominate because each cable has a huge capacity and there is some incentive to lay excess capacity in order to preempt potential rivals. For example, Cable & Wireless and Tel Optik (a small U.S. firm which, like Orion, was led by former government insiders) announced plans for PTAT 1 and 2 as privately owned transatlantic fiber optic cables. NYNEX later bought out Tel Optik, thus marking the potential entry of regional Bell operating companies into facilities services internationally.[17] Many observers see TAT 9 as a preemptive effort to discourage PTAT 1.[18] Certainly, TAT 8 and TAT 9 plus PTAT 1 would raise the number of undersea circuits from 14,000 (voice equivalent circuits) to a minimum of 210,000. Yet total demand (including satellites) is predicted to be only 80,000 circuits by 1990 unless substantial cost cutting triggers the demand for new enhanced services.[19] This suggests greater pressure on prices in the Atlantic. As the next section indicates, there will be similar pressures in the Pacific.

More important, there are many policy questions about how to leverage this new capacity for the purpose of advancing competition in international markets. Chapter 4 noted that indefeasible rights of use are one important question. How vigorously will the United States support entry by American satellite carriers into other countries? What will these proceedings imply for entry by foreign satellite systems into those countries? Will the United States eventually decide to grant U.S. entry to new, foreign common carriers—say, a French satellite system—and if so will it demand strict reciprocity for American carriers? And how will it handle the question of proportional loading between satellites and cable?

The most closely analogous case of this sort before Orion was the U.S. effort to secure increased competition in the North Atlantic airline market. Breaching united European opposition, however, required a combination of vigorous bilateral diplomacy and the threat of withdrawing U.S. antitrust immunity from the International Air Transport Association (IATA). And although Intelsat's defenders have argued that the United States wasted its diplomatic energy in this case, the results have benefited transatlantic air travelers.

JAPAN: REFORM AND INTERNATIONAL CHANGE

The uninhibited U.S. spree with deregulation may only be symptomatic of a political system given to economic excesses, but such a conclusion is not self-evident because that most disciplined of economic-political systems, Japan, is also experimenting with domestic and international deregulation. And, as in the United States, the opening of competition in services brings enormous pressure for experimentation with facilities.[20]

Briefly, a neat intersection of international trade politics involving the United States and Japanese domestic industrial politics led to the Japanese experiment with greater competition in telecommunications. For a decade, the United States has believed that it possessed a comparative advantage relative to Japan on telecommunications equipment. Washington argued that only the Nippon Telegraph and Telephone's (NTT) restrictive procurement policies, which favored four principal Japanese suppliers (NEC, Fujitsu, Hitachi, and Oki), and the restrictive conditions on the sale and attachment of customer premises equipment to the public network stopped the United States from selling vigorously in the Japanese market. Subsequently, the United States identified the ability to sell value-added and information services as another priority for the U.S. telecommunications and computer industries in Japan.[21]

The U.S. pressure, which eventually won Presidential attention and backing, created a constituency for change in Japan among those most worried about the relationship with the United States. This included the Ministry of Foreign Affairs (MOFA) (never a prime player on industrial policy), the Ministry of International Trade and Industry (MITI), which runs foreign trade policy, and Prime Minister Nakasone himself. This coalition forced progressively stronger Japanese commitments to opening the procurement policies of NTT to the United States. But this alone would not have produced deregulation.

The politics of industrial policy had to join foreign trade politics. On this front two separate movements joined in a domestic campaign for liberalization. One was directly tied to telecommunications; the other was a broader effort to redefine the role of the state and public enterprises in Japan. Both were rooted in the heart of the Japanese business community, the Keidenran, not in consumer, labor, or other "outsider" groups.

The marriage of telecommunications and computers had increasingly made NTT a prime backer of critical public research support for microelectronics, computers, and telecommunications. (It is important to realize that Japanese funds for these activities are not large by U.S. standards.) And NTT's cozy relationship with its family of suppliers meant that a large

136

number of Japanese firms were being cut out of some research projects, and, more vitally, excluded from large markets for their electronic goods. Mitsubishi, Sony, Toshiba, Matsushita, and other eminent firms were not family members. These firms wanted a chance to compete in the telecommunications markets and a research system that was more supportive of their needs. They also wanted a chance to experiment with new ways to let telecommunications services supplement their thrusts in the computer market. For them, the coming of competition in telecommunications opened markets at home and new techniques for advancing their technology.[22]

Just as this discontent was rising, a split between MITI and the Ministry of Posts and Telecommunications (MPT) became prominent. One important boost for MITI action came, as in other countries, from large users. The evidence gathered by one set of foreign consultants to a major Japanese automobile firm was that the efforts of large users in Japan to obtain more attractive terms for leased lines yielded this auto firm a cost savings equal to 1.5 percent of its cost of sales, a substantial figure. At the time, large users calculated that the introduction of more competition would yield at least an additional 20 percent savings in circuit costs.[23]

A second traditional and powerful clientele for MITI were the Japanese trading companies. At this stage in Japanese development the trading companies were increasingly being bypassed by their own "families" and were looking for new lines of business. Mitsubishi Trading and C. Itoh, for example, decided to become information (and hence communications) companies as part of their effort to forge a new identity. For example, C. Itoh formally created its Information Systems and Technology Committee in August 1983, when it was certain that communications competition would occur. It had been working on the issue for some time.[24]

Even more critically, MITI wanted to use telecommunications as an instrument to boost overall Japanese competitiveness in microelectronics computers. It thought that telecommunications had to be a sacrificial lamb to quiet the United States and, more fundamentally, it considered a faster rate of innovation and

137

much lower prices in telecommunications services to be indispensable to innovation in electronics and the rationalization of the growing Japanese manufacturing and business operations overseas. Thus, it was willing to accept more competition in telecommunications—especially since it would confirm its supremacy over computers.[25]

MPT resented MITI's intrusion into its traditionally sleepy bureaucratic domain. It was a deceivingly dangerous foe because it was a traditional career stop for powerful politicians, and is especially associated with powerful former Prime Minister Tanaka. Moreover, it had attracted some bright new talent who articulated a new ideology for Japan that combined more flexible regulation with another state-sponsored campaign for the creation of a comprehensive "information society." Ironically, this notion supported NTT's aspirations to build an integrated services digital network (called an information network system, or INS) on the model of the Bundespost. But MPT used the idea for arguing that it had to become a much more powerful overseer of NTT than it had in the past, particularly if there was to be more competition.[26]

The other domestic movement for competition was aimed more broadly at the role of the state in the Japanese economy. Japanese companies had become vociferous in arguing that there was an urgent need for more flexibility in the regulation of the economy and greater prudence in public spending. The attack on regulation can be seen as part of the receding support for MITI's guidance of an economy that is increasingly diverse in its competitive interests.

The criticism of the budget deficit, which was much steeper proportionately than in the United States, reflected a straightforward concern that such a deficit could only drive up taxes or draw unduly on Japan's large stock of national savings. In short, Japanese business wanted a rollback of government spending. And a prime target of their ire was the huge deficits being run up by such government corporations as those that ran the railroads and highways. While NTT (and its international counterpart, KDD) made money, critics of NTT argued that expenditures were rising faster than revenues, and the $125 billion spending program for its INS program threatened to make NTT a major financial burden in the future.[27]

The resolution of foreign confrontation and domestic intrigue was a major reform of the Japanese telecommunications system. No one doubts that a rejuvenated MPT will play an active role in supervising the market. Nor should one miss the fundamental fact noted by the Berkeley Roundtable on the International Economy: Deregulation is part of a broader government effort to introduce innovation in equipment and services. This effort includes many interventionist programs, especially to serve medium-sized to small users in innovative ways. But strong pressure from the United States on trade issues at a critical juncture in 1984–1985 ensured that the rules governing customer premises equipment and enhanced services became much more liberal than the early MPT drafts on liberalization of competition suggested.

The structure of the domestic marketplace will feature several new competitors in domestic, basic facilities and communications services with NTT. Four of these competitors have been licensed to provide domestic, terrestrial service. Japan Telecom Ltd, which is 36 percent owned by the Japanese National Railway, began operation in August 1986. It used the national railway's bullet train road bed to lay an optical fiber cable between Osaka and Tokyo. Kyocera, the ceramics group, has a 28 percent share in Daini Denshin Denwa (Daini Denden), which began operations in October 1986. Sony and Mitsubishi are also among its owners. Daini Denden serves the Osaka-Tokyo corridor with a microwave network and is expected to be the strongest of the long distance competitors. Teleway Japan system, which began operations in November 1986, is based on fiber optic cables run along the Japanese Highway Authority's motorways. The Japan Highway Authority and Toyota Motors are both 6 percent shareholders. Each of these new ventures is aiming for a 5–8 percent share of the lucrative Osaka-Tokyo long-distance market, but informed estimates suggest that these companies will capture about 5 percent of the long-distance market for the prime Japanese metropolitan region by 1990. In contrast, Tokyo Telecommunications Network, 48.5 percent owned by Tokyo

Electric Power, has so far offered service only as a backup to NTT and only in Tokyo Electric Power's operating area around Tokyo.[28] However, TTN could emerge as an important player.

None of these Type I carriers can be more than 33 percent owned by foreign interests, and Japanese companies have not been overly enthusiastic about complicating their domestic politics by seeking such links. Japan Telecom Ltd rejected an investment offer from Cable & Wireless. Only the new satellite networks (discussed later) have foreign ownership.

As of September 1987 all three of the long-distance competitors were offering domestic long-distance services between Tokyo and Osaka for about 25 percent less than NTT for comparable service. MPT forced all three new competitors to offer their services at the same price.[29] Nonetheless, Daini Denden, which reportedly had been willing to offer much deeper discounts, appears to have signed up more customers than the other two new long-distance competitors combined. Furthermore, NTT has an incentive to allow its competitors some success in order to ensure that the Diet does not decide to break it into pieces as happened to AT&T.

There are two unique features of the Japanese formula for Type I carriers. First, MPT continues to regulate total capacity in the market, and thus the number of entrants. Second, MPT encourages the formation of consortiums among other common carriers that represent a mix of specialized interests, including electronics firms, service firms, and sophisticated users. This may encourage more efficient bargaining about the design of the network of the future and about the transfer of know how among the participants.

The enhanced services market will be even more competitive than basic services. There are presently about 300 Type II carriers, and their numbers are expected to grow. (MITI expects information service exports to grow from 4.8 billion yen in 1984 to 1,800 billion yen by the year 2000. In the same period information service imports are expected to rise from 23.2 billion yen to 3,000 billion yen. The average annual rate of growth of information services is expected to average 13.3 percent for the rest of the century.)[30] Resale of leased circuits will be permissible, and these networks may even offer voice services as long as they are combined with other service offerings. Japanese regulators even hint that they may adopt some equivalent to the FCC's open network architecture and comparably efficient interconnection to ensure that network architecture is fully open to all competitors.[31] Indeed, MPT refused to accept the first tariff proposal by NTT on its version of an integrated services digital network because it did not conform closely enough to international standards.

Most significantly, networks that lease transmission and switching facilities, rather than own them, may be majority owned by foreign firms. Given the interest of Japanese firms in experimenting with options for global computer and marketing strategies, foreign firms (especially IBM and AT&T) are playing major roles as leaders of consortiums with major Japanese partners. IBM, much to the dismay of the Japanese computer industry, has even signed an agreement with NTT to look into establishing a value-added network with NTT using IBM's SNA standards.

As in the United States, domestic deregulation cannot be the stopping point for change. For example, Japanese firms soon formed joint ventures with U.S. companies to open their own value-added networks in the United States. Concomitantly, MPT worked with the U.S. government to bend CCITT restrictions on the shared use and resale of international leased circuits in order to lower the costs for VANs. At the same time, when Japan privatized NTT and broke up its monopoly, it gave Kokusai Denshin Denwa (KDD), its private monopoly for international services, a short reprieve (in part because KDD has been especially important for the financial dealings of Japanese political factions). But in late 1987 the hard bargaining about competition for KDD was resolved. The same political coalition that pushed domestic change broke KDD's monopoly. Japan granted franchises to two new international service companies for basic transport services.

As with the domestic services market, foreign trade policy and industrial policy intersect when choices about how to introduce competition are made. And facilities will be closely connected to the key politics of the decision.

In response to persistent pressure from the United States, Japan finally abandoned its insistence that its satellite system could be sole-sourced from Japanese suppliers. (The rationale for the policy was a combination of national security, industrial development, and claims of special technical needs.) As a result, Japan bought two U.S. telecommunications satellites to complement its domestically produced satellites.

The U.S. satellites were purchased by consortiums of Japanese companies that presumably believed they could pick up expertise by partnering with U.S. firms and could complement their general move into more sophisticated information services. The ownership patterns confirmed this presumption. Japan Communications Satellite Company featured two leading trading companies—Mitsui (also a key partner in AT&T's Japanese value-added network) in partnership with C. Itoh, and Hughes Satellite (a General Motors subsidiary) to launch a satellite built by Hughes. The other consortium, Uchu Tsushin Company, is a joint venture dominated by Mitsubishi, Mitsubishi Electric Industries, and Ford Aerospace. It will launch a Ford satellite. (Mitsubishi is a major Japanese builder of satellites.)[32] Mitsubishi Electric also is partnered with IBM in a value-added network and Mitsubishi has an equity interest in several of the domestic other common carriers.

So far, everything would be straightforward except for the problem of missing demand and cross-cutting partnerships. Solving the problem of missing demand was simple; few believed that Japan would have enough demand for leased circuits from the domestic satellite facilities to support an investment in two satellites. So, why do it? Either the purchasers thought the satellites so superior that they could win a showdown for traffic in a glutted market, an unlikely event in such a politically sensitive market, or they thought that new avenues of demand would open up.

MPT has suggested that one use of the satellites might be for specialized government agencies, such as the defense program. But many believe that Japan might approve commissioning the satellite systems as an alternative to Intelsat in the international market once the United States broke the ice. Certainly, Mitsubishi floated a trial balloon in a paper describing a satellite-to-satellite system (combining the Ford satellite with one built by Mitsubishi) for transmission between the United States and Japan.[33] And, several authorities reported that Intelsat and Japan held talks about Intelsat leasing one of the Japanese domestic satellites as an alternative to Japan approving an independent system.

So far, Japan has elected not to sanction an alternative to Intelsat. But it has decided to allow two new competitors to KDD, at least for the time being. (Some of the domestic OCCs believe that one day they will be able to challenge this decision, but they will not risk MPT's ire early in their operations.) As we shall soon explain, the decision to create a second KDD soon became entangled with questions about international facilities.

The first question about the "second KDD" was who would receive the franchise? The politics of this choice were textbook cases of coalition politics. One group, International Telecommunications Japan (ITJ) was composed of Mitsui, Mitsubishi, and Sumitomo—three of the four largest Japanese trading houses—plus Matsushita Electric Industrial Company, Marubeni Corporation, Nissho Iwai Corporation, and the Bank of Tokyo. The other group, International Digital Communications Planning (IDC), was led by C. Itoh, the other major trading house. Its technical advisor was NTT, the giant domestic phone company that MPT was refusing to allow in international markets. Its partners initially were Toyota, two major computer firms (NEC and Hitachi), General Motors and, most critically, Cable & Wireless (which owns the Hong Kong phone company and British Mercury and is trying to become the first company with truly global facilities). Later, the 33 percent foreign equity (the maximum permissible) was split up among Pacific Telesis International (a subsidiary of a regional Bell operating company) with 10 percent, Merrill Lynch with 3 percent, and Cable & Wireless with 20 percent.[34]

MPT was by all accounts so determined to exclude the Cable & Wireless group that it chose to organize its rival. MPT reportedly feared that the efficient Cable & Wireless switching operations in Hong Kong could press KDD very hard while moving crucial switching operations out of Japan. At the same time, it was determined not to let NTT sneak into the international long-distance market.

The facilities question reinforced the conflict over the "second KDD." MPT has long worried about creating excess capacity in facilities when introducing competition. Even though there is competition in domestic facilities, all parties expect MPT to try to keep some limits on total capacity by informal means. It also preferred companies that accepted the Japanese style of informal consultation and oversight. This made it prefer a Japanese consortium for the second KDD, and it preferred that the newcomer lease KDD facilities for its operations. (KDD and Cable & Wireless were members of the consortium creating Transpacific 3, a fiber optic cable for common carriers connecting the United States, Japan, and such countries as Hong Kong and South Korea. It will cost $700 million.) ITJ's ownership and business plan fit this goal.

Cable & Wireless immediately raised the stakes by convincing Pacific Telecom, a utility company based in the state of Washington, to assume a significant share in a new Transpacific Fiber Optic Cable for "non-common carrier" services on another trans-Pacific fiber optic link. Cable & Wireless would have a 20 percent ownership share. International Digital Communications Planning promptly announced its decision to use the new cable for its operations. If IDC and the cable project succeeded, Cable & Wireless might someday own equity interests in the major carriers at both ends of major international transmission facilities. This development would make the traditional notion of facilities jointly provided by independent national entities largely obsolete. This prompted MPT Minister Karasawa to complain, "we must maintain impartial and equal relations with the carriers of each country, and it is therefore impossible to deal with only one special foreign carrier, such as Cable & Wireless, for example."[35] It also meant that the IDC consortium could promise its customers an all-fiber route from Japan to Europe via the Cable & Wireless fiber optic network in the United States and

North Atlantic. This might severely squeeze KDD, the traditional darling of Japanese politicians.

Keidenran stepped in at this point as a would-be mediator because the U.K. and U.S. governments had become active in their protests about the telecommunication situation. It appointed a mediator to see if the two consortiums could somehow be merged. After consultations, including discussion with MPT, ITJ invited foreign participation in its consortium as long as they did not directly provide telecommunications services. Ten multinational firms sent a joint letter expressing a wish to belong: General Electric, Ford, Citibank, Bank of America, American Express, Salomon Brothers Asia, Boeing Computer Services, Unisys, Société General (France), and Deutsche Bank. This ploy obviously sought to quiet the British and U.S. governments.[36]

The Keidenran mediatory called for sixty-six companies to put up the capital for the second KDD. Seven foreign firms, including Cable & Wireless, Pacific Telesis International, and Merrill Lynch would be in the core group while the primary Japanese leadership would come from Mitsubishi, Mitusu, C. Itoh, and Tokio Marine and Fire Insurance. The arrangement would make the equity share of U.S. firms minuscule, and the Senate promptly passed a resolution by 93–0 to protest the idea. Moreover, Cable & Wireless reacted to the merger with skepticism and declared (with the backing of its government) that it would not reduce its 20 percent equity share and would insist on rotating its executives through ITJ's management. It also insisted that the second KDD should use the Pacific Telecom cable.[37] AT&T and KDD then proposed yet another transpacific cable under their own sponsorship, an idea that challenged MPT's argument that there is no need for another cable. Their counterattack also illustrated another dimension to this struggle. Both Cable & Wireless and the AT&T-KDD venture wanted to control the new cable because the controlling interest could swing lucrative suply contracts (for example, cable-laying services) to their own subsidiaries and dominate the allocation of circuits, a much-prized planning advantage.

After Prime Minister Thatcher protested, the MPT licensed both consortiums and will probably authorize the new cable.[38]

The lessons of this story are fourfold. First, there is growing skepticism that monopoly services can make the best selection of the optimal set of facilities for domestic innovation in telecommunications. Limited competition in the provision of basic transmission facilities and services is one way to reform the process. Second, domestic deregulation quickly becomes entangled with international competition. The form of the linkage varies according to the country, but the spillover is substantial. Third, there are many important players that are primarily interested in the choice of facilities and will push the rules governing domestic and international services to favor their facilities. Fourth, as the number and types of international facilities expand, there will be significant pressures on monopoly pricing and for greater ease of entry for services that promise to fill excess capacity. Any strategy for altering the terms for the provision of telecommunications services globally must pay careful attention to issues concerning facilities.

NOTES

1. As of mid-1987 Intelsat operates sixteen satellites. Other satellites are used for domestic (civilian and military) purposes and by several regional satellite consortiums. The Soviet Union's Intersputnik consortium is considerably smaller than Intelsat.
2. Telephone traffic can be sent over cable or satellite. In general, satellites are better for thin routes or for multiple point to multiple point transmission. New fiber optic technology plus the one-quarter second delay as transmissions are bounced off a satellite generally make cable better for heavy route traffic. In general cables are superior for data transmission and satellites for broadcasting. The FCC has begun an inquiry into possible modifications of its balanced loading policy. Most analysts expect that this rule will be relaxed. However, in the spring of 1987 the United States expended considerable political capital to help elect an American to head Intelsat. The FCC may choose not to precipitously drop balanced loading and offend Intelset at this juncture.

3. The work of Stanley Besen and others shows that there is no reason to believe that the market will automatically lead to the optimal mix of technologies from the viewpoint of maximizing social welfare.

4. Much of the material on the separate satellite controversy is adapted from our article, "The Great Satellite Shootout," *Regulation* (May–June 1985):27–35. Also see Richard R. Colino, "A Chronicle of Policy and Procedure: The Formulation of the Reagan Administration Policy on International Satellite Telecommunications," *Journal of Space Law* 13, no. 2 (1986):103–56.

5. Richard R. Colino, "An Inside Look at the 'New' Intelsat," *Telephony*, September 22, 1986, pp. 50–52.

6. We thank Gregory Staple for this information. For a broad view of international satellite developments see his "The New World Satellite Order: A Report from Geneva," *The American Journal of International Law* 80, no. 3 (July 1986):699–720.

7. As it turned out, the chief financial problem for these systems appears to be convincing bankers that they can win approval to operate. Although there is no proof that they will offer a reliable quality service, there doesn't appear to be much of a problem convincing the financial community that they can launch a satellite and offer a competitive system. This assumes of course that the problems plaguing launch systems in the United States and Europe are resolved successfully.

8. IBS requires adaptation of European earth stations to handle Ku and C band signals for the service. See Michele Ellis, "Earth Station Makers Hesitant about IBS Market," *Communications Week*, May 5, 1986, p. 20.

9. Contel is the tenth largest phone company in the United States. Some said this decision was motivated by Comsat's weakened position. (Others, more cynically suggested that the allure of the golden parachutes for top Comsat executives was the real stimulus.) In any event Contel, shaken by its own management problems, called off the deal in the spring of 1987. See "Comsat, Contel Set Merger Pact of $2.47 Billion," *Wall Street Journal*, September 30, 1986. Significantly, this was not the first time Comsat has struck out on its own. For a decade the company tried to diversify into related fields with decidedly mixed results. In 1973 it started Comsat General to provide design and consulting services to national satellite systems. In 1976, with Intelsat's permission, it launched a series of maritime communications

satellites (Marisat), as well as satellites to serve the domestic market (Comstar). And it is starting a specialized service network for NBC, Holiday Inn, and other clients. Some of its ventures have been spectacular failures. It sunk large amounts into a direct broadcasting service that is now on hold. It also lost substantial sums in Satellite Business System before selling its share to its partners. Furthermore, AT&T, which has already launched its own satellites, could decide to deprive Comstar of its main customer.

10.   For a detailed chronology of the infighting and particularly the role of Congress see Richard R. Colino, "A Chronology of Policy and Procedure."

11.   The FCC tentatively approved applicants included International Satellites, backed by United Brands and TRT, an international telegram and telex network, which like Orion wanted to offer specialized service to Western Europe; Cygnus Satellite Corporation, which wanted to serve the Caribbean as well as Europe (and later decided to merge with PanAmSat); Columbia Communications, which planned to serve the Pacific; MCCaw Space Technologies, a Pacific system hubbed on Guam; and Financial Satellite Corporation, which planned Atlantic and Pacific services for data, voice and video for the finance industry. All had to prove that they had a foreign partner and adequate financing before receiving a final FCC approval. See *International Communications Week*, "Here's Status of the Other Six Private International Satellite Systems," January 16, 1987, pp. 4–6; *Communication Daily*, April 3, 1986, p. 3; *International Communications Week*, April 4, 1986.

12.   In July 1986 the Intelsat Board declared that the United States and PanAmSat had not provided enough documentation to allow for a coordination process to begin. The resulting delay imperiled the company's financing. The United States again lost badly on this issue in the September meeting although it provided substantial new data on the European transponders. After a breakdown in the discussion in October, the Intelsat Board approved the system in December 1986 although the staff reported PanAmSat would cost Intelsat 3.2 percent of its potential revenues. See *Telecommunications Reports*, September 15, 1986, pp. 102 and 24–26; November 3, 1986, pp. 29–30; December 15, 1986, pp. 15–16 and 34–36; *International Communication Week*, April 10, 1987, pp. 2–3. Interviewing confirmed these reports.

13. *Telecommunications Reports*, April 6, 1987, p. 6 and July 20, 1987, p. 51.

14. PanAmSat has vigorously protested a number of new Intelsat discounts and offerings to little avail with the FCC. But it has done much better in fighting the politically beleaguered Comsat's innovations for Caribbean services. See *Telecommunications Reports*, September 15, 1986, pp. 24–26.

15. *International Communications Week*, April 3, 1987, p. 9 and *ibid.*, April 17, 1987, "Contel Seeks End to Comsat Merger, Citing Pending FCC Actions" and "Fowler Signals Approval of Transpacific Fiber Optic Cable" both start on p. 1.

16. The FCC has proposed to change Comsat from the sole signatory to Inmarsat to a new consortium including Comsat. This would make the marketing of new Inmarsat services more competitive. The FCC also indicated sympathy to new satellite ventures in this field. Comsat said it did not object to a separate ARINC system so long as it did not delay approval of its own system to be offered through Inmarsat. *Telecommunications Reports*, March 2, 1987, pp. 25–26; April 6, 1987, p. 14. "AVSAT and TRT Communications Plan Aeronautical Satellite Systems," *International Communications Week*, March 6, 1987, p. 8; *FCC WEEK*, June 15, 1987, pp. 10–11.

17. Although NYNEX's waiver to participate in Tel Optik will be considered separately, Judge Green's September 1987 decision denying regional Bell operating companies permission to sell their own value-added services was seen as a major setback for NYNEX.

18. TAT 9 is a $350 million deal scheduled to begin operation by 1991. AT&T has a 30 percent share. Spain's Telefonica is the largest European owner, which angered West Germany and especially France (which wanted the landing). Teleglobe also has a 10.1 percent share, but this is expected to decline later. *Fiber Optic Weekly*, April 10, 1987, p. 1.

19. Data would constitute 15 percent of the 80,000 circuit total. Stephanie Cooke and Lee Mantelman, "Gbit/s Glut Possible, as Transatlantic Titans Tangle," *Data Communications*, August 1986, pp. 56–58.

20. We could equally well have looked to Britain for a second case.

21. Timothy J. Curran, "Politics and High Technology: The NTT Case," in I.M. Destler and Sato Hideo, eds., *Coping with U.S.-Japanese Economic Conflicts* (Lexington, Mass.: Lexington Books, 1982).

22. William H. Davidson, "Japanese Telecommunications Policy, New Directions and Old Dilemmas," *Telecommunications Policy* (June 1987):147–60; Daniel Okimoto, Takuo Sugano, and Franklin B. Weinstein, eds., *Competitive Edge: The Semiconductor Industry in the U.S. and Japan* (Stanford, Calif.: Stanford University Press, 1984); Youichi Ito, "Telecommunications and Industrial Policies in Japan: Recent Developments," in Marcellus S. Snow, ed., *Marketplace for Telecommunications* (New York: Longman, 1986), pp. 201–30.

23. Interview, Ottawa, Canada, October 1986.

24. C. Itoh had been the agent of Hughes for over twenty years. It soon entered the satellite communications business. "Key Management Strategy Based on CS Business," *The Telecom Tribune*, December 1986 and January 1987, p. 3. Part of this account is based on interviewing data with consultants to the trading companies.

25. This account has profited immensely from the study by Chalmers Johnson although it does not quite agree in his degree of emphasis on bureaucratic control over the changes in the market and lack of fundamental changes (especially in VANs): "MITI, MPT, and the Telecom Wars: How Japan Makes Policy for High Technology," (Berkeley, Calif.: Berkeley Roundtable on the International Economy, 1987).

26. Traditionally NTT was part of MPT. In fact, the brightest engineers went to NTT, not MPT, so that the NTT tail wagged the MPT dog. Once NTT was separated from MPT on April 1, 1985, MPT could exercise greater regulatory influence than was possible previously. Johnson notes MPT's political clout in being a career stop for future prime ministers.

27. "The Next Generation — INS — Japan's Information Network System," Nielsen Dataquest Japanese Research Newsletter, October 1984, p. 5; David Friedman, "The Misunderstood Miracle: Politics and Economic Decentralization in Japan," Ph.D. Thesis, Department of Political Science, M.I.T., 1985 (Ithaca, N.Y.: Cornell University Press, forthcoming). For a general history see Jerry L. Salvagio, "An Overview of the Privatization of Japan's

NTT," International Communication Association, May 22–26, 1986.

28. "How Japan Has Opened Its Lines of Communication," *Financial Times*, March 3, 1987. NTT's revenues in 1983 were $18.4 billion: about $7.5 billion for long distance, $1.4 for leased lines, $2.9 for local service, and a huge $6.6 categorized as other (including pay phones) (interview data). *Dataquest* estimated that NTT had data revenues of about $2 billion on 1984 revenues of $18.9 billion (October 19, 1984). Combined revenues for NTT and KDD for the year ending March 31, 1986 totaled 5.307 billion yen.

29. *The Economist*, September 11, 1987.

30. "21st Information Industry Vision Report," *Telecom Tribune*, July 1987, p. 3.

31. There have been controversies about circuit resale. But see an interview with a reseller: "Circuit Resale Business Proceeding Smoothly," *The Telecom Tribune*, March 1987, p. 6. The consideration on ONA and CEI is tied to whether NTT should be required to have a structurally separate subsidiary for data communications after the introduction of ISDN: "Toward a More Internationally Open ISDN Market," *The Telecom Tribune*, November 1986, p. 2.

32. A group led by Sony which intended to use RCA satellites was denied Type I carrier status by MPT on January 8, 1986. The lack of anticipated capacity was the reason given for this decision. William H. Davidson, "Japanese Telecommunications Policy," p. 156.

33. N. Takahashi, "Pacific Regional Communications Satellite System," concept proposal, mimeo.

34. Interviewing in Japan, Hong Kong, and the United States from June through August 1986 provided information for this account. Also see "Fowler Signals Approval of Transpacific Fiber Optic Cable," *International Communications Week*, p. 1. However, because the Modified Final Judgement barred former AT&T units from offering international phone services, to participate Pacific Telesis must win a waiver from Judge Greene.

35. "Fears of Protectionism in the U.S. Congress," *The Telecom Tribune*, March 1987, p.1.

36. *Telecommunications Report*, April 20, 1987, pp. 8–9; "FCC Grants Landing License to Pacific Telecom Cable for U.S.-Japan Link," *International Communications Week*, May 1, 1987, pp.

6–8; "U.S. Firms Join British in Telecom Venture Bid," *Japan Economic Journal*, April 4, 1987, p. 2.

37. *International Communications Week*, April 3, 1987, pp. 3–4.
38. "Japan Grants Cable & Wireless Access to Phone Market After Intense Lobbying," *Wall Street Journal*, September 24, 1987, p. 23.

6

IS COMPETITION CONTAGIOUS?
The Case of Canada

On October 3, 1987, U.S. and Canadian negotiators agreed to a comprehensive trade agreement. Telecommunication services are an important element of the pact, which must be approved by Congress and Parliament before taking effect. This chapter examines the degree to which this agreement and future trade negotiations might advance the reformulation of domestic regulation governing basic and enhanced services. It also explores how governments and corporations sort out the linkages between their positions on services and related equipment markets.

The U.S. regulatory bargain helps clarify special features of the Canadian market and political system that should influence the Canadian response to technological change and "transnational economics." The analysis in Chapter 3 suggests four major hypotheses. (1) The reorganization of the U.S. market raises competitive challenges for all service industries in Canada. Greater competition in enhanced telecommunications services is already more attractive and this may soon be true for long-distance voice services as well. (2) Canada's interests in the equipment industry suggest that it will make concessions to avoid a confrontation over telecommunications trade issues. (3) Canadian telephone companies have varying degrees of sensitivity to the world market and these differences could create room for political innovations in regulatory and trade policy. (4) The politics of Canada's federal system suggest that in contrast to the United States, Canada's federal regulators will try to preserve a monopoly in facilities while advocating full competition in enhanced services and nibbling away at the formal limits on competition in switched voice services.

WILL CANADA CHANGE ITS POLICIES?

The U.S. experiment suggests that most countries will react to pressures arising from four major issues discussed in Chapter 3.

First, to what extent should countries encourage new providers of basic and enhanced telecommunications services in order to encourage greater efficiency and innovation? The U.S. answer is that there should be great freedom except for local basic services, but the share of the market controlled by newcomers is less important than that their potential for entry is credible.

Second, what is the balance of the distribution of benefits between small and large users, and between users and telecommunications equipment suppliers? The United States has moved to reduce substantially the previous advantage of small users and equipment suppliers. This decision gives all public switched telephone networks (PSTNs) an incentive to target their largest customers as their key growth and profit center. To do so, they want to follow their large customers to wherever they do business. It also gives the providers of services an incentive to subsidize the providers of equipment less generously so that they can offer large users lower prices and more flexible mixes of equipment.

Third, how much freedom should there be in the provision of telecommunications equipment? The United States believes that customer premises equipment should be fully open for competition and that transmission and switching equipment (collectively known as network equipment) should be open to the threat of entry (although there was little expectation that AT&T would lose its dominant position). This dynamic situation was an incentive for those in the computer business to experiment with wide-ranging new packages of communications, software, and equipment. Thus, the lines between computers and communications are becoming even more blurred. At the same time, the makers of network equipment became more attuned to exports and designing their equipment to global standards (instead of idiosyncratic U.S. network standards).

Fourth, to what extent will countries favor very smart, centralized integrated services digital networks in the future? In the United States the ISDN will be a much more flexible and limited set of designs for data and voice communications. This means that telephone companies will not have a strong advantage when competing against computer firms in those spheres where their businesses overlap.

Although the U.S. experiment provides a baseline against which to measure regulatory change, the United States has not embraced completely free competition. And, there is no reason to believe that a U.S.-Canadian telecommunications agreement will do so. The short negotiating deadline set for U.S. negotiators by Congress and the Mulroney government's sensitivity to criticism in Canada of the talks limited the range of outcomes significantly. However, a close examination of individual market segments may suggest whether and to what degree specific features of Canadian politics and economics ultimately will follow or diverge from the U.S. approach.[1]

THE POLITICS OF THE EQUIPMENT MARKET

Although the relative success of Canada and the United States varies according to the market segment, one constant is that the Canadian equipment markets are far less vital to United States firms than vice versa. (The scale of the two countries' markets is vastly different; in 1989 Canada's telecommunications equipment market will be about $2.5 billion while the U.S. market will be close to $40 billion.) Politically, greater vulnerability makes it easier to organize Canadian firms for action on U.S.-Canadian trade than is the case for U.S. firms, especially smaller U.S. firms specializing in high technology.

Canada traditionally runs a large surplus on trade in telecommunications equipment with the United States. The surplus increased as newly independent Bell operating companies doubled their orders from Northern Telecom (in part to diversify and become less reliant on AT&T); it settled at over $200 million per

155

year by 1986. In addition, Northern Telecom is now the second largest *domestic* telecommunications equipment manufacturer in the United States.[2] Of its total sales of $2.8 billion, about half are generated in the United States.

No Canadian firm is a major international player in the computer market. Therefore, the United States enjoys a balance-of-trade surplus with Canada on computers and related equipment. In 1985 Canada suffered a trade imbalance in computers, semiconductors, and electronic components in excess of $3.5 billion Canadian, part of a large continuing deficit in high-technology trade for Canada.[3]

Protecting Network Equipment and Computers

In general, the Canadian government restricts competition in their equipment market more than does the United States although the Canadian tariff on telecommunications products is markedly higher than that of the United States (17.8 percent in Canada versus 4.3–8.5 percent in the United States).[4] Nominal tariff levels, of course, tell only part of the story. This is especially true in the Canadian computer market. Smaller Canadian firms are higher cost producers with narrow product niches. The extensive efforts of the Canadian government to respond to their vigorous lobbying raised the costs of computing equipment in Canada substantially above U.S. levels.

In addition to customs evaluation methods that boost the effective tariff protection on computers, the Canadian government has a "Buy Canada" program for government procurement in the telecommunications and computer markets. (Foreign firms can "rationalize" their operations with significant Canadian production in order to qualify for the preference system for Canadian firms. AT&T does not qualify as a rationalized firm.)

The combination of policies led to a variety of claims about the cost of computing equipment in Canada. Some estimated that it was 40 percent higher than in the United States. However, when adjusted for the greatly weakened exchange rate of the

Canadian dollar since 1984, a more realistic estimate is a net difference of 5 to 20 percent.[5] This figure is large enough to cause domestic tensions between the producers and users of computers that is spilling over into telecommunications debates (see below).

Nominal tariffs and government procurement practices also do not fully summarize the policy choices about the telecommunications equipment industry. The two dominant firms, especially in network equipment, are Northern Telecom and Microtel. Each firm is owned by a major telecommunications network—Bell Canada owns 51.9 percent of Northern Telecom and Microtel is wholly owned by British Columbia Telephone, which is itself a subsidiary of the U.S. firm GTE.

The two firms are vastly different in size and health.[6] Northern Telecom is an international leader while Microtel had such serious financial troubles in the 1980s that the Canadian government used its procurement policy informally to assist the firm. These difficulties partly stemmed from problems in the equipment business of its U.S. parent (GTE) and partly because British Columbia Telephone's telephone network provides a much smaller market for its equipment than does Bell Canada for Northern Telecom. British Columbia Telephone has 13.5 percent of Canadian traffic while Bell Canada controls about 60 percent of the Canadian telecommunications market. This opens the way for a potential division between the two firms concerning a key policy that hinders foreign competitors.

The Canadian government has sanctioned a preferential buying system by Bell Canada. Bell Canada in essence gives Northern Telecom a right of first refusal for network equipment. As a result, 85 percent of Bell Canada's procurement is from Northern Telecom; this was about 75 percent of Northern Telecom's Canadian revenues in 1984. U.S. firms argue that the prices charged by Northern Telecom are sufficiently high to subsidize its global operations outside Canada.

The boost for Northern Telecom from Bell Canada procurement threatens to become even more significant in the future. Private forecasts of the Canadian market suggest that purchases of network equipment will rise from $835 million to $1 billion per annum from 1985 through 1990.[7] At the same time, the total share of Bell Canada in the procurement market for central office switching equipment will rise because it has not modernized its switching network as much as the other large telephone companies. (However, Bell Canada will not exercise a similar purchasing power in the 40 percent of the equipment market dedicated to transmission equipment, especially fiber optic cables.)

Northern Telecom's preferential buying policy is coming under severe attack from U.S. suppliers. GTE, Rockwell, and AT&T have formed a lobbying coalition and requested that the vertical integration and buying policies of Bell Canada be made a central issue in the free trade negotiations. Northern Telecom, naturally, denies any problem exists.[8]

The United States also argues that Canada's policies for setting technical standards are unnecessarily burdensome and fall short of the spirit of the GATT Code on Technical Barriers to Trade (the Standards Code). However, it is not clear that U.S. companies care deeply about this issue.

Even if neither side really expects completely open competition in network equipment, some minority share for foreign competition is a credible U.S. demand. Northern Telecom's heavy involvement in the U.S. market makes it especially vulnerable to threats of reprisal if trade talks on telecommunications make no progress. However, one problem for the United States will be that Canada may choose to cloak its telecommunications equipment policies under the umbrella or "informatics" to argue that the United States enjoys an overall advantage in the computer and customer premise equipment markets.[9] But the evolution of the Canadian equipment market may again cause a growing division in Canadian ranks.

Linking Computers and Customer Premises Equipment

The biggest data-processing equipment makers in Canada are all U.S. based. They supported more competition by arguing that lower tariff barriers would permit their local subsidiaries to become cost-competitive producers of specialized equipment and peripherals for their parent companies' global operations and sales.[10] However, these firms reportedly were cautious when advocating particular new policies when issues of customs valuations were negotiated, because they suspected they might do better with individual arrangements. Meanwhile, small, low-cost producers exporting from the United States also favored trade-policy reform. However, they found it difficult to organize for effective political action, because the Canadian market was such a small piece of their business.

In short, restrictions on trade seemed to favor Canadian electronic firms at the expense of U.S. firms. But the merger of computer and communications markets has started to blur this logic. A look at the customer premises market explains why.

Although the customer premises equipment market is technically open to everyone, the Bell Canada-Northern Telecom influence is so great that U.S. firms (and some Canadian suppliers) complain that it is difficult to achieve entry in the crucial private branch exchange (PBX) market. The IBM-Rolm venture has been the greatest success of the newcomers after outside vendors were allowed for PBX systems in 1981, but its share is less than 5 percent of the market.

The true significance of the PBX market for domestic Canadian politics is clear only when the deepening alliance between Northern Telecom and Apple Computers to abet Northern Telecom's thrust into office automation products is understood.[11] Although the agreements presently are primarily tied to sharing design information, there is considerable speculation that the two will look at joint PBX and computer products in the future. The success or failure of this particular pairing matters less than that the pressures for integrated computer and communications offerings are on the rise, and are leading Northern Telecom into major deals with the stronger computer firms outside Canada. Such an arrangement will force other Canadian players to further reassess their interests. It also makes it more important for rival computer firms in the United States to organize to attack Northern Telecom's stronghold.

159

Users and the Equipment Market

Just as important, the interests of PSTNs may change in the future. They are critical both as major equipment customers and because of their considerable influence concerning regulatory policies. As a prosperous parent, Bell Canada may not challenge its sibling, Northern Telecom, and thus not fit the trend toward less support of equipment makers by PSTNs. But if other Canadian PSTNs become engaged in a more actively competitive relationship with Bell Canada, they may find it in their own interest to challenge arrangements that shelter the revenues of their competitor's equipment subsidiary.

Meanwhile, other large users will also influence the political game. User's strategies for quality control and cost control for consumers are tied to computerization. So too are value-added networks that provide computer processing services. As a result, major users of computer equipment have an interest in persuading government to liberalize its policies. Users helped to shape the government policies that kept nominal tariffs low. They undoubtedly will continue to favor competitive policies. Meanwhile, users' attention have also turned to the rules governing basic network services.

The agreement reached by trade negotiators on October 3, 1987, covered two U.S. proposals concerning telecommunications equipment. One focus was on reducing tariffs on telecommunications equipment. Northern Telecom was forced to bend because of its large U.S. market. Only small details on content remained to be worked out. Canada received U.S. concessions in other areas in return for a quick tariff cut. The second focus was on efforts to make certain that regulated public monopolies followed open procurement policies. (The U.S. government first called for open procurement by regulated commoncarriers but then opted for a monopoly standard after AT&T complained vigorously.) The U.S. government accepted a generic agreement but remained troubled by the cozy procurement relationship between Bell Canada and Northern Telecom.

In summary, a great deal remains to be negotiated concerning telecommunications, computer, and customer premises equipment. Much of the debate will relate to trade talks, but practical action may grow out of revisions in domestic regulatory policy. The split between Microtel and Northern Telecom raises the possibility of sharp questioning of the vertical integration of Bell Canada and Northern Telecom. Meanwhile, Northern Telecom (along with all other manufacturers) is going to have to shop for new partners in the computer industry to complement its line of customer premises equipment. This will raise new questions about the alignment of interests in the Canadian computer market.

Large users have every incentive to encourage more competition and flexibility. And the other PSTNs of Canada have to worry more and more about how to keep those large users happy. As they seek to offer these users better deals they will have a greater interest in getting better terms for purchases of network equipment. This development bodes well for those advocating a more open equipment market.

BACK TO BASICS: THE POLITICS OF TELEPHONE NETWORKS

The Petition for More Domestic Competition

The market for common carrier telecommunications services in Canada is about $6.8 billion per year. At first glance, the ownership and regulation of the phone services in Canada is "Balkanized." However, the federal government has direct regulatory power over the two largest companies, which together provide over 70 percent of Canada's phones. Therefore, the practical control of the federal authorities is greater than the nominal division of power suggests.[12]

The federal and provincial authorities largely contented themselves to traditional oversight "policing" of the telephone companies until 1968. The creation of the Department of Communications in that year marked an effort by the Trudeau government to develop an "industrial policy" for telecommunications and information. This immediately set off a battle for power between Ottawa and the provinces that has proven a political embarrassment for everyone. Ottawa has favored more standardization of policies and greater freedom of competition in order to stimulate modernization of the network and the related equipment industries.[13] The federal government wanted freedom of competition in customer premises equipment and freedom of competition in private voice services, value-added, and infrastructure services. Until July 1987 the federal government left the door open to competition in long-distance voice services, but it resisted competition in facilities. In July it announced that effective immediately it would permit competition in long-distance services and facilities among licensed Type I carriers. This decision came after a gradual process of liberalization and as part of a general effort by the Mulroney government to bolster its business support in the midst of the trade negotiations.

Although the Canadian courts gave every sign of sanctioning the federal government's modest claims for greater authority over telecommunications, no prime minister wants to use this power without reaching some accommodation with the powerful provincial prime ministers (who have a political stature somewhat akin to major U.S. senators).[14] Many of the regional politicians from provinces that might benefit most from competition also have national political ambitions. They did not want to fight with their peers on such a touchy issue. Therefore, the Canadian prime minister confronted a generally unified front of resistance on telecommunications issues from regional prime ministers whose interests ought to diverge more. In 1987 Ottawa and the provinces continued to hold summit conferences on telecommunications in an attempt to "bless" an increase in federal authority in return for federal pledges of discretion in promoting competition.

On balance, Canadian telephone and record services are less open than those in the United States or Japan, but competition is considerably more open than in most of Europe. In Canada each common carrier has a monopoly on its local phone service. Canadian National Canadian Pacific Telecommunications

(CNCP) is the monopoly provider of telex and telegraph services. However, since 1979 the federally regulated firms had to interconnect with private lines offered by CNCP Telecommunications for clients that wish independent local voice and data services. This has not seriously threatened the local monopoly on voice traffic.[15] CNCP had revenues from telecommunications services of only around $15 million in 1984.

Most of Canada's long-distance traffic travels over Telecom Canada, an association of the phone companies operating in each province plus the national satellite carrier, Telesat Canada. Regulators have justified the monopoly on grounds of efficiency and the benefits of cross-subsidization for the consumer. Long-distance traffic subsidizes local users of phone services. (The size of the transfer is disputed.) Larger, lower cost providers of long-distance services also subsidize provinces with higher costs and lower volumes. The size of this transfer is determined by a formula set by the member companies under a unanimous consent rule. As greater competition threatens profits, this formula will more and more be attacked by the lower cost phone companies.[16]

On October 25, 1983, CNCP asked the Canadian Radio-television and Telecommunications Commission (CRTC) for permission to interconnect its system with the PSTNs of Bell Canada and British Columbia Telephone. This amounted to seeking entry into the long-distance voice market. CNCP argued that consumers would benefit from competition and claimed that its existing market in data communications would erode badly unless it could match Telecom Canada and offer both phone and data services. CNCP also promised to match the existing carrier's degree of cross-subsidization to local users while providing alternative long-distance service. It sought a duopoly where a continued commitment to cross-subsidization would limit savage discounting of prices.[17]

In August 1985 CNCP's application was turned down because of fears of higher costs for local household services, a decision it promptly appealed.[18] Much to the surprise of the industry, CNCP lost the appeal in October 1986, but the CRTC affirmed that competition in long-distance services was accept-

163

able in principle. Even as the CRTC temporized, independent analysts were identifying other potential competitors.

As Japan is learning, electric utility companies could make strong potential entrants in the phone industry because of their rights of way, household metering systems, and strong political clout. At present, some of Canada's largest utilities have private telecommunications systems and are in the process of modernizing them.

In addition, in 1985 the Canadian government authorized the privatization of Teleglobe Canada, Canada's major international long-distance monopoly. The purpose of the proposed sale was to increase its efficiency; the government estimates that prices will go down by at least 13 percent under private ownership. It also opens the way eventually to competition. (Teleglobe retains a monopoly on cable landing licenses and international earth stations, and it no longer has a legal monopoly over non-U.S. international traffic.) Foreign ownership of up to 20 percent of Teleglobe Canada was sanctioned and British Telecom expressed interest. After rumors had made CNCP and Telecom Canada the leading contenders (with Bell Canada a dark horse threatening to enhance its dominance of the Canadian telecommunications market) the government awarded the sale to Memotek, a small firm ($83 million in assets) that specialized in data communications products and services in the United States and Canada.[19] The deal finessed forcing a choice among the major telecommunications companies. It also fit the general trend toward blurring the lines between services and equipment.

Perhaps the most significant development for the future of the politics of Canadian telecommunications is the growing rift between Bell Canada and the other carriers. Once there is a strong suspicion that greater competition will be permitted, all parties start to wonder on what terms they should manage their relationship with Bell Canada. The U.S. experience of AT&T relations with the regional Bell operating companies hints at what could happen. Already there is a rekindling of old histories of predatory pricing against small telecommunications firms.[20]

The Changing Role of Users and Policies for Services

The politics of basic services will be even more complicated in the future. As telecommunications costs rose as a share of corporate operating costs and became more vital to controlling operating costs for many large companies, large users favored more competition to widen their service options and lower rates. This group's costs for long-distance voice and private data communications circuits were, respectively, about 40 percent and 50 percent higher than their counterparts in the United States.[21]

Moreover, for a while some users in British Columbia circumvented the Canadian long-distance system when calling from Canada to the United States through resale companies that rerouted Canadian calls to less expensive WATTS lines going anywhere in the United States. This cut prices by 14 percent to 52 percent. The resellers planned to expand operations to handle discounted calls to Eastern Canada via the United States.

Finally, in April 1985 Canadian PSTNs won important regulatory victories that allowed them to rebalance their rates in such a way as to kill off the challenge of the resellers.[22] But the option of using U.S. facilities to cut costs in delivering long-distance services by Canadian carriers remained if more competition was introduced in Canada. The heavy North-South flows of long-distance traffic across the U.S.-Canadian border amounted to $730 million in 1985 and the East-West traffic in Canada parallels routes where ample and cheap transmission capacity exists in the United States.

Large users started to favor federal approval for new long-distance carriers from the United States. For example, they supported CNCP's arrangements with AT&T to provide a greater availability of private leased lines to the United States. Targeting traffic in Ontario and Quebec increased pressure on authorities in other provinces to change their policies.[23] As noted previously, in July 1987 the federal government reached a sufficient compromise with the provinces to announce competition for long-distance services and facilities for interprovincial and international traffic. As in Japan, the government would designate a group of Type I carriers. Except for GTE's existing holdings, foreign ownership would be restricted to 20 percent of the equity of Type I carriers.

Canada's treatment of U.S. other common carriers emerged as an early issue in the bilateral trade negotiations. Although MCI and US Sprint could transmit calls from the United States to most major Canadian markets, they did not receive incoming traffic from Canadian carriers. This made the Canadian traffic unprofitable for the OCCs although they had to provide the service in order to win attractive U.S. customers (Canada is one of the top three destinations for U.S. international calls). US Sprint in particular protested. It claimed potential losses of $50 million in 1985–1988.[24] Although Canadian carriers worried that the entry of the OCCs would open the way to ingenious bypass of the domestic Canadian long-distance network, no sooner had the issue hit the trade agenda than Canada modified its policy to end the complaint.

Future negotiations about domestic and international long-distance services will be complicated because, just like state regulators in the United States, the provincial regulatory authorities are articulate defenders of small residential users. (Moreover, the provinces most insistent on retaining past practices are also those with comparatively smaller clusters of large businesses to oppose protection.)[25] However, provinces have comparatively greater political power in Canada than do state politicians in the United States. Moreover, the provinces have local phone companies (often owned by the provincial governments) with comparatively higher cost structures for long distance than the ones in federally regulated areas. Therefore, in many cases they also are representing the interests of their phone companies.

The biggest potential for disrupting a trade agreement and regulatory arrangements for telecommunications services would be an effort by Bell Canada to emulate the U.S. model and pursue its largest customers abroad. Bell Canada recently purchased a pipeline transmission company that has holdings in the United States as part of a diversification program. Although the economics must have looked good, observers noted that Bell Canada also was buying valuable rights of way over which they could establish transmission facilities. If Bell Canada entered the U.S. long-distance or value-added market successfully, it would force a reexamination of all other arrangements governing both the equipment and service markets.

It became clear by the summer of 1987 that a Canadian move into the U.S. services market was in the cards. Bell Canada had reached a tentative agreement with Ameritech, a regional Bell operating company, for a joint venture in information services.[26] More important, the Canadian negotiators demanded a unilateral right for Canadian firms to build facilities or resell long-distance services in the United States. The Canadians would not offer U.S. firms a reciprocal privilege and justified their position by noting concessions on other issues.

U.S. negotiators resisted Canadian demands to include international basic services in the bargain, limiting the agreement to enhanced and computer services. U.S. negotiators won access to the telecommunications transport network for American providers of enhanced and computer services on a national treatment basis. (Canadian firms received identical guarantees in the U.S. market.) Some provisions to assure that monopolies did not abuse their position were included, but the U.S. industry wanted more. They sought guaranteed minimum rights for enhanced services providers. U.S. firms fear that Bell Canada will try to dominate Teleglobe and then push for control of Telecom Canada as well. If this occurred U.S. value-added network providers would have to rely on a facilities system controlled by their strongest competitor, Bell Canada (now that Bell Canada is free to offer VANs).[27]

THE POLITICS OF VALUE-ADDED NETWORKS: ALL IN VAIN?

Canadian data-services companies are not large and the market is highly fragmented. Databases are a bright light in Canada's international enhanced service trade. In 1987 two of the fifteen largest database companies in the world (judged by the number of on-line bases offered), I. P. Sharp and QL Systems, were Canadian. Of 1,802 listed database producers and vendors, 111 were Canadian.[28] However, overall the Canadian picture is much less favorable than the one in the United States because the higher costs of transmission and equipment prevent exploitation of Canada's lower labor costs.

Value-added services are significant because they are the key to other segments of the telecommunications market. The views of Bell Canada and British Columbia Telephone concerning value-added services are similar to those held by their U.S. counterparts, but their regulatory position is somewhat different. They are similar in that both serve areas in which large, expected growth in demand for newer enhanced services will partially offset the sting of losing their monopoly on basic services. (Estimates of the market for value-added services are notoriously unreliable, but in Canada the market may grow from about 10 percent of all telecommunications services to 15 percent by 1990.)[29] However, the situation differs from the one that once faced AT&T because Canadian law always allowed them to provide enhanced services. Therefore, they need not give away something on basic services to enter the enhanced market.

In August 1984 the government in Ottawa ruled in favor of freedom of entry into enhanced services. This does not automatically mean that the provinces will follow, but it gives interested users and would-be entrants into the business a useful precedent on which to build. Freedom to compete limits the cost of computer equipment because if cost differentials become too great, customers will curb processing data in Canada and switch to U.S. networks. It also threatens the price of basic services because major users will eventually find it profitable to combine their voice and data into enhanced services (for example, if voice calls could be "enhanced" by introducing such features as message storage and forwarding of phone calls and the combination of voice and data for business conferences). As in the United States, a small percentage of all users generates the bulk of the long-distance traffic—banks, for example, are particularly heavy users. So, their exit from the public network would greatly reduce volumes and force the public to pay for the fixed costs of the remaining facilities.

The Canadian policy did not lead to a boom in independent providers of value-added services because of continuing restrictions on competition in facilities and on shared use and resale of circuits. The new competitive policies announced in July 1987 promised to remedy many of these problems. They authorized complete freedom of competition in value-added and information services by Type II carriers. Although Type II carriers may not own transmission facilities, they will be allowed to lease and use facilities services as they wish. Furthermore, Type II carriers may be owned totally by foreigners.

Two problems involving trade issues remain. On May 22, 1987, the CRTC decided that it had the authority to decree a service (Call-Net) either basic or enhanced according to its "primary" function, even if it contained enhanced elements by both Canadian and U.S. standards. (In this case, telephone customers received an automatic voice mail system among other items.) U.S. negotiators concluded that even similar definitions of basic and enhanced services may yield to divergent administrative practices. This suggests the need for even greater ongoing attention to the link between domestic regulation and trade rules.

A second barrier to free entry is the limits on bypassing Canadian networks by using U.S. based value-added networks. Canada insists on local data-processing in some sectors such as banking.[30] Thus, even free access to U.S. value-added networks would not end all required local data-processing. The U.S. financial industry continued to register complaints on this topic throughout the bilateral free trade negotiations. More fundamentally, the government and phone companies have longstanding policies that limit the crossing points for telecommunications from the United States to Canada to official network carriers. Current federal rules and phone companies' practices make it impossible to rely on U.S. value-added networks to handle data shipped from a Canadian origin to a Canadian destination. (One-way transit in either direction is permissible.)

Canadian regulators, in short, tried for a long time to protect the basic network while slowly opening data services to greater competition. The smaller Canadian providers of enhanced services feared potential competitors from the United States as much as they opposed any domestic barriers to competition. But a significant base of support for competition emerged. Loopholes in the old regulations permitted larger users to bargain aggressively about the terms and prices of services. Yet these users still faced significant cost disadvantages compared to their U.S. counterparts. This made them a constituency for futher reform that may push harder for lower rates through increased competition in basic services while reinforcing their commitment to international free trade in value-added services.

The major example of a private sector initiative on transborder computer services was launched by the Royal Bank of Canada, a major user of transborder data networks. The Royal Bank sought a Canadian-U.S. agreement to allow much freer competition in data-processing services and free movement of information between Canada and the United States. This initiative received considerable attention, including quick positive reactions from U.S. trade negotiators.[31] But it did not prove sufficiently compelling to lead either side to choose it as the basis for a special quick agreement that would set a "favorable tone" for the general bilaterals.

The initiative was consistent with the position of many trade organizations. For example, the Canadian Business Equipment Manufacturers Association, a group with a substantial number of local subsidiaries of multinational firms, favors freer trade in data services so members can become specialized niche suppliers of computer equipment and services for their parent companies. Equally predictably, smaller computer services firms resisted free flow in international computer services. One executive has claimed that 15 percent of Canada's unemployment is due to transborder data flows.[32] So far, the Canadian government has clearly tilted toward the larger users and producers. An IBM Canada executive chaired its advisory group on computers and communications for the bilateral trade talks.

On balance, the political coalition for reform raises questions about the government's ability to maintain strong distinctions between basic and enhanced services in the long run. Larger users and equipment makers benefit from a blurring of the boundaries. Trade relations will reinforce the pressures eroding the dividing lines. Yet the Canadian experiments strongly suggest that the Japanese formula for competition may prove a more appealing guide for many countries than the path followed by the United States. And to the degree that Canadian policy reforms resemble the Japanese approach, it also is possible that Canadian political battles also will follow the lines of struggle in Japan. This suggests that Canadian government authorities may actively experiment with a large number of public development programs to boost services for smaller commercial users of the communications network even while competition improves the situation of large users.

SUMMARY

Canada has already experimented with greater competition in telecommunications, and the trade talks will allow advocates of liberalization a chance to promote still more innovations. The degree to which the United States and Canada will achieve freer competition in telecommunications equipment and services will depend in part on the changing arrays of interests in Canada's domestic regulatory arena, particularly in the federal government's ability to override provincial objections to competition. Trade in value-added services in the long run will alter the terms for domestic basic services. It is not yet clear whether the U.S. government's complaints on telecommunications equipment have led to a deal that is consistent with the United States' own regulatory bargain on equipment. But the degree of competition in equipment is most likely to increase if Canadian regulatory changes also promote more competition in services and a rift among Canadian telephone companies.

Trade talks are usually blunt instruments, and particularly so in this case. In order to put the agreements on a "fast track" approval process in Congress and to bolster the troubled Mulroney government, the talks had to be concluded quickly. This meant the tougher conceptual questions had to be fudged with an eye to bolstering positions at the Uruguay Round.

On balance, even these flawed trade talks contributed to regulatory innovation. Clearly, significant differences in national practices will continue, but the trade talks (at least in telecommunications) permit the systematic review of both nations' domestic and international policy commitments. The purpose was less to achieve clear and detailed rules than to alter the incentives of the commercial interests in both countries in such a way as to give them substantial stakes in increasing the scope of international competition. This is not so much a campaign for free trade as it is social engineering of interests in the two countries.

NOTES

1. We also assume that the trade negotiations will force some changes in U.S. policy. For example, the U.S. government discriminates in its procurement codes and U.S. law places greater restrictions on the foreign ownership of PSTNs than does Canadian legislation. Moreover, the United States has not accommodated Canadian wishes to put new mobile satellite services on UHF, a source of great irritation to Ottawa. But the focus here is on Canada. Additional details on Canadian telecommunications can be found in Jonathan D. Aronson and Peter F. Cowhey, "Trade in Telecommunications and Information Services," in Robert Stern, ed., *Trade and Investment in Services: Canada/U.S. Perspectives* (Toronto: University of Toronto Press for the Ontario Economic Council, 1985); Peter F. Cowhey, "The Informatics Sectors," *International Journal* (Winter 1986/87).

2. Several Northern Telecom employees in the United States seem to spend all their time insisting to American officials and journalists that Northern Telecom is a U.S. company. This was particularly evident in September 1985 when NTT picked Northern Telecom over AT&T on a $200 million contract for switching

equipment. NTT and the Japanese both stressed that all the switches would be manufactured in the United States.

3. Computer trade statistics are from a release of the Electronic Directorate, Statistics Canada, dated April 1986. The telecommunications trade balance is cited in Wilson P. Dizard and Lesley D. Turner, "Telecoms and Canada-U.S. Free Trade Talks," *Transnational Data and Communications Report* (July 1987): 15–18.

4. Fiber optic cable has a tariff in both countries of about 11.5 percent. In both countries the tariff on computer hardware is about 4.0 percent while peripherals and software are duty free. Our discussion of equipment, basic services, and value-added services draws heavily on a working paper prepared by the National Telecommunications Information Administration (NTIA) of the U.S. Department of Commerce in 1984.

5. We estimate the higher end of the range of costs for computing equipment by combining the Canadian federal sales tax of 10 percent and a combination of the nominal tariff and the Canadian government's method for determining the customs' valuation of the equipment. Some parties claim that Canada's valuation method greatly increases its level of effective protection. Interviews with representatives of IBM Canada, and Telecom Canada, Toronto and Ottawa, November 28, 30, 1984.

6. The Canadian federal government directly regulates Bell Canada, British Columbia Telephone, Canadian National Canadian Pacific Telecommunications, Teleglobe Canada, and Telesat Canada. The ten other telephone companies, three of which are provincially owned, are provincially regulated.

7. Interview data, 1986.

8. Based on correspondence from Northern Telecom to the Office of the U.S. Trade Representative dated September 8, 1985.

9. Dizard and Turner, "Telecoms and the Canada-U.S. Trade Talks," also note that some provinces have preferential procurement policies for suppliers from their territories. It is not clear if their practices are under federal jurisdiction, or how great a problem this constitutes.

10. CBEMA, "Transborder Data Flow," pp. 1–10.

11. "Northern Telecom and Apple Join Forces in the Office Automation Field," *Wall Street Journal*, September 15, 1986, p.4. For more analysis on the consequences of international corporate arrangements see David Mowery, *High Technology Partnerships and the Transfer of Technology* (Washington, D.C.: American Enterprise

Institute, 1986) and Peter F. Cowhey and Jonathan D. Aronson, *International Corporate Alliances* (Cambridge, Mass.: Ballinger, forthcoming).

12. Bell Canada, operating in Quebec and Ontario, owns significant portions of each of the main telephone companies in the Atlantic provinces. British Columbia Telephone is indirectly owned by GTE. The principal telephone companies in Alberta, Manitoba, and Saskatchewan are provincially owned and regulated. The remaining four are privately owned and provincially controlled. Telecom Canada (Department of Public Relations), *Statistics 1983* (Ottawa, 1983).

13. We have used interview materials to supplement the insightful analysis of Richard Schultz and Alan Alexandroff, *Economic Regulation and the Federal System* (Toronto: University of Toronto Press, 1985).

14. The key case is CNCP vs. Alberta Government Telephone. Ultimately this case will probably establish the right of the federal government to override provincial objections to the introduction of new competition in the long-distance market.

15. Evidence of J. G. Sutherland, president and chief executive officer of CNCP Telecommunications, prepared in support of the Application for the Interchange of Traffic with the Public Switched Telephone Networks, Before the Canadian Radio-television and Telecommunications Commission, April 9, 1984, especially pp. 19–23.

16. Interviews in Toronto and Ottawa, November 28–30, 1984.

17. CNCP Telecommunications, "Telecommunications Policy: Riding the Waves of Change," prepared for the Telecommunications Policy Review, Department of Communications, Ottawa, May 1984; CNCP Telecommunications, Application for Interchange of Traffic with Public Switched Telephone Networks, Before the Canadian Radio-television and Telecommunications Commission, Filed October 25, 1983.

18. Some Canadian scholars are actively repeating estimates concerning the loss of service for the poor in the United States that the data do not support. One estimate is that 150,000 subscribers (or 400,000 people) would lose phone service in Canada if rates were merely rebalanced. This argument is based on the mistaken estimate that the U.S. local rates could jump 50 percent and cause the degree of universal access to drop about 8 percent to 84 percent of U.S. households. See Robert Pike and Vincent Mosco, "Cana-

dian Consumers and Telephone Pricing — From Luxury to Necessity and Back Again," *Telecommunications Policy* 10, no. 1 (March 1986): 17–32.

19. *Telecommunications Reports*, February 23, 1987, pp. 22–23; "Canada to Sell Teleglobe to Memotek," *Telephony*, February 23, 1987, p. 13. Bell Canada subsequently purchased a minority interest in Memotek.

20. See the following exchange: Steven Globerman, "Predatory Pricing and Foreclosure in Telecommunications," *Telecommunications Policy* 9, no. 4 (December 1985): 319–28; Robert E. Babe, "Rejoinder: Predatory Pricing and Foreclosure in Canadian Telecommunications," ibid.: 329–33.

21. Interviews, Ottawa, October 1986.

22. See the discussion of Schultz and Alexandroff, *Economic Regulation and the Federal System*.

23. According to our reconciliations of data provided in interviews by major carriers, private leased lines services account for at least 20 percent of the value of U.S.-Canadian long-distance traffic.

24. OCCs typically spent over $10 million for facilities to handle Canadian traffic. USTR announced that it would press for acceptance of basic principles about the right of entry rather than fight on behalf of a specific carrier. USTR had to be sensitive to the concerns of AT&T, which had invested in the expectation that the U.S. government was not going to take sides among U.S. carriers.

25. The phone companies disagree among themselves about the amount of competition to accept. Bell Canada argued that it costs $1.93 to generate $1.00 of local service revenue, versus $0.32 to generate $1.00 of long-distance revenue. CNCP disputed Bell's computation. Joseph S. Schmidt and Ruth M. Corbin, "Telecommunications Policy in Canada, The Regulatory Crisis," *Telecommunications Policy* 7, no. 3 (September 1983): 215–27.

26. A joint venture of Bell Canada, Ameritech, and Telenet Communications intends to provide a network gateway to databases and electronic messaging services. The service, Inet, will use Telenet packet switching. Ameritech paid $5 million for 15 percent of the venture, subject to getting a waiver from Judge Greene. Mitch Beits, "Trio Targets Info Services," *Computerworld*, August 31, 1987, pp. 14–15.

27. Interviews, August and September 1987.

28. I. P. Sharp was purchased by Reuters, a British firm, in 1987. *Directory of Online Databases* 8, no. 3 (New York: Cuadra/

Elsevier, 1987); "Networks Bring Useful Benefits," *Financial Times*, Special Survey on Computers in Business, April 11, 1983, p. 18. Canada appears to be a comparatively weak player; with total exports of data services to the U.S. of about $10 million annually, Canada is a major importer of these services.

29. Our estimates are based on data concerning the volume of access lines devoted to different services. Interviews suggest that demand growth for basic services will be about 5 percent per annum, while those for enhanced services could be three to four times that rate.

30. The Canadian banking act of 1980 allows U.S. banks to process data on Canadian citizens outside Canada but requires that a complete set of records on Canadian transactions be maintained within Canadian borders. Kenneth J. Friedman, "The 1980 Canadian Banks and Banking Law Revision Act: Competitive Stimulus or Protectionist Barrier?" *Law and Policy in International Business* 13, no. 3 (1981): 783–810 or Ronald L. Plesser, "Issues of Data Flow Across National Borders Must be Faced," *ABA Banking Journal* (February 1982): 71–78.

31. The Royal Bank acknowledged that some Canadian value-added networks might face competitive difficulties from free trade. Therefore, it favored combining tax relief and R&D assistance for the value-added networks. Rowland Frazee, "Trade and Technology, It's Canada's Move," a speech prepared for delivery to the Canadian Club of Toronto, November 7, 1983, published by the Royal Bank of Canada; Rodney de C. Grey, "Traded Computer Services, An Analysis of a Proposal for Canada/U.S.A. Agreement," Grey, Clark, Shih and Associates for the Royal Bank of Canada, 1983.

32. CBEMA, "Transborder Data Flow," presents a general view on transborder data flows. The criticism is found in remarks of Mr. Loewen of the Canada Independent Computer Services Association, as reported in "Conference Report: Joining the Information Club," *Telecommunications Policy* 10, no. 1 (March 1986): 72–76.

7

CAN COMPETITION BE REPULSED?
Setting Standards in Europe

Domestic regulators and international trade negotiators have devised many ways of using the design or application of technical standards to block competition. Standard setting is essential for the design of telecommunications and information services, but many analysts worry that, by adroitly mixing pricing and design policies, dominant phone networks can undercut the potential for competition in telecommunications and information markets. This chapter examines the potential for repelling international competition by rigging the design of the next generation of the telecommunications network.

Using the debate about the future of European telecommunications and computer policies as a test case permits us to examine the potential for modernizing the sector when there is no commitment to a free trade or deregulation model along the U.S. lines. Europe trails Japan and the United States in data processing and microelectronics but is reasonably competitive in telecommunications and broadcasting equipment. Many European business and government leaders see telecommunications and broadcasting as Europe's last chance for competitiveness in advanced electronics this century. For them the key question is: How can Europe and each country in it become more competitive in telecommunications in high-technology sectors more generally, and ultimately across sectors?[1]

Obviously, postal telegraph and telephone authorities can use their monopoly control over the network (including procurement practices, research funds, and rules governing what equipment customers may hook up to the network) to support national equipment makers. More elaborately, PTTs can manipulate

177

pricing, technical standards, and permission to provide independent data communications services in ways that *alter the demand for competing types of customer premises equipment in the short run*. These same actions can *give market cues to suppliers about what features to design for a particular product line in the long run*. For example, in the short run, PTT manipulations might influence a firm's choice about whether to spend more on new switchboards or on computer terminals. In the longer run firms might be signaled about whether to build low- or high-powered communication satellites.

THE EUROPEAN ALTERNATIVES

To date, European choices have indicated that they will abandon the most rigidly nationalistic forms of mercantilism for telecommunications. However, the PTTs of Europe are still a long way from renouncing the old system of national monopoly linked to an international cartel for services—a classic set of national mercantilistic policies. The PTTs adapted slowly and awkwardly to the merger of computers and communications. Most European PTTs continued to cling to their traditional postal, telephone and telex monopolies. Some even hoped to expand the scope of their monopolies by extending the notion of technological "national champions" to the data communications network.

To achieve their ends, the more aggressive PTTs

1. require some local processing of information (thus reducing savings that users could realize by employing remote data processing networks);

2. advocate abolition of private leased lines (in order to force users onto the public switched network where they could then be charged on a volume-sensitive basis);

3. forbid the resale or shared use of capacity on private leased lines (thus making it uneconomical for users with smaller communication needs to consider leased lines).

For similar reasons some PTTs

4. prohibited connecting a private leased line to the public switched network;

5. banned the establishment of independent transmission facilities;

6. required use of PTT supplied equipment for the "first phone" on a line or the modems for data communications;

7. make testing and "type" (generic testing) of customer premises equipment very difficult;

8. run essentially a closed procurement policy for network equipment to support suppliers that are national champions in both telecommunications and computers.

The Deutsche Bundespost has come to symbolize national mercantilism. Despite growing pressure from domestic and international users, other German ministries, the United States, and the European Community, the Bundespost continues to follow a national, protectionist policy with regard to equipment, basic telecommunications services, and enhanced services. The Bundespost stubbornly insists that a subscriber's premises is inseparable from the network. It consistently argues that it must put the good of the customer before the good of the manufacturer. All primary instruments (although not all private branch exchanges) are supplied to users by the Bundespost to protect the customer and the network. The Bundespost once based its policies on three unquestioned assumptions:

1. The market for services is essentially static.

2. The Bundespost is more technologically competent to judge and serve the needs of its users than the German users.

3. Liberalization will inevitably lead to cream skimming and substantial revenue losses.

Therefore, while almost all other PTTs have been moving slowly toward liberalization and competition, the Bundespost has been backtracking.

On the equipment side, the Bundespost has stated that between 1988 and 1992 it will annually buy about DM 5–6 billion in sophisticated central office switching equipment, but only from two sources: Siemens and SEL (ITT's German subsidiary that is now owned by France's Alcatel). Approval procedures for attachment of equipment have grown more, not less complicated, making it particularly difficult for foreign firms to succeed in selling sophisticated customer premises equipment in Germany.[2] Although the Bundespost promised U.S. officials in December 1985 that they would work to liberalize in these areas, in March 1987 the United States remained extremely dissatisfied by the absence of any significant progress. There was considerable discussion in Washington of retaliating against West Germany by subjecting regional Bell operating companies' purchases of Siemens' network equipment to severe scrutiny.

Germany long refused to grant operating agreements to more than one international long-distance carrier. Thus, British Telecom, but not Mercury, could send and receive telephone traffic between Germany and the United Kingdom. In September 1987 the Bundespost announced that, like AT&T, MCI would be granted its own gateway. In addition, despite protests from smaller U.S. carriers, US Sprint was chosen to operate a common gateway for other U.S. providers of long-distance services.[3]

As of September 1987 the Bundespost still flatly refused to allow private parties to provide value-added and information services to the public over private leased lines from the Bundespost. Although the Bundespost promised in December 1985 to liberalize the provision of enhanced services after the harmonization of tariffs in 1988, the United States remains skeptical. The United States worries (1) that the Bundespost has resisted setting a date on which parties may provide new services to the public via private line circuits; (2) that the Bundespost's proposed new pricing structure for leased lines will perpetuate the Bundespost's monopoly by charging third parties substantially more for private line circuits than it charges itself; (3) that even if the first two issues are overcome, competition may still not arise because proposed prices for domestic and international leased lines are unreasonably high.[4]

However, there was finally some reason for optimism in September 1987 when, after two and one-half years of deliberation, the twelve-member Witte Commission presented to Chancellor Kohl some surprising liberal proposals for deregulating the Bundespost.[5] The Commission found that contrary to Bundespost claims, its monopoly position was not protected by the West German constitution. Although it may be unconstitutional to privatize the Bundespost, the constitution does not prevent allowing competition. This parliamentary report recommended the separation of the post and telecommunications businesses of the Bundespost. By a six to six vote the Commission decided against a proposal that would have allowed competitors to the Bundespost in the provision of the basic network service. Instead, a new body, to be called Telekom, would retain the monopoly on the basic network and on the telephone service. However, competition would be allowed in the provision of value-added network services, mobile radio, and satellite television. It appears that private enterprise would be able to provide all telecommunications services except voice. However, competition in the provision of voice mail would be permitted, and the Witte Commission appears to favor eventual competition in the provision of voice services. For now, Telekom would retain the monopoly over leased lines, but the Witte Commission indicated that unless it provided leased lines at satisfactory rates, a competitor could be licensed after three years. (This is a step behind but somewhat akin to the Japanese Diet's threat to break up NTT if its new competitors did not win a reasonable share of the Osaka-Tokyo long-distance market.) The Commission sought closer regulation of Bundespost tariffs and urged that tariffs decline. The prospects for volume-sensitive tariffs, due to be introduced in January 1988, were ambiguous. In addition, if the Witte Commission recommendations are accepted, the Bundespost would lose its exclusive right to provide the first telephone instrument.[6]

Not everyone was happy with the recommendations. Elements of Bundespost management, the left-wing postal union, the right-wing Bavarian government, and some favored equipment suppliers remained opposed to significant deregulation. On the other hand, some in Germany doubt whether the Witte Commission is more than a pro forma bow toward outside pressures. Some believe that once this report is filed, it will be ignored or discounted. But although the Bundespost remains the largest employer in Germany and has great influence, Bundespost management may decide to accept many of the Witte Commission recommendations.

One factor favoring this prediction is the increased push by the Commission of the European Community for European telecommunications integration. On June 30, 1987, the Commission released a Green Paper that provided the first official written statement of Commission policy on the development of a telecommunications regime in Europe.[7] In 1986 the Task Force on Telecommunications and Information was upgraded, becoming Directorate General XIII (Telecommunications, Information Industries, and Innovation), indicating the importance attached to this area. However, this finding was issued as a Green Paper rather than a more action-inducing White Paper.

In an effort to promote "the completion of a Community-wide market for goods and services by 1992" the Green Paper advocates liberalization and competition, but it envisions controlled liberalization and far less radical deregulation than in the United States. Public monopolies could continue to provide the basic network infrastructure and all voice services would remain exempt from competition. At the same time, the Green Paper stresses the necessity of expanding competition in the provision of enhanced services and terminal equipment and advocates the development of an integrated European market for services. (Given continuing disagreement among EC member countries, it is not surprising that the line dividing basic and enhanced services is not clearly drawn.) At the core of the Green Paper are ten proposed positions. Although its language is more careful and precise, in essence the paper sees a Europe in which:

1. PTTs continue to control and operate the network infrastructure but competitive, two-way satellite systems are allowed on a case-by-case basis
2. No new competition in the provision of voice telephone service
3. All other services provided on an unrestricted basis within and between Member States (for own use, shared use, or provision to third parties)
4. Strict standards for network infrastructure and services for all service providers including PTTs
5. By Community Directive, all requirements imposed by PTTs on providers of competitive services for use of the network to be clearly defined
6. Unrestricted provision of terminal equipment including Receive Only Earth Stations (Provision of the first telephone set could be excluded.)
7. Separation of regulatory and operational activities of PTTs
8. Strict continuous review of commercial activities of PTTs, particularly regarding cross-subsidization of services and manufacturing
9. Strict continuous review of all private providers in newly opened sectors to avoid the abuse of dominant positions
10. Full application of the Community's common commercial policy to telecommunications. Information to be provided to build up a consistent Community position for GATT negotiations and relations with Third Countries[8]

Overall, the Green Paper seeks liberalization to achieve a common market in telecommunications equipment and services without totally alienating the PTTs. By calling for unrestricted provision of all telecommunications services other than telephone voice service, the Commission has taken an important step. Nonetheless, the Green Paper would allow PTTs to maintain their position with regard to voice services, which generally account for more than 85 percent of PTT revenue. The Green Paper even concedes the first telephone instrument to the PTT. In addition, "the Commission states that both the prohibition of voice resale and the form of tariff for leased lines must remain the

183

prerogative of the PTT in each Member State."[9] Similarly, some of the provisions regarding technical standards and the protection of the network could be interpreted in ways that would limit non-European competitors.

In short, the Witte Commission report indicates clearly that the German (as well as Swiss and Austrian) nationally based mercantilist policies are unlikely to be maintained over the medium or long term. The European Communities Green Paper reinforces this conclusion, calling for a departure from many old PTT practices. New policies will be crafted. But the Green Paper can be interpreted in many ways and its recommendations are still far from being implemented. Many alternatives still can be envisioned. We consider two simplified models for change over the next five years: Europe-wide "benign mercantilism" and selective liberalization.[10]

Europe-wide "Benign Mercantilism". Europe could decide to integrate its national markets into a European market without significantly liberalizing competition. This would require a mix designed to restrict competition by non-European manufacturers and service providers, some sharing of costs and markets throughout the European Community by European firms, no competition in telecommunications facilities and very limited competition in enhanced services. For example, the European Community, through common R&D projects, might encourage European joint ventures for supply of network equipment, some liberalization of customer premises equipment, and extensive control over data services by the PTTs. The goal would be to create a friendly milieu for European information equipment and services firms; but each country would primarily rely on its own national supplier. If the PTTs also dominated the new services areas of data processing by constructing a highly centralized version of an integrated services digital network in order to promote European computers firms, an EC-wide policy of benign mercantilism could emerge (see below).

Selective Liberalization under the Auspices of the EC. Following this approach, the EC would systematically choose pro-competitive programs from its existing menu of initiatives.[11] PTTs' monopolies on basic services and transmission facilities might continue, but perhaps in modified form. The main objectives would be to set some common minimum technical standards for digital communications, open competition in the customer premises equipment market, permit limited competition by non Europeans for network equipment, encourage much greater competition in the provision of enhanced services, and retain freedom of competition in computers.

To date, the initiatives of the European Community have preeminently focused on breaking up the rigidly national organization of the European telecommunications market. They could ultimately be consistent with either benign mercantilism or selective liberalization. This chapter asks if the political and economic conditions would permit a policy of benign mercantilism in the market possible. It concludes that even if Europe attempted to implement benign mercantilism in the design of the network it would likely make compromises that would deviate significantly from the strategy. Europe should carefully consider selective liberalization of regional and international competition.

COMPETITIVE PROBLEMS

Europeans worry that they are falling dangerously behind in the critical fields of microelectronics and computing. Underlying Europe's problems in information technology is its poor performance in the semiconductor and computer sectors. "Europe produced less than 5 percent of world integrated circuit output in 1982, against 70 percent for the United States and 25 percent for Japan."[12] The IBM grip on the European market particularly galls European policymakers. Although experts believe that Europe is better positioned to compete in telecommunications, even there it is vulnerable.

On the positive side in services markets, the PTTs have begun introducing a wide variety of new value-added services.

France's Minitel is considered the most successful videotex service in the world.[13] The five Scandinavian countries adopted a common standard and surged to an early lead in cellular mobile telephone services. The Spanish were among the first to introduce a public packet switching network in the late 1970s.

Problems are equally widespread. For example, the German Bundespost's Datex P network was so notoriously expensive and poor in performance that there was a substantial flow of illegal communications traffic to Belgium where users could buy alternative data processing services. Overall, the European market for information services lags significantly behind the United States. Using the narrowest definition of information services, the U.S. market in 1982 was $2.6 billion while that in Europe was roughly $530 to $750 million.[14]

Europe's lagging market in information services is a serious problem because only by combining data communications in packages with telecommunications and computer equipment that appeal to large users can leadership be established. Europe is responding by aggressively modernizing its network. By 1995 European expenditures to expand and modernize their telecommunications networks could reach $130 billion. By the end of the century an additional $240 billion could be spent for terminals and associated equipment.[15]

Spending by European PTTs will grow rapidly because European per capita investment in telecommunications facilities trails the United States and Japan. (Per capita investment for telecommunications is about $57 in Europe, $72 in Japan, and $90 in the United States.) Already, after long delays, European officials have accepted that their industries suffer from problems of scale in production. European companies are having to realign their strategies (through price cuts and strategic alliances among European firms) to catch up in global competition. (In addition, European firms are banking on the potential of a smart ISDN under PTT control as the target market for their switches as the building blocks for a smart centralized network. This network will also support a complete line of highly standardized customer premises equipment.) As a result, the EC and the PTTs have started to encourage collaboration among their national equipment suppliers for the next generation of switching. (France's Alcatel bought the largest European switch maker, ITT, and offered to make Spain, Italy, and Belgium partners.) These alliances reduce the size of cross-subsidies to equipment makers for any individual nation and assure enough cooperation to facilitate standardized digital services.[16]

In short, Europe's strategy for network equipment is closely tied to the PTTs' strategy for handling challenges from the information industry. Yet, so far the overall European record on equipment and enhanced services leaves much to be desired. This opens the possibility that Europe will turn to "benign mercantilism" in an effort to bolster its competitive position.

A STANDARD SOLUTION

Most efforts to capture markets by rigging technological standards build on a seemingly bland mixture of efficient technical design and endorsements of the benefits of standardization. Often, they contain a number of sensible and praiseworthy elements, but the total package can have pernicious consequences.

To illustrate this phenomenon, this section examines how a benign mercantilist might structure a proposal for the creation of an ISDN in Europe. Then it contrasts the rhetoric that would surround such a proposal with a description of the hidden objectives that could underlie such a technical program.

The Purposes of the Policy

All countries are moving to some form of an integrated services digital network. The question is what form the ISDN will take. The purposes of a mercantilist ISDN would be threefold: equity, efficiency, and industrial policy.

Equity. The annual revenues of the largest European PTTs are about $15 billion, somewhat smaller than NTT, about the same

187

size as GTE, and about a third again as large as the U.S. regional Bell operating companies. In a competitive market will PTTs be able to continue to heavily cross-subsidize smaller users and still generate adequate research funds to keep national equipment makers competitive in the expensive race to develop the next generation of technology? (PTTs would be vulnerable on this account if they implement an ISDN design that extends fiber optic cabling into residences.)[17]

If, as expected, competition pulls the fastest growing, most profitable new services away from PTT monopoly control, how can the PTTs remain profitable and true to their missions?[18] PTTs are especially worried about possible cream-skimming that could arise if users could pay lower rates for sharing leased lines than they now pay on the public network. Thus, a mercantilist ISDN would force customers to pay the cost of supporting both the basic and advanced systems. By manipulating prices, users could be forced to migrate from existing data networks to the public ISDN. Pricing systems could be designed to prevent large users from engineering their own leased channels to gain significant advantages.

Efficiency. Some economists and communications experts assert that there may be economies of scale and scope involved in the installation of the next generation of digital transmission and switching euipment that can only be realized by a monopoly. What works in a market the size of the United States may be inefficient for the French or German market. Further, it is sometimes argued, that technical efficiency may be possible only if all interconnections within a network are managed by a monopoly (see Chapter 3).[19]

Industrial Policy. The merger of computers and communications always poses a fundamental question about where the intelligence of the combined system should reside. To be blunt, *a mercantilist, European industrial strategy would have two primary purposes: (1) To undercut IBM's position by increasing the market share of European computer and software firms and*

(2) to standardize the network of the future in order to bolster European manufacturers of central office switches.

To some, the key obstacle preventing the establishment of European-designed technical standards is IBM's dominance of the European mainframe computer market. IBM is more European in approach than any national computer firm in Europe. Mercantilists believe that in the absence of government intervention IBM's own standard for communicating among computers, Systems Network Architecture (SNA), would probably emerge as the de facto standard for all data communications systems.[20] Mercantilists and many others want to prevent this outcome. They have many sympathizers in the U.S. computer industry.

European firms complain about weaknesses in the SNA. More fundamentally, European competitors believe that IBM's influence will be reinforced if it is the *primary* designer of the next generation of standards. Europeans are still upset about their failure in the 1970s to develop a viable European manufacturer of mainframes to compete with IBM. Those fearing IBM are skeptical that IBM's agreement to support other interconnect standards for equipment in addition to SNA and its pledge to make earlier announcements of its plan for new products will suffice to deter SNA. (These were the two important conditions of the settlement of the EC antitrust suit against IBM in 1984.)

The Technical Design

Both a liberal and a benign mercantilist strategy would begin by promoting common standards for some minimum core configuration of ISDNs being developed in different countries.[21] This would require encouraging common technical standards for digital switching and transmission systems that could use existing copper cables. For example, by providing for at least two 64 kbit/second channels and a 16 kbit/second control channel (the "D" channel), planners could implement a uniform European approach that could handle the transport of digital services and allow the combined transmission of voice and slow- to medium-speed data. Later, Europe might move on to a "broadband" ISDN using fiber optics that could handle voice, high-speed data and video services (such as broadcasting and videoconferences that require a huge flow of bits per second).

An ISDN becomes mercantilist when its terms for entry, pricing, and systems architecture are designed to make sure that the PTT will be the dominant (not necessarily the sole) source and designer of value-added services. The PTT could discourage all independent provision of telecommunications facilities. It also could provide all data communication channels and charge each user on the basis of the number of bits transmitted (instead of by the number of lines used). Special communication services, such as data bases or videotex, would be carried (or supplied) by the PTT and be listed on a single public directory. By making the system as smart as possible and by excluding alternative approaches to combining communications and data, the system pushes the PTT (and the communications system) to standardize much of the information industry. In short, the PTT would try to use its control over a vital part of the combined information and communications industries to set technical standards that would give it competitive leverage over the information industry.[22]

The key technical vehicle for turning an ISDN into benign mercantilism is the marriage of ISDN to Open System Interconnection (OSI), a standard for computer communications worked out by the International Standards Organization (ISO). OSI attempts to ensure that any end user can interconnect with another. A brief, technical description of the linkage between OSI and ISDN will help clarify the politics and economics surrounding its adoption.[23]

OSI has seven layers (or levels). The lower layers, 1–3, define how the network interconnects with users' data terminals and manage the transmission of data. Layer 4 is a halfway house. Layers 5–7 define how a particular program or piece of equipment for using data will translate the communicated data into the task at hand. It *is* possible to design an efficient data communications network that standardizes the lower levels but leaves the higher levels up to individual users or suppliers. (Control Data, for example, is most concerned about level 2 standards.) Substantial international agreement already exists on how to implement most of layers 1–3. (Layer 3's X.25 standard for packet switched data networks is perhaps the best known. However, there are several variations of the X.25 standard, some of which are not fully compatible.) Negotiations continue on standards for layer 4, but significant variations are already emerging.[24]

The central question about ISDN's technical design is Who should manage the format for advanced communications and provide the new enhanced services and customer premises equipment to the network? Should it be the central network, the major users, or the independent suppliers of enhanced services? *A more mercantilist ISDN would work to extend PTT control past layer 3, to layer 4 and if possible into layers 5–7.*[25] It would also give the PTT control over much of the customer premises equipment that links the central network to the premises of the user (the so-called network termination equipment). A more pro-competitive policy would limit PTT control to the lower layers and would worry less about standardization of the upper levels than about achieving a clear, flexible agreement on layers 1–3. It would also allow users and vendors to own and design much of the network termination equipment.

A mercantilist strategy might help the European telecommunications and computer equipment industries in three ways. First, if they can agree among themselves, European companies would strongly influence the writing of standards and software. This means that equipment makers would find it much easier to compete against SNA and IBM. Large domestic users (as opposed to U.S. multinationals) will have a local, or European, alternative to IBM for its information system.

Second, data communications will develop somewhat more slowly because the pace of installation of the ISDN would determine the growth of data communications. Europe lags in this market. This would give it time to catch up, especially if others also adopt mercantilist ISDNs.

Third, and most important, *an ISDN can alter the mix of equipment sales and influences who buys what in ways that favor national producers.* In short, an ISDN moves a larger share of the data processing tasks of the information industry to the

191

PTT-controlled public network. Therefore, "smart" switches and data processing equipment appropriate for massive sophisticated phone companies increase as a share of total demand of the information industry. In general, equipment will be more standardized, longer in its life span, and more geared to centralized information processing.[26] The specialized, highly innovative technology produced by smaller firms for distributed processing and telecommunications systems (such as smart computer terminals to manage telecommunications) becomes less salient in this environment (partly because the PTT controls the network termination equipment). The buying power of the PTTs becomes much more important for the information industry, and the major European telecommunications-data processing firms (which overlap) are likely to do better in an environment stressing reliability rather than rapid innovation geared to many diverse groups of users. Of course, this development may most favor Japanese equipment makers, which specialize in high-quality, low-cost standardized equipment.

LIMITATIONS ON THE OSI AND ISDN PROGRAMS

Could Europe reach agreement on the standards needed for a benign mercantilist strategy? If it did, would it ease its problems? Our answer to the first question is no.[27] Our reply to the second query is that the strategy for OSI confuses two related objectives: the reduction of an existing disadvantage and the creation of a new competitive advantage. A mercantilist strategy that established standards such as OSI could help reduce some old liabilities. It might lessen the degree to which European suppliers are hampered by the lack of a unified European market. But we doubt that such a strategy could create new commercial advantages for European firms because the new standards would not serve as the basis for altering the balance of industrial power.

To illustrate our argument and underscore our hypotheses we examine one key case of competitive standard setting in detail. Supporters of OSI are encouraged by the progress to date on levels 1–3; but is agreement likely on the higher levels? For a mercantilist strategy to work, it is not enough to build a slow, gradual consensus on standards. Instead, agreements would need to arrive quickly at *detailed standards* that carefully define all of the key parameters for the technology. However, overcoming difficulties in communicating between networks usually requires settling on *general standards* that define a broad approach but leave many important options unresolved during the early development of a technology. General standards increase the likelihood that conflicts of interpretation will arise that will require later revision.[28]

We offer four hypotheses about conditions that could prompt the setting of detailed standards. But in each instance the conditions that could lead to standardization also contain perverse disincentives that could provoke opposition to standardization.

All four hypotheses reflect a few common dynamics. It is difficult to get collective action to set standards because the benefits of standards flow to many, and the aggregate benefits far exceed the returns to the average supplier or user. Therefore, it takes a buyer or seller (or government) with an unusually large stake in the issue to assure action. These special players may have individual agendas that deviate from the optimum preference of all market participants. Moreover, standards for dynamic technologies frequently do not emerge out of some process of universal consent. Instead, actors will set strategies to lure a minimum core of the market, which will tilt the market in a way that latecomers will follow.[29]

Hypothesis 1. If a dominant supplier unilaterally establishes de facto standards, then it may later find it useful to help customers by formalizing the standards. However, this same supplier will be less enthusiastic about setting standards if it loses unilateral control over their definition or if a clear standard makes it easier for competitors to enter into related product lines that the supplier also dominates.

Hypothesis 2. If standardization would especially benefit a few major international buyers in the market (for example, through smaller inventory costs), then the buyers may cooperate to impose a common system design and other standards. However, these same buyers may not choose to cooperate on standardization because it hinders specialization of equipment and services that could provide them with significant competitive advantages. Many buyers in the information industry are interested in becoming sellers of value-added versions of these inputs.[30]

Hypothesis 3. If a few major sellers have roughly equal power in the market, then they may benefit from standardization if it expands the total size of the market (by making people more willing to buy a new technology) or if it makes economies of scale easier to achieve on products involving high development costs. However, standardization may also open the customer bases of producers to rivals with the resources necessary to contest it.[31]

Hypothesis 4 (a variant of Hypothesis 3). If there is a dominant firm and a few major firms in the second tier of the market, the second tier firms may benefit from creating an alternative to the standards of the dominant firm. However, the creation of an alternative set of standards may open their own customer base to rivals and a collective effort to set standards may be too slow to take advantage of a principal competitive strength of second tier firms, their ability to move more quickly in pursuing new niches than the larger dominant firm.

Despite the complexity of figuring out the interests of the major competitors, these four hypotheses may help illuminate the prospects for OSI/ISDN. The first hypothesis suggests why IBM has mixed motives about OSI.

IBM is the dominant company in mainframe computers. Therefore, it could aim to set a de facto standard (SNA) unilaterally. But its weaker grip on microcomputers and its poor position in minicomputers made it hard to block other suppliers from collaborating on an alternative system (see below). Moreover, IBM was under considerable antitrust pressure from the EC. Therefore, it moved in three directions at once.

First, it is making SNA an attractive integrated system in order to hold onto its customer base. It has announced plans for major value-added network and information systems in Japan, France, and the United Kingdom based on SNA. In addition, in 1985 it introduced modifications to SNA that make the system much more thoroughly integrated as an architecture and much more flexible in interconnecting networks originating out of several mainframe computers simultaneously. Then in 1986, IBM introduced a local area network (LAN) for microcomputers and workstations, including those of other makers, that can be connected to SNA.[32] A plan for its Rolm PBX to integrate voice and data over SNA followed quickly. Its new line of personal computers introduced in 1987 featured prominently new protocols for standardizing software writing and communications capabilities (Systems Applications Architecture), including ties to IBM mainframes.

Second, IBM has committed itself to compatibility with all OSI layers. But, as it has little incentive to make its own system too easily open to competitors, will IBM, in fact, support transparency at every level? (Hypothesis 1) Some observers suspect that even if IBM eventually conforms, it will drag its feet on interconnecting to the higher layers. More crucially, IBM has elected to connect SNA to OSI through "gateways" that do not introduce OSI into the internal SNA architecture. Although IBM is opening up its SNA and LAN architectures, mostly so that outside suppliers can design products for them, IBM will always have the greatest mastery of SNA. At the same time, IBM is working with NTT and others on ways to establish data communications systems that will open up non-SNA systems more easily to IBM penetration.[33]

Third, IBM will work aggressively to expand its data communications business because it is a vital auxiliary to the software growth that is central to IBM's plans. Achieving leadership in selected segments of the information services industry will also preempt this technology-market segment from serving as a staging ground to assault IBM's dominant position in the mainframe industry. In short, IBM will not reject OSI. Indeed, properly handled, OSI provides IBM with a legitimate excuse to position SNA as the leading data communications architecture without risking an antitrust action for abuse of market power.[34] But IBM's strategy does depend on forcing the PTTs to make available basic transport services for telecommunications at low costs in order to make them viable for users. And, it requires IBM to attack any effort to impose rigid standards for the higher OSI levels.

IBM is only part of the story. Hypothesis 2 suggests examining large corporate buyers. Some U.S. firms, such as Boeing and General Motors, are prominent supporters of OSI. General Motors used its massive buying power to force a major consortium of companies (including IBM, Hewlett-Packard and Motorola) to collaborate in working out a comprehensive system of protocols (Manufacturing Automation Protocol or MAP), which may become the industry standard.[35]

Large corporate users' support for OSI does not automatically translate into support of ISDN. It is not so easy to get detailed agreements on how to tie software protocols to plans for communications networks. For example, European automakers have resisted proposals for a common data network even though they are exploring MAP. There are three reasons for this phenomenon.

First, the overwhelming bulk of traffic is still voice. The economics of mixing voice and data is still tricky. IBM and AT&T's designs for LANs manage both voice and data, but they usually segregate these flows in important ways. It is not clear that an ISDN is the optimal way to mix them. Second, no single user's communication needs are distributed in a way that fits the "average user" that the ISDN seeks to serve. For example, bandwidth, speed, and formatting needs may vary greatly. A third reason for U.S. corporate resistance to an ISDN is that, until recently, the United States regulatory system significantly restricted the RBOCs from selling many enhanced services. Therefore, large users learned to manage many of these tasks through their own resources. They want to do the same thing in Europe. (A prime case is General Motors.) Moreover, to assure reliability and security, many large users insist on providing or duplicating functions at some OSI layers in their own system. They are not interested in an ISDN design that makes them pay twice.[36]

Finally, Hypotheses 3 and 4 point out the role of major nondominant suppliers. No other computer company can match IBM. But do second tier computer companies and the leading telecommunications firms share an interest in common standards? The answer is yes, up to a point. These companies, including several large American firms that developed their own network architectures, now support OSI as a way to counter the existing IBM advantage. The most dramatic development along this line was the creation of the Corporation for Open Systems (COS) by twelve U.S. firms that compete with IBM to accelerate OSI's development. IBM and many others later joined the group.

A particular benefit of COS for its members is its effort to centralize product testing and certification for all industrial countries. This process has been a particularly troublesome problem for U.S. firms trying to sell in other countries. Japanese and European firms have negotiated with COS about possible membership. (Reportedly, COS demanded access to more data about Japanese technology as a price for Japanese entry.) But the response of a key European computer official is noteworthy for what it tells us about standardization: "Even if we [Europeans] do our best, we will not prevent the telecommunications environment from being different than in the U.S. We cannot be in absolute agreement in the upper levels of the seven-layer Open Systems Interconnect model, although we will have more facility in the lower ones."[37]

In short, the biggest and most easily achieved benefit from OSI cooperation comes at levels 1–3 which are critical to many small and medium-sized customers. Cooperation at the higher OSI levels is technically and politically harder to achieve, especially for new technologies. The higher OSI levels are critical to new markets where innovation is rapid, such as videotex and automated manufacturing. The market for these services is not fully defined because it is just taking off and many new firms are entering the market. The large number of new players makes it harder to coordinate standards and gives each player an interest in building up its early market share by marketing exclusive software programs.

One of the most important characteristics of the market today is the race by Digital Equipment Corporation and other makers of minicomputers to attack IBM by declaring that they now have systems that support all seven OSI levels. But these systems have divergent philosophies lodged under the structure of OSI. (For example, DEC openly criticized General Motors' MAP protocols in 1987 as being unnecessary. Many large users and vendors heatedly rejected DEC's claims.) Equally important, the vendors solution does not necessarily support the pricing, speeds, bandwidths, and other specifications desired by the PTTs.[38]

How likely is it that companies and governments will create detailed common standards as an alternative to SNA? Recalling the distinction between detailed and general common standards, the analysis suggests four conclusions.

First, the biggest gains come from supporting OSI levels 1–3. Detailed standards for these layers are already providing the foundation for a credible alternative to SNA because they assure a *minimum* level of compatibility among the alternatives to SNA. To the extent that detailed standards for layers 1–3 are not developed, actors will search for flexible, inexpensive ways to manage remaining incompatibilities (for example by offering special software programs to interconnect networks).

Second, if companies and governments try to develop standards for the higher OSI levels early in a technology or market's development, they will create loose general standards. If first they write detailed standards, later major revisions will be required.[39] This makes it possible to adhere to standards and still experience many of the problems that would occur if no standards existed.

Third, if standardization occurs at the higher OSI levels, it will most likely take place under two circumstances. Very specific standards for particular applications may be imposed by large users in some cases (such as the GM and Boeing efforts). Or, more comprehensive standards may occur later in the cycle of market and technological development. In the future, when this stage is reached, one or two technological leaders will probably dominate the market, and all other competitors will have an incentive to cooperate in writing standards to make their systems compatible with the leaders.

Fourth, the first three conclusions suggest that OSI and an economically efficient design for value-added networks and information services will largely evolve out of multiple experiments and approaches at creating new ways to combine computers and communications. A master plan can lay out the basic outline of a future system, but it cannot at this stage impose a detailed list of specifics.

These four conclusions suggest that the prospects for creating new competitive advantages by installing detailed OSI standards and an ISDN are limited.[40] The strategy could reduce some existing competitive disadvantages faced by firms competing with IBM and it would limit some risks on new products in selected cases, but there also would be liabilities.

CONCLUSIONS ABOUT THE INFORMATION INDUSTRY

Everyone agrees that some form of an ISDN will dominate the future of telecommunications. This chapter has discussed how a benign mercantilist strategy might try to exploit technical standards. The analysis suggests three observations about how the delivery of network services affects competition.

First, if a mercantilist strategy were successful, this strategy would *change the mix* of the equipment needed in the market. IBM and all other data processing firms would lose market share to telecommunications corporations in the information market. This helps explain why many computer companies support OSI but oppose a mercantilist ISDN. (Obviously, this is a less serious problem for firms equally strong in both businesses.) Moreover, prospects for longer lived and centralized switching and processing installations would work against those with rapidly changing technologies. Ironically, this outcome might benefit IBM because

199

it is rarely the market leader in technological innovations. It would most certainly help the Japanese.

Second, the economic incentives and emphasis on preemptive setting of standards of the mercantilist ISDN could *send misleading cues* for technological innovation. Designing for an ISDN only makes sense if it will be replicated globally. Yet neither the American nor the Japanese markets are moving to a highly centralized ISDN, despite European claims to the contrary. Liberalization in both countries has made centrally designed and engineered systems impractical.[41] Furthermore, European high-technology companies have been plagued by their inability to predict the future market even when they commit ample financial and scientific resources. Designing for an ISDN system used only in Europe (or part of Europe) would reinforce European weakness.

Third, suppose that a minimum ISDN is adopted. Then producers and users (but not the PTTs) would have a *growing interest in* the sophisticated value-added and information services offered as *alternatives* to the public communication system. Value-added and information services can help reconcile divergent communication and equipment standards. Providers can configure their mix of software services and users' equipment to ensure quality and minimize costs for voice and data communications for specialized users. For example, the McDonnell-Douglas MacAuto services cater to medical clients. These services also could be an increasingly important tool in helping equipment makers to sell their products. For example, the enhanced service partners of AT&T and IBM in Japan are major Japanese electronic firms, which traditionally have not been major suppliers to NTT. Similarly, General Electric is configuring its value-added services to handle firms, using Apple computers, which GE is now stocking for resale to new clients.

Still, there is an important role for European collaboration in the information industry. Any politically acceptable strategy for the industry will include a strong element of governmental guidance. Moreover, if benign mercantilism threatens premature and excessively rigid standards, the pure American model for telecommunications may suffer from excessively conflictual standards. A more promising strategy would be to use the EC as a catalyst for selective liberalization in Europe.

Any liberalization strategy probably will be built on the recommendations of the EC Green Paper. The initial EC legislation probably will force all member countries to establish independent regulatory bodies for their communication affairs. Presumably this would deprive the PTTs in the EC of some of their power.[42]

They would also begin by breaking the narrow national boundaries on research and development and on procurement subsidies for network equipment. Well before the release of the Green Paper, the EC began to move in this direction with the establishment of the European Strategic Programme for Research and Development in Information Technology (Esprit). Esprit is a ten-year collaborative research program (1984–1993) "designed to help provide the European information technology (IT) industry with the key components of the technology it needs to be competitive on world markets within a decade." Esprit was designed to transfer technology across the EC by fostering collaboration and paving the way for standards. It is meant particularly to focus on pre-competitive R&D in five key areas: advanced microelectronics, software development, advanced information processing, office systems, and computer integrated manufacturing.[43]

The hallmark of the Esprit program is that EC funding is used to supplement projects identified and 50 percent funded by companies that are within the overall priorities of the program. This leads to substantially more flexible experiments with transnational collaboration than do programs largely designed and funded by the EC itself. However, the PTTs do not participate directly in Esprit, and the program was not designed to substitute an EC-wide program with implicit national quotas for the existing national preference systems. Accomplishing this would mean the extension of the Esprit program for information technologies to telecommunications.

This was one objective of the program for R&D in Advanced Communications technologies in Europe (RACE) which was established in 1985. RACE is designed to foster research and development necessary to allow for the introduction of EC-wide integrated broadband communications by 1995 in conjunction with the evolving ISDN. RACE is meant to clarify the potential for technology options, facilitate choice, and reduce uncertainty. RACE is more "system-driven" than Esprit and the R&D it will concentrate on is located between the precompetitive R&D which is the focus of Esprit and work on competitive development of technologies.[44] PTTs are involved with RACE. It is not yet clear, as some European critics have already noted, whether RACE will follow a pro-competitive strategy. (Indeed, for a time in 1987 RACE funding was on hold because the British refused to release EC R&D funds until EC budgetary differences are worked out.)

In addition to its push for unrestricted provision of all telecommunications services except voice services, the Green Paper makes clear the Commission's desire to foster greater economies of scale and competitive discipline for European firms by opening up significant shares of each national procurement market to other European firms. It began in 1985 by asking each PTT to open 10 percent of its telecommunications equipment procurement to firms from other EC members. It also sought the easing of barriers imposed by standards for testing equipment to be attached to the telecommunications network. The Green Paper urged increasing the percentage of open procurement to 40 percent. Ultimately the Commission wants open telecommunications procurement within the EC.

Following the Green Paper, there also is likely to be more support of standardization of the basic standards for digital transmission and switching, more open procurement, easier testing and certification, and uniformity of the basic services network for digital transmission in order to raise the size of the market available to all EC producers. This is not only economically desirable, it also would produce an important political consequence: larger markets for smaller makers of customer premises equipment give these producers an incentive to challenge existing restrictions on competition. This would bolster the EC by making the European political economy more like the United States, where the large and technically integrated market made it lucrative for small innovators to fight for the right to provide new services and equipment.

Ultimately, however, the most important initiatives proposed by the Witte Commission and the Green Paper involve liberalization of the provision of enhanced services. Even if the PTTs maintain their control over the basic network and over voice telephone services during the first round of liberalization, the establishment of a more open international market for enhanced services is also vital. It will help extend the political coalition in support of limited liberalization within the EC and serve as a catalyst for further reexamination by PTTs of their vested interests. Judging by the experience of the United States, the PTTs may decide that their best long-term strategy is change that extends well beyond even the proposals of the Green Paper. Consider the following three cases in the United States.

1. AT&T is redesigning its network to fit the ideal of Global Information Movement and Management. This system would provide global corporations with a single bill and a single customer service center for their global operations. Just as important, it would reconfigure the network to give the user a transparent, software-defined network. Practically speaking, this means that the customer can work out arrangements with AT&T to have almost any mix of speed, bandwidth, and services. It might have a value-added network for most of its data and a leased circuit for certain designated days of the week. From the viewpoint of the user, it might use AT&T facilities for its own private network for one function and be a passive provider of data for an AT&T value-added network on another function.[45]

2. US West (a regional Bell operating company) is proposing a radical new idea on how to break its monopoly on the local loop in return for greater freedom in new services. Under OSI competitors would "have access to the telephone network 'at any reasonable interface point.' . . . [A competitor] could set up a central office switch and have users on US West local loops connected to this switch [for basic or enhanced services]."[46] US West would charge its rivals the same price for access as it charged its own subsidiary. In return, US West could enter such

new fields as brokerage and insurance services, marketing research, and consumer electronics sales where its strengths as a large service firm could give it a competitive advantage in selected niches.

3. Ameritech (another RBOC) has designated computer software for LANs as a key growth market. It has decided to build its offerings around a system centered on IBM PC compatible machines rather than minicomputers (such as DEC or AT&T). If Ameritech is to offer an integrated communications and computer services strategy, then it will be interested in designing a smart network to work with sophisticated customer premises equipment consistent with an IBM standard.

No one knows which approach to designing networks is best. Instead, we want to stress that large public networks should start to look for new ways to blend computer and communications capacities once some competition enters the system. Greater international competition in telecommunications services complements any future EC strategy to promote more experimentation with the proper mix of intelligent communications systems. The fatal flaw of a mercantilist ISDN is that it would have to preempt the future in regard to too many key design elements before sensible compromises are possible.

NOTES

1. See, for example, M. Albert and R. J. Ball, "Towards European Economic Recovery in the 1980s," report presented to the European Parliament, Working Documents 1983–1984, August 31, 1983, particularly Chapter 6, "Creating a European Area for Industry and Research," pp. 71–82.

2. The Bundespost notes that U.S. firms (mostly subsidiaries operating in Germany) get about 4 percent of the Bundespost's annual procurement budget. In response, U.S. authorities note that almost all of these sales went to firms with "preferred supplier relationships" or were sales that went to U.S. military and government facilities in Germany.

3. The Bundespost, content with its dealings with AT&T, did not want to deviate from its preferred monopoly-to-monopoly dealings. Moreover, until the Witte Commission report was officially submitted to Chancellor Kohl in late summer 1987, the Bundespost had little incentive to announce concessions. Why should they give ground and get no credit for their action? However, in the spring of 1987 the Bundespost agreed to meet with four U.S. carriers—US Sprint, MCI, TRT, and FTCC—to consider operating with alternative long-distance carriers. Ultimately, the Bundespost agreed to allow two additional gateways for telephone traffic between West Germany and the United States that would not be routed via AT&T. US Sprint was chosen to operate the common gateway, and MCI was promised that it could operate its own independent gateway as long as it maintained at least a 13 percent share of the U.S.–West German traffic. If the protests of the smaller carriers are quelled, trial operations for subscriber traffic could begin in early 1988. Return traffic from West Germany to the United States will begin about six months after the successful opening of trial operations. (Telex from the Deutsche Bundespost to MCI, US Sprint, TRT, and FTCC, September 22, 1987; *Communications Daily*, September 29, 1987 and September 30, 1987.

4. U.S. government memorandum, 1986.

5. The Bundespost delayed making any concessions to competition before the Witte Commission report was filed. However, before the report was filed, the Bundespost became more aggressive on integrated services digital networks and on broadcasting. Broadcasting is more closely linked to telecommunications in Europe than in the United States because the PTTs, unlike their American counterparts, own the underlying broadcast facilities. By laying extensive amounts of new cable, the Bundespost, in effect, was forcing the German states to reconsider their policies against private broadcasting in order to utilize the new cable that was put at their disposal.

6. "West Germany ponders radical deregulation plan," *Telephony*, September 21, 1987, p. 12; "Witte Commission Report on Future of West German Telecommunications Presented to Kohl," *Telecommunications Reports*, September 21, 1987, pp. 28–29.

7. Commission of the European Communities, *Toward a Dynamic European Economy* COM(87) 290 final, Green Paper on the development of the common market for telecommunications

services and equipment (Brussels, Commission of the EC, June 30, 1987). Also see "An Analysis of the Draft EC Green Paper on the Development of the Common Market for Telecommunications Services and Equipment," Washington, D.C., U.S. Department of State, Office of Planning and Analysis, Bureau of International Communications and Information Policy, July 16, 1987, mimeo.

8. Green Paper, Section VI of the Summary Report and Section 10.3 of the full text.

9. Department of State, "Analysis of the Draft EC Green Paper," p. 5.

10. Neither of these models fully describes the current EC program, which contains a mix of pro-competitive and anti-competitive policies. Unlike traditional mercantilists who favored the maximization of national growth at the expense of other countries and therefore preferred strong government controls over the economy, many analysts now suggest that groups of governments (like the EC) can devise "benign" forms of mercantilism that permit greater government control of world markets as well as continued international economic growth, equity, and political harmony. Miles Kahler, "European Protectionism in Theory and Practice," *World Politics*, 37, no. 4 (July 1985):475–502. American economists are also reexamining whether protectionism may be beneficial under some circumstances. See Paul Krugman, ed., *Strategic Trade Policy and the New International Economics* (Cambridge, Mass.: MIT Press, 1986).

11. Judgments about what is pro-competitive or anti-competitive are ours. EC officials might disagree.

12. Europe has increased its share of semiconductors only to 15 percent "Chip Battle Grows in Europe," *New York Times*, May 11, 1987, p. 26Y. Stephen Woolcock, Jeffrey Hart, and Hans Van Der Ven, *Interdependence in the Post-Multilateral Era: Trends in U.S.-European Trade Relations* (Lanham, Md.: Center for International Affairs, Harvard University and University Press of America, 1985), p. 102.

13. Once notorious as a poor performing lazy monopolist, the French PTT has shown great energy and initiative in the last decade. Minitel is one of the few viable videotex services now in operation due to several clever ploys by the PTT. But, how much is Minitel really costing the French PTT? How much activity is not accounted for by directory services or by dating/sex bulletin boards and services? How long will it take for the system to be

profitable? Will the long-term changes in the way the French interact with computer terminals be worth the expense?

14. U.S. Department of Commerce, "A Competitive Assessment of the U.S. Data Processing Services Industry" (Washington, D.C.: DOC, December 1984), p. 9.

15. The EC estimates that in 1984 world public and private expenditures for telecommunications reached $125 billion, about $90 billion of which was spent by PTTs. Investment figures can be found in the ITU's annual *Yearbook of Common Carrier Telecommunications Statistics*. See also Research and Development in Advanced Communications Technologies for Europe, "Why RACE? draft working paper (Brussels: RACE, EC, 1985).

16. Although Siemens, Plessey, CIT-Alcatel-Thomson, and Italtel agreed to pursue joint development of a central office switch, most analysts doubt that this collaboration will succeed. The development of a switch involves too much sharing of core electronic and services technologies unless there is a wide-ranging and fundamental business partnership. Instead, European manufacturers favor selective strategic alliances (rather than a common front). No doubt some of the PTTs hope for a broader set of ties among the firms. This would explain why ITT was not included, because it was considered American even though its System 12 switch was developed in Europe. Philips was excluded because of its alliance with AT&T. Ericsson was left out because Sweden is not an EC member. For a brief overview of EC efforts to promote cooperation, see "European Telecommunications Cooperation: Wishful Thinking or an Achievable Reality?" *Telephony*, October 28, 1985. For a more detailed picture of the telecommunications collaboration that the EC wishes to encourage, see "Report of the Commission to the Council on R&D Requirements in Telecommunications Technologies as Contribution to the Preparation of the R&D Programme RACE" (Brussels: Commission of the European Communities, March 25, 1985), COM(85) 145 final. We will focus on these issues explicitly in our forthcoming *International Corporate Alliances* (Cambridge, Mass.: Ballinger).

17. It is hard to imagine how a household could generate the traffic to support a 2.048 megabyte/second connection. Calculations suggested by A. Michael Noll indicate that such a cable could handle about 500 pages of text every second! Therefore, a massive cross-subsidy will be required. The Arthur D. Little report, *Telecommunications Regulations Policy In the European Com-*

munity, USA and Japan, prepared for the EC in 1982–1983, estimated that the cost of lines for high-speed data connections to residences would be triple that of existing connections (p. 147).

18. There is a middle ground between monopoly provision and private free-for-all. Private firms could be sanctioned to compete with the PTTs in the provision of enhanced services (see Chapter 9).

19. Remember, however, that there are two ways to solve problems of equipment incompatibility. Either the equipment can be made compatible by adopting and enforcing common standards. Or, it may be that translation programs (protocol conversion) becomes so sophisticated that with little loss of efficiency, formally incompatible equipment can be made to talk to each other. Solutions that take some from each approach are, of course, also available.

20. IBM built its leadership in computers in part because it "bet the company" in the 1960s. It made the expensive commitment that all generations of its products would be compatible. SNA (and its successor SAA) was the result.

21. Everyone defines an ISDN differently. Our definition is more political than technological. We consider a system to be a minimum ISDN if it seeks primarily to allow digital switching and transport services in such a way that many different suppliers of value-added networks and information services can build their own proprietary systems while building on the basic digital services. Such a minimum ISDN (which may include broadband transmission) is consistent with a competitive system. To get a range of views on ISDN see Warren G. Bender, "Is the ISDN a Future Fact or Current Fancy?" *Telephony,* February 21, 1983, pp. 108–13, 164; International Chamber of Commerce, "ISDN—A Future Universal Telecommunications Network: A Business User View," ICC Policy Statements on Telecommunications and Transborder Data Flows, Position Paper 6 (Paris: ICC, November 1985).

22. Janusz A. Ordover and Robert D. Willig, "An Economic Definition of Predation: Pricing and Product Innovation," *Yale Law Journal* 91 (1981):8–53. On the German design see Helmut Schon, "The Deutsche Bundespost on its Way Toward Setting the ISDN," (Bonn: Bundespost, no date), mimeo; Anne Brit Thoresen, "Infrastructural Change: The Digitalization of the European Public-Switched Communication Infrastructure: How Will ISDN Emerge in Europe," (Berkeley, Calif.: Berkeley Roundtable on the

International Economy, 1985), mimeo. According to Robert Bruce, Jeffrey P. Cunard, and Mark Director, the Bundespost wishes to design the system so that technology defines the types of services rather than trying to maintain the CCITT's conceptual equivalent of basic and enhanced services, bearer and teleservices: *From Telecommunications to Electronic Services*, pp. 561–66.

23. The key organization developing recommendations for OSI standards is the CCITT of the ITU. See Ernst Weiss, "ISDN—User and Social Aspects," paper presented to the World Telecommunications Forum, 1983, and *Datamation*, April 15, 1985, pp. 67–70 for useful explanations.

24. An ideal European industrial strategy would also design and implement a common set of European computer operating systems that provided a viable alternative to IBM's SNA. The most likely prospect would pair the Unix operating system developed by AT&T and the OSI/ISDN standards championed by the CCITT and by CEPT. IBM's SNA evolved as a series of expedient compromises. In contrast, from the start AT&T designed Unix to integrate multiple users doing multiple tasks. Data communications was a key concern of the developers of Unix. This sophisticated operating system is fully backed by AT&T Labs. But, because AT&T is not powerful in the computer market, Unix is an attractive rallying point for companies looking for an alternative to IBM. A consortium led by Siemens and also including Bull, ICL, Nixdorf, and Olivetti is promoting the development and use of AT&T's System V and Microsoft's Xenix Systems 3 and 5, the major commercial versions of Unix. Microsoft, the designer of the most popular version of the DOS operating system, also has signed up to work with AT&T on cooperative research on Unix. The EC's Esprit Rose data network also chose Unix as its operating system. See *Datamation*, March 1, 1985, pp. 36–46.

25. At present most activities of European PTTs are restricted to layers 1–4. Discussions are underway to decide the extent to which layer 4 will become PTT-dependent because of the requirement for coordination through the so-called D-channel protocol, which has now become an international standard: (CCITT recommendation T.70). We thank the Commission of the European Communities, Directorate General for Telecommunications, Information Industries and Innovation for this input. Whether in the future European PTTs might try to extend their influence to layers 5–7 is not clear.

26. Ann Hutcheson Reid, "The Economic Stakes of the Integrated Services Digital Network" (Paris: OECD, 1984), mimeo.

27. The cellular mobile radio illustrates the problem of getting unity. Although Scandinavia was the early world leader in this technology, only the Benelux countries adopted the standard agreed to by Denmark, Sweden, Norway, Finland, and Iceland. The United Kingdom, France, West Germany, and Italy each adopted their own standard that was incompatible with all the others. See Kari Karaima, chairman of Nokia, (the Finnish pacesetter), Speech at the European Services Industry Forum, Brussels, April 24, 1987.

28. For example, to communicate between networks using different variations of the X.25 standard often requires special software or hardware engineering. And, agreement on X.25 standards is far more harmonious than in other cases where national telecommunications standards clash in Europe. For example, supporters of RACE concede that the first generation of European narrowband digital networks that are now being developed will not be fully compatible because each PTT has spent so much on individual national variations. PTT hopes for a fully compatible network rests on broadband transmission scheduled for the 1990s. On this last point see Robert Rosenberg, "OSI Protocol Products Proliferate; But Will They Talk to Each Other? *Data Communications*, May 1987, p. 58 and Marvin Sirbu and D. L. Estrin, "Standards," mimeo of a paper for Airlie House, 1985.

29. For a detailed, complementary analysis of standards, see Stanley M. Besen and Leland L. Johnson, *Compatibility Standards, Competition, and Innovation in the Broadcasting Industry* (Santa Monica, Calif.: Rand, November 1986), R-3453-NSF; Michael L. Katz and Carl Shapiro, "Network Externalities, Competition, and Compatibility," *American Economic Review* 75 (1985):424–40. Our specific hypotheses rely extensively on: Marvin Sirbu and Laurence E. Zwimpfer, "Standard Setting for Computer Communication: the Case of X.25," *IEEE Communications Magazine*, 23, (March 1985):35–45; Ashraf M. Dahod, "Local Network Standards: No Utopia," *Data Communications*, March 1983, pp. 173–80.

30. For example, Citibank sells financial data services that modify and enhance information provided by others over leased lines.

31. For example, if Wang had supported the Xerox-DEC LAN, Ethernet, it would have opened its bigger customer base to the other firms.

32. Leila Davis, ed., *IBM in Communications* (Capitol Publications, 1985); Stanley Gibson, "IBM Unveils New Net Plan," *Computerworld*, September 22, 1986, p. 1.

33. "The company's next move with regard to X.25 may be to actually provide a facility for embedding SNA in an X.25 network in a way that allows communications involving SNA protocols," Davis, *IBM in Communications*, pp. 2–6; John Pickens, "ISDN in an SNA World," *Computerworld Focus*, September 9, 1987, pp. 47–50.

34. Although it is possible to communicate between a SNA and OSI network at the higher OSI levels, users will find it easier to keep an all SNA equipment base but will not be penalized when it has to communicate with an OSI system. It should be noted that IBM has already open research centers in France and Italy to support work on OSI and telecommunications systems. It has also launched joint ventures with many foreign firms (such as Nissan and Fiat) to design computer-integrated manufacturing software and value-added networks targeted to individual industries. *Datamation*, January 15, 1985, p. 69 and February 1, 1985, pp. 98–104; *The Report on IBM*, March 18, 1987, p. 5.

35. IBM's design for the front office network of large corporations does not neatly fit the MAP system. Therefore, it has designed a variant to fit MAP. IBM controls over 40 percent of the data processing market for factory automation. The world market for factory automation by 1990 was estimated at $38 billion.

36. See Ann Hutcheson Reid, "The Economic Stakes in the Integrated Services Digital Network"; Lawrence Bolick, "Insight into On-Site Telecom," *Datamation*, March 1, 1985, pp. 76–92. Several studies indicate that an ISDN will work best when traffic volumes are lower and spread over longer distances. Ironically, most European data traffic is in the form of high volumes on short distances where leased lines at fixed rates are cheapest. Philip Black, "The State of Affairs in Worldwide Packet Networks," *Data Communications*, February 1983, pp. 97–100. IBM has real long-run advantages on on-line transaction processing, Unix, and data management. See "What Could Bring DEC Down?" *Computerworld Focus*, September 2, 1987, pp. 47–52.

37. The official was Emmanuel De Robien, a director of Bull and former head of a major European computer association. Quoted in Amiel Kornel, "U.S. Standards Efforts Receive European Reception" *Computerworld*, September 15, 1986, p. 112.

211

38. For example, DEC is interested in winning the market for sophisticated distributed intelligence systems. Many of the computer scientists designing for this segment consider the trade-offs between reliability under a ISDN and performance characteristics to be unacceptable. They favor refinement of the Interconnect Protocol that allows for a high probability of interconnection of networks while assuring other favorable performance characteristics. (Based on interviews with one of the authors.) DEC's criticism of MAP is reported in Clinton Wilder, "Olsen Slams GM's MAP, Touts Decnet," *Computerworld*, April 16, 1987, p. 12.

39. Sirbu and Zwimpfer, "Standard Setting for Computer Communication."

40. In essence this is an argument about why Europe should avoid any attempt to establish a policy of benign mercantilism. It is not a critique of efforts by the EC to encourage more competition.

41. It may take some time for NTT to admit the change. NTT's Information Society Network, the Japanese version of ISDN, was pioneered by Yasusada Kitihara, the head of research for NTT. The strong Tanaka faction of the LDP favored Dr. Kitihara as head of NTT, but Prime Minister Nakasone, backed by the powerful Japanese business federation, installed Dr. Shinto, an executive who made his name in businesses not connected to telecommunications. It will take some time before internal NTT doubts about the ISDN's practicality surface. Yasusada Kitihara, *Information Network System* (London: Heinemann Educational Books, 1983).

42. In Europe, postal and telecommunications services are provided by different organizations in Belgium, Greece, Ireland, Norway, Spain, Sweden, and the United Kingdom. However, in Belgium the post and telecommunication organizations report to the same minister and in Spain telex and telegram services are still provided by the PTT. The PTT still provides both services in Denmark, France, Germany, Italy, Luxembourg, the Netherlands, and Portugal. However, the Netherlands has announced that there will be more separation between postal and telecommunications organizations starting in 1989, and separate telecommunications services providers also exist in Denmark, Italy, and Portugal. *Transnational Data and Communications Report* (July 1987), pp. 20–21; "PTTs Could Become History," *Data Communications*, January 1987, p. 15.

43. Commission of the European Communities, Information Technologies and Telecommunication Task Force, "The Esprit Programme" TFITT/179/85-EN (Brussels: EC, February 1985).

44. Commission of the European Communities, "Report of the Commission to the Council on R&D Requirements in Telecommunications Technologies as Contribution to the Preparation of the R&D Programme RACE" COM(85) 145 final (Brussels: EC, March 25, 1985); Commission of the European Communities, Information Technologies, and Telecommunications Task Force, "Advanced Notice on the Definition Phase of the Programme RACE" (Brussels: EC, no date). The eight areas selected for exploratory R&D under RACE are (1) high-speed integrated circuits, (2) high-complexity integrated circuits, (3) integrated optoelectronics, (4) broadband switching, (5) passive optical components, (6) components for high bitrate long-haul links, (7) dedicated communications software, and (8) large area flat panel display technology.

45. New York Telephone is following a similar approach to large customers inside its service area. See Dave Rovnan, "NY Tel Offers New Net Service," Communications Week, May 5, 1986, p. 28.

46. Paul Kemezsis, "US West's Blazing Spirit: An RBOC from the Frontier," Data Communications, August 1986, p. 63. See also Wall Street Journal, July 22, 1986, p. 4 and September 24, 1987, pp. 1, 20.

III

Options for the Future

8

FOUR MODELS OF THE WORLD MARKET

Barriers to entry vary, but few, if any, segments of the world telecommunications and information markets are still natural monopolies.[1] Cumulatively, these economic and political barriers influence the form that future international competition will take.

So far U.S. negotiators have offered only cautious guidelines for managing trade in services. They realize that free trade in services is so controversial that they must begin with modest proposals. Not surprisingly, other countries want to know where these suggestions will lead.

If carried to its logical conclusion, the U.S. views would transform telecommunications into a classic commodity market, with highly standardized and interchangeable goods, subject to the rules of free trade. But many countries want only minimal moves towards freer trade, preferring to maintain a system of national monopolies linked by a cartel centered on the International Telecommunication Union's International Consultative Committee for Telephones and Telegraph (CCITT). These countries will try to quarantine a small island of free trade in an ocean of monopoly, thereby hoisting a diplomatic initiative on its own petard.

Free trade and monopoly are the two leading models on the table, but other alternatives exist. This chapter explores four models for organizing the international telecommunications and information markets: monopoly, free trade, international vertical integration, and international corporate alliances. The third and fourth models are related. Both emphasize the role that direct foreign investment could play in organizing the global market. But the underlying image of the market and of politics in each model is different.

The models crystallize the choices contained in the variety of national experiences reviewed in Chapter 1–7. Although these models will never exist in pure form, they help show how economic and political trends could shape the broad contours for the market.

The four models raise the same considerations. They all contain explicit ideas about the competitive potential inherent in different mixes of services and facilities. They highlight contrasting visions of the proper role of government in domestic and international markets. They specify market entrants and their services. They suggest the type of leading firm that will emerge from these competitive arrangements, probably a good indicator of the nature of competition and government control of the market. Moreover, each model indicates which economic interests win most often under its rules. (To simplify the analysis, the fate of large users, carriers and electronics firms is used as a benchmark and as a common denominator.)

THE MONOPOLY/CARTEL MODEL

The ancien regime of telecommunications consisted of national monopolies tied together by an international cartel that legally sanctioned administered prices, equal splits of international revenues, and rules that forbid competition for international traffic. Strictly controlled entry was one critical factor that allowed postal, telegraph and telephone authorities to run international exchange in an administered economy by lowering transaction costs. It reduced the incentives for fighting over prices. This assured that prices were not being perpetually renegotiated (a nightmare for administrators) and made it much easier to plan investment (by reducing worry about sudden shifts in market share).

The monopoly/cartel system had its political roots in a coalition of support from households, postal and telephone labor unions, the publishing business (whose mailing fees were usually heavily subsidized by the post office), government finance ministries (for which PTT earnings were a lucrative source of invisible tax receipts), the telephone monopolies themselves, and the equipment manufacturers.[2]

Economists argue that cartels, especially global cartels, are highly precarious. They disintegrate if members have substantially different discount rates, if there is no dominant member of the group, and if it is difficult to monitor and enforce their arrangements. But, this PTT- and ITU-supported system for telecommunications is remarkable for its longstanding continuity. Legal sanction helped monitor and enforce the cartel. National regulatory arrangements made all PTTs value capital intensive and long-lived investments (hence keeping the discount rate similar). Until recently, U.S. adherence to the monopoly model meant that the bulk of transoceanic traffic was controlled by AT&T. When satellites became available in the 1960s, the United States prompted the organization of a single cartel organization for the market.

Times have changed. Many key countries have switched to some version of a competitive model. The United States has aggressively sought loopholes in the international monopoly model. Moreover, domestic competition has affected significantly how capital investments are evaluated. Much of the U.S. rate increase for local users since competition is the result of newly accelerated write-offs of capital investments by the telephone companies. Preferred rates of return began to diverge because competition increased risk. Variations in the degree of domestic competition created disparities among firms when they calculated necessary rates of return for investments (because expected utility includes a risk factor). Finally, as soon as competition becomes credible, all major players are tempted to start defecting from current cartel arrangements and to court major customers with the promise of lower rates. The offering rates for new international fiber optic cables already show signs of this phenomenon.[3]

The changes in international telecommunications suggest that the old monopoly/cartel system is in trouble. The PTTs' last hope is that there are indeed significant economies of scale and scope and that risks from sunk-cost investments do make competition less attractive. So far, these claims look dubious for virtually all long-distance facilities and enhanced services and for selected basic service markets (see Chapter 7). Still, competitive possibilities do not automatically become political realities because legal barriers do not crumble in the absence of active political organization.

So, the continuation of the national monopoly model depends partly on neutralizing the transnational, pro-competition coalition of large users, service industries, and certain electronics firms (which were not the preferred PTT suppliers). How could the coalition lose? Perhaps, in Europe there may be much higher concentration of national electronics industries than in the United States or Japan, which might result in fewer attacks by competitors on the leading firms supplying the PTTs. Or, perhaps the PTTs could be saved because many countries emphasize highly centralized bargaining involving all major industries, labor, and government. This pattern of "corporatist" bargaining could discourage "end runs" on the PTT, especially if labor objects and the service industries reach compromises with the PTTs. (But labor supported "privatization" of the national network in the Netherlands and Japan.)

To the extent that the old monopoly model accepts competition, it is primarily for the provision of information services. Typically PTTs argue that they should have administrative power over information services but largely choose not to monopolize them. Instead, PTTs prefer to provide all, or most, value-added services and some information services. The packet-switched public networks, subsidized videotex systems, and the centralized integrated services digital networks of the future would provide a single set of standards and pricing guidelines for independent suppliers of information services. If permitted, free trade in services would allow foreign firms to sell only information services in national markets.

THE FREE TRADE/COMPETITIVE MODEL

The free trade/competitive model has a long history of application to commodity trade. The question is How applicable is it to services? The free trade regime assumes that governments play a small role in shaping individual markets. (Macroeconomic policy is the government's forte.[4]) Each market is ideally a commodity market in which subtle differences in labor, capital, and other factors lead to highly specialized trade and competition. The GATT bargaining process makes it easier to strike cooperative bargains covering trade by requiring transparency in trade regulations and careful supervision of retaliation against other countries and by encouraging packages of equivalent concessions rather than item-by-item reciprocity.

So far the U.S. government has pushed free trade in services in a limited way. It supports the right of U.S. companies to bring their domestic competitive assets to bear in selling value-added and information services in foreign countries. (The asset supplied might involve tapping items such as U.S. based data banks, software programming, or management personnel.) This approach targets segments of telecommunications where the barriers to entry are lowest because of smaller investment costs or because assets may be easily converted from one set of customers to another (for example, the same software programs can often meet customer needs in many countries).

In practical terms, the United States implicitly argued that value-added and information service providers should have the right to offer both global services connecting different countries and sales of value-added and information services in individual countries. This approach poses a conceptual problem because the second item closely resembles the right to foreign investment. This raises difficulties for the General Agreement on Tariffs and Trade.

As Chapter 3 noted, in the absence of competition in underlying facilities, the United States also must insist on strict rules governing the provision of facilities services such as leased circuits and the architecture for protocol conversions. Typically, this has led to demands for flat rates for leased circuits (or rates set equal to those charged to enhanced services operations of the local PTT). These arrangements alone may be inefficient, but they allow potential providers of services the freedom to configure value-added networks to deliver information services. Without such possibilities, many information services will never materialize.

The opening U.S. position is designed to buy off large users and providers of enhanced services by giving them greater latitude to operate. It also provides some benefits to the electronic firms by making sure that no PTT can control the terms for computer communications and hardware choices (see Chapter 6). Fundamentally, it pushes for the discipline of free trade in only two pieces of the market. It will tend to produce a world of "loose multinationals"—companies with many international operations and holdings that are not integrated into a global network capable of challenging for a central position within the world telecommunications industry. This would be the equivalent of a world of Electronic Data Services and GEISCOs, not one equivalent to a world girdled by a global AT&T for telecommunications or an American Express for financial services. Significantly, IBM's joint ventures for value-added networks in Japan, France, and Italy make it a likely winner in this scenario.

A bolder approach to free trade that conforms more closely to the pure model of trade can be imagined. In this variation the United States would insist on competition in international facilities and basic services. To date, the United States has voiced only cautious interest in establishing the right of its other common carriers to deliver and receive traffic from foreign PTTs. In essence, the United States has stated that MCI or US Sprint should be able to directly route calls to, say, France and should receive return traffic from France proportionate to the share of U.S. calls it delivers. It also supports some international facilities competition for the provision of "private" line services (see Chapter 5).

Ultimately, pure free traders would want something more. On international long-distance services, for example, users might freely choose among carriers when calling France. More vitally, France would acknowledge an obligation to let any competent company offer long-distance services from France to the United States. All U.S. carriers electing to operate in France would be guaranteed the right to compete freely for international traffic. France would guarantee that international calls be freely connected to the domestic network, charging only a reasonable access fee for the connection. The access fee could be treated as a tariff for the purpose of GATT negotiations. The rules governing the existence and bargaining over tariff reductions would follow traditional GATT logic.

This broader approach would pose a more extreme challenge to the PTTs than the current U.S. position. A "bold" free trade approach also must include something beneficial to the PTTs. If the United States pushes for the right to create networks for the provision of value-added and information services between countries, it might also have to concede that domestic information services were not purely tradable goods. In that case, information services could be subject to whatever local telecommunications arrangements prevail. Although each country would have an obligation to make value-added services available on terms that would not constitute an invisible trade barrier for information services, there would be no guaranteed right to allow domestic value-added networks.

The national domestic loop remains a PTT monopoly. It poses a possible bottleneck for those competing with the local PTT for the country's international market. However, the general opening of the international services market constrains the exercise of national monopoly powers. High prices or discriminatory service terms would presumably drive many international users' operations elsewhere, and anger large domestic users. In short, if the international market is fully open, monopolistic control over domestic facilities and value-added services is less worrisome.

THE DIRECT FOREIGN INVESTMENT MODEL

But what if governments cannot resolve their disputes about how much competiton should be injected into international telecommunications? Firms still have to operate internationally and want to do so as widely and as efficiently as possible. They are already starting to take matters into their own hands.

In this new era of communications and computer capabilities there are numerous philosophies about how to engineer an optimal system. It is clear, however, that investment levels for renovating the major networks are on the upswing and that PTTs worry that the financing of these investments could undermine their control over the fastest growing services.

This book has focused on the transaction costs that arise from tough negotiations over the right to operate and be paid fair prices. Examining the engineering problems and costs associated with efforts to provide global services over networks, we have asked the following types of questions: To provide long-distance services, should a network rely on fiber optic or satellite transmission facilities? How can carriers assure that their circuits are of consistently high quality? (Whether because of gremlins or precision engineering woes, seemingly similar circuits vary in quality.) Given that quality declines as the number of switching points rises, how can carriers reduce the number of interconnect switching points? Or, how can value-added networks cooperate with facilities providers in working out interconnections without giving up valuable proprietary knowledge (on either side) or without insisting on the insertion of obtrusive or specialized value-added network switching equipment on the premises of the facilities owner?

Some firms are dreaming of a whole new approach to global communications and information systems. They are frustrated by high bargaining costs, by the difficulty of engineering networks on a cost effective basis and by the complexity of providing services to users on a global basis in today's environment. They want to be global communications companies with the freedom to operate everywhere they choose. As they grope for ways to do so, they are pushing governments into experiments that may ultimately provide an alternative to both monopoly or classic free trade.

It is neither possible nor desirable for a single entity to serve every town worldwide over its own facilities. But what if AT&T

or NTT could offer basic and enhanced international services anywhere and domestic long-distance services among key cities around the world?

The operating rights of global carriers would be subject to rules set by multilateral and bilateral agreements. The global agreement might assure that global carriers could own and operate any facility or service between countries while also obligating each signatory to offer reciprocal rights to other countries' global carriers wishing to establish their own facilities and domestic long-distance services on a reciprocal basis.

The precise terms governing foreign entry into domestic markets would be negotiated bilaterally, subject to guidelines in the multilateral agreement. This bilateral bargaining would need to establish two sets of reasonable limitations. First, countries might develop a nondiscriminatory way of limiting the total number of foreign networks. Presumably, this would require some parity in bilateral entry rights and a minimum obligation to allow at least one foreign entrant. (A country could insist on some degree of local content.) Second, the host country could limit the foreign operators' business to certain gateway cities. Gateways are a familiar concept in aviation and could be replicated in telecommunications for vertically integrated carriers. A gateway would be a city where foreign carriers are allowed to pick up and deposit traffic. Any call that does not start or end at an international gateway would be guaranteed "transit" to its local destination by one of the domestic carriers on a nondiscriminatory basis.[5]

As with airlines, an international agreement could establish general principles, but the total number of international carriers and gateway cities could be subject to bilateral bargaining. Unlike the current airline system, international telephone carriers would be guaranteed the right to pick up and deliver phone calls among a country's gateway cities and to deliver traffic to any other international destination. This would permit the phone carriers to assure their large users of the ability to deliver integrated global services.

This model is particularly appealing for larger users and well-situated providers of telecommunications services. It would

225

benefit large users as consumers of the services but would discourage them from operating bypass networks. (Limits on the total number of foreign carriers would give a priority to establishing the rights of "full service" global carriers.) It would also assist a few of the major electronics firms whose products became closely linked to the major carriers.

The closest current approximation to the model is the strategy of Cable & Wireless. It is the most international of all telecommunications service providers. Indeed, in its quest to be able to deliver a message around the world on its own facilities, it has recently formed a series of local partnerships to build fiber optic networks to span the United States and both the Atlantic and Pacific oceans. With its ownership shares in other telephone cables and its likely equity participation in the new Japanese international phone company, it is emerging as a global telecommunications company.

Cable & Wireless is not the only firm capable of playing this game. For example, France's PTT (Direction Générale des Télécommunications) has created a series of subsidiaries geared to more competitive segments of the market. One of them already owns equity shares in U.S. telecommunications companies. Similarly, Bell Canada owns potential right-of-ways in the United States and British Telecom has increased its U.S. investment activity.

This approach to organizing the world market would also offer some important rewards to governments. Some level of cross-subsidy from long-distance to local users is easy to retain because governments could charge the equivalent of an access fee for connection to the local network. Moreover, in practical terms, it is hard to dislodge the PTT as a principal competitor in its home market simply because of its superior ties with customers. Under this model the PTT could pursue its own clients overseas. Moreover, the country could implement an industrial policy for telecommunications equipment as long as it did not interfere with the foreign carrier's right to use equipment of its own choice and did not restrict the right of customers to choose customer premises equipment.

THE INTERNATIONAL CORPORATE
ALLIANCE MODEL

There is probably no firm that would rush to install facilities and establish its business in every major market. And, integrated global firms trying to enter even the most desirable domestic telephone markets would confront fierce resistance from those involved in long-entrenched political bargains. Inevitably, under the third model, joint ventures that appease local regulators and benefit from carriers with strong local positions will emerge. These joint ventures could evolve into international corporate alliances and become the basis for organizing the market.

The international corporate alliance model could emerge if most governments recognized (or were forced to recognize) the desirability of substantial competition in all forms of services. But, fearful of what it could do to various cross-subsidy commitments, governments still hesitate to permit unlimited competition. Moreover, many governments are convinced that there are still important benefits to be derived from economies of scale (or scope) and dangers associated with surplus capacity in telecommunications that require market oversight. Therefore, governments would want to adequately represent all of the diverse interests in telecommunications policy without allowing unlimited competition. Governments would force greater efficiency and innovation, but assure a balancing of interests among the carriers, electronics firms, and large users. As in Japan, governments might then choose to create managed competition that guaranteed all major players, including major equipment firms and users, representation.

The international corporate alliance model is adumbrated in two recent negotiations. First, there is Japan's experiment to create a second international telecommunications carrier. Internal and external pressures finally persuaded the Japanese government to allow a second entrant to be owned by a broad range of major domestic and foreign users, firms wanting to specialize in information services, and a few firms such as Cable & Wireless that dream of being global carriers (see Chapter 5). The second example is the ARINC satellite system, which the FCC put on hold at least temporarily in September 1987. ARINC, a planned communications and information system for airlines, was to be owned by fifteen international airlines in partnership with an independent satellite company and would have competed directly with Intelsat and Inmarsat. ARINC's proponents still hope to introduce new facilities for international services and form the basis of a new international alliance of users and providers.

Like the foreign investment model, the international corporate alliance model implicitly resolves trade problems by emphasizing the virtues of investment as the key to market entry (although trade is permitted). But here foreign investment takes the forms of pools of representative interests implicitly or explicitly approved by governments. Companies that do not develop ongoing business partnerships will be left out. To assure that a cross-section of interested parties is represented, the most politically significant ventures will need a large pool of partners.

In time the partners should develop broader, international working relationships. Only rarely will arrangements be exclusive, however. Like royal court politics in medieval Europe or the collaborative arrangements among Japanese families of companies (*keiretsu*), the international corporate alliance model places a high premium on developing relationships that can be a continuing source of advantage in global competition. Firms should seek preferred, not exclusive, partners in many markets. Thus Philips, Olivetti, and AT&T are trying to rationalize their relationships systematically in a number of markets. France is trying to use Alcatel's purchase of ITT to build alliances with Spanish, Italian, and West German telecommunications firms. AT&T's partners in its Japanese value-added network include major users of data communications and prestigious local firms interested in building data communications know-how into their product lines.

The mixture of winners and losers in this scenario differs in subtle ways from the other alternatives. The other scenarios expect that some mix of new carriers, large users, and, to a lesser extent, various equipment makers will be the primary winners. This scenario predicts representative mixes of interests operating as consortiums. The marketplace is more competitive than in the past but still more guided by government oversight over entry than in the United States. In contrast to the previous scenario, the new international carriers and large users are not the big winners. Although the consortium lower costs for users almost as much as "bold" free trade or international integration, its main innovation is the use of increased competition and flexibility to improve technological innovation.

The consortium transfers know-how and assure coordination of groups of users, service suppliers, and equipment manufacturers during the evolution of an information era. For example, companies like DEC or NEC are building equity shares in and close ties to major network providers. In this scenario bargaining over which firm gets the right to enter eventually forces more cooperation among key interests, which usually argue that innovation is slowed by their deep divisions. In a sense, this scenario reduces the role of the network provider (an AT&T or an IBM) as a major leader in the world information market. It enhances the skills and capabilities of the individual equipment makers by making them more efficient at network communications. And, it assists large users primarily by spurring more flexible mixes of new communications and information technologies.

Any international corporate alliance is difficult to maintain over time because individual firms have many incentives to "shirk" or "defect" from the common effort of the alliance. Instability becomes an acute problem as collaborative ventures move into varied commercial projects. But international alliances can survive if governments' market intervention forces cooperation, or if the firms enter arrangements that put them under similar political constraints at home. For example, the British-French alliance to build the Concorde lasted because the two governments controlled procurement and because the labor unions in both countries "captured" the effort.[6]

The international corporate alliance model is a middle ground between the free trade/competitive model and the monopoly/cartel model. It implicitly recognizes that it is no longer possible for any country to unilaterally run its regulated domestic market. An international agreement is needed to set the terms of domestic regulation and to designate who has a right to compete in major markets. Participation in these international alliances provides firms with an opening wedge into new markets and improve their ability to monitor foreign markets. Therefore, governments are entitled to insist on reciprocity when allowing joint venture partners to invest in their domestic markets. That is one way for governments to assure that their domestic firms receive roughly equivalent treatment in the home countries of investing firms.

SUMMARY

This chapter sketched four alternatives for organizing the global telecommunications market. We argued that the national monopoly/cartel model is an anachronism. If countries stick closely to that model, competition could be restricted to a fairly narrow niche in the market.

So far, the United States has pushed for freer trade only in enhanced services. It also has called for the equivalent to a right of foreign investment in these services—a position difficult to sell in GATT negotiations. For the United States to win, important new GATT precedents involving investment issues must be created. Or, alternatively, the free trade model could be extended to facilities and to all services between countries, while at the same time restricting the right of foreign firms to sell information services in domestic markets.

Ultimately, the complexity of conflicting political claims and the economic and technological risks associated with offering global services may persuade both governments and companies that free trade is not the best way to serve customers. All players may be forced to move toward the foreign direct investment model to manage international telecommunications and information services. This could lead to rules that permit the creation of global telecommunications carriers entitled to compete under rules not unlike those emerging in the aviation sector. Or international corporate alliances could become the operative model. Broad consortiums representing a wide variety of users, manufacturers, and carriers could proliferate. Government supervision would be blended with a substantial dose of new international competition.

NOTES

1. Remaining barriers include the costs of negotiating entry with acceptable operating conditions, the initial investment requirements, the risks associated with the pursuit of a relatively small number of demanding clients, and the cost of managing ongoing relations with the local PTTs.
2. Eli Noam, "International Telecommunications in Transition," (Washington, D.C.: Brookings Institution, 1987).
3. At a major conference one U.S. user noted a 30 percent drop in rates for 1.5 megabits/second circuits since late in 1986. A Norwegian corporate executive also reported a price war in Europe. *Telecommunications Reports*, May 18, 1987, pp. 36–37.
4. John Gerard Ruggie, "International Regimes, Transactions and Change: Embedded Liberalism in the Postwar Economic Order," *International Organization* 36 (Spring 1982): 379–415.
5. Daniel Kasper's book in this series, *Deregulation and Globalization: Liberalizing International Trade in Air Services* (Cambridge, Mass.: Ballinger, forthcoming), provides a clear analysis of the airline regime. We see no reason why, in principle, a country could not charge a reasonable access fee for interconnection to the local domestic networks.
6. Elliott J. Feldman, *Concorde and Dissent: Explaining High Technology Project Failures in Britain and France* (New York: Cambridge University Press, 1985).

9
GATT NEGOTIATIONS AND TELECOMMUNICATIONS SERVICES

If the monopoly/cartel model is no longer adequate, what can be done? How can current trade rules be extended to cover telecommunications services? This chapter looks at the prospects for incremental change led by the GATT (the limited free trade model) and then explores how "common law practices" of evolving national regulatory arrangements, bilateral negotiations, and new approaches by other international organizations could produce more far-reaching changes (the vertical integration and corporate alliance models).

Government leaders and government bureaucracies have limited time and energy. Leaders need to cut to the heart of what is important; details can be cleaned up afterward. Trade in services is a gordian knot awaiting its Alexander.

The reasons for putting services on the trade agenda are clear. The long-term goal is to promote growth and development by expanding trade in services. The short-term aim is to promote trade expansion in services by reducing existing barriers, preventing new barriers, and developing and implementing a system of principles, rules, and procedures that apply to as large a percentage of trade in services as possible.[1]

Negotiators anticipate that telecommunications will be at the core of any general agreement on services. Therefore they want to write the rules in such a way as to bolster the general services framework. This will have to be accomplished in the context of increasing efforts by the U.S. Congress to monitor and protect key sectors including telecommunications. As of October 1987 it appeared that when a trade bill emerges from the congressional conference committee, it would allow enough presidential discretion to make it veto-proof. There almost

233

certainly will be a telecommunications section of this trade bill, drawn mostly from old bills introduced by Senator John Danforth (R. MO) and Congressman Robert Matsui (D. CA), that will again call for guarantees of market access for U.S. telecommunications firms. It will cover value-added networks but not the international provision of basic services. The demand for sectoral equivalence (mirror reciprocity) will probably be dropped because U.S. industry now acknowledges that each national network system has a sovereign right to some distinct characteristics. Instead, the bill will mandate greater precision in specifying and achieving U.S. negotiating objectives. It is also likely to call for periodic (preferably annual) reviews to assure adherence to agreed to objectives. Like the NTT pact, success would be measured in terms of sales volumes but, despite opposition from the labor unions, overseas sales of U.S. subsidiaries are likely to be counted toward sales totals. The new twist this time is that the telecommunications industry is prepared to accept remedies identical to the ones under the general trade legislation (which, of course, are getting tougher). Whether or not this trade bill becomes law, it illustrates the mood under which services and telecommunications service negotiations will be conducted.

THE STRUCTURE OF AN AGREEMENT ON SERVICES

Table 9–1 lists our main recommendations for structuring a services agreement. Our first and very important contention is that the GATT should and will win the authority to negotiate an international agreement on services, including telecommunications and information services. The GATT has already won preliminary turf battles with the UNCTAD and the OECD.[2] But the ITU continues to view the GATT as a trespasser. It is trying to preserve its domination over telecommunications services by striking preemptively to extend its control. Thus, during the work of the Preparatory Committee for the 1988 World Administrative Telegraph and Telephone Conference (WATTC) many countries with strong PTTs argued for extending the CCITT's

234

Table 9–1. The Structure of a Services Agreement.

I.	GATT competent to negotiate on services
	A. Telecommunications services central
	B. Pricing and standards relevant to GATT
II.	General framework agreement on services
	A. Attach agreement to existing articles and codes
	B. Cover as broad a range of services as possible
	C. Only umbrella signatories can sign sectoral codes
	D. Some telecommunications principles in umbrella
III.	Sectoral telecommunications services code
IV.	Negotiating fundamentals
	A. Conditional most-favored nation treatment
	B. Exchange legal, not economic concessions

authority far into the realm of value-added and information services.

We believe that the United States, was right to try to limit the scope of the proposed new WATIC regulations that would extend the PTT's regulatory jurisdiction to enhanced services that are provided on an unregulated basis in the United States.[3] *The future management of the trading system requires that the new rules for trade in telecommunications services take precedence over the rules of other international institutions.* Even though the GATT does not possess much telecommunications expertise and it is not perfectly suited to dealing with services, GATT must be able to trump the ITU because its vision and grasp are much broader.

Trade negotiators must make sure that GATT agreements take precedence over other international arrangements. GATT language should obligate signatories to make their international agreements in the ITU and elsewhere consistent with their obligations under GATT. The CCITT and CEPT cannot be allowed to introduce anti-competitive measures via the regulation of the international telecommunications network.

The United States should try to pinpoint international practices about pricing, the definition of which services fit under which regulatory framework, and should establish the interna-

tional setting of technical standards as issues of importance to the GATT.[4] Most items can be pursued through regulatory policy, but the GATT process forces these issues into a broader, and perhaps more congenial, policy milieu.

Presuming that the GATT establishes itself in the telecommunications arena, a services agreement could take several forms. Three generic types of agreements could emerge from the Uruguay round. First, existing GATT Articles and Codes might be amended and extended to cover services. This is improbable not only because of the technical problems of applying rules designed for goods to services, but also because unanimity among the contracting parties would be required. However, important service issues could be treated by extending and strengthening key Tokyo round codes. Second, new agreements on services could be attached to the GATT (like the Codes negotiated during the Tokyo round) without requiring changes in the existing GATT articles. In theory, all ninety-two contracting parties could participate, but to do so a country would need to explicitly accede to them. We expect this outcome. Third, a separate "General Agreement for Services" (GAS) could emerge from trade talks. Although the GATT and GAS might share offices and staff, the GAS would be a completely separate organization existing outside the GATT. Every country would be free to participate or not.[5]

Bilateral agreements will also have a role to play. The United States used its bilateral negotiations with Israel and Canada to learn what could be done and to set useful precedents for multilateral negotiations. The Uruguay round will continue developing agreements on services. These agreements, in turn, could set the stage for more ambitious bilateral liberalizing efforts outside the Uruguay round among countries that wish to establish more far-reaching arrangements.

Regardless of the exact relationship between existing GATT rules for goods and new ones for services, the outline of the emerging Uruguay round services bargain is already emerging. First, negotiators will try to develop a general framework (or "umbrella") agreement relevant to as broad a range of services as possible. As the umbrella nears completion, negotiations to develop separate sectoral codes will accelerate.[6] *Only countries that accede to the umbrella code could sign on to individual sectoral codes. Any country that accedes to the umbrella accord could choose to participate in one or more of the sectoral codes.* (We do not favor a package deal that would assure that the total number of signatories per code did not dip significantly by demanding that countries that sign one code sign the others.) We expect certain generic problems related to telecommunications services to be addressed in the umbrella agreement.

Reliance on conditional most-favored-nation (MFN) treatment is controversial but will be necessary. Some worry that fragmentation could arise without unconditional MFN treatment.[7] We expect that the experience of the Tokyo round codes will mute these doubts and that changing international competitive conditions will require more flexibility for services than is currently provided by unconditional most-favored-nation treatment. The regulatory nature of most restrictions to trade in services and particularly telecommunications services also complicates matters. Conditional MFN treatment should provide for the extension of negotiated benefits to all signatories of the umbrella agreement and of the sectoral codes, but not to nonparticipating countries.

Furthermore, *to reach agreements negotiators should trade legal (not economic) concessions.* This procedure was used to negotiate the Tokyo round codes and will be even more critical at the Uruguay round because of the links between these negotiations and domestic regulatory policies and because of the difficulty of measuring economic concessions on services. But U.S. negotiators constantly should remember that not all sectors are created equal and that there are complicated interconnections between sectors. U.S. strategists must develop a clear understanding of the real economic importance of possible concessions.[8] At the same time, governments should work to assure that regulations are adopted in the least restrictive manner possible. As a beginning, governments might individually review the impact of their regulatory practices on foreign service providers.

THE CENTRAL ISSUES[9]

With the structure laid out, we turn to four issues of substance that will dominate the general services discussions. First, there are issues of definition and coverage. How will services and trade in services be defined? What sectors will be included in the talks? Second, there are issues of international management and national regulation. How will negotiators balance the need to build international cooperation with the obligation to respect legitimate national regulatory objectives? Third, there is the development issue. How can liberalization be made to promote development as well as growth? Finally, there are issues of enforcement and evolution. Can a dynamic agreement be reached which includes an acceptable dispute settlement mechanism. Table 9–2 serves as a guide for this section.

Definition and Coverage

Negotiators and leaders are paid to make decisions under circumstances where there is incomplete information. If subsequent data show that those decisions were flawed, they can be altered. All services that can be traded should be covered by a new GATT agreement even though this will force the GATT to extend its reach into traditional investment issues. Industrial countries led by the United States should flex their muscles early in the negotiations to reach closure on this set of issues. It is important not to let the service exercise bog down in arguments over definition and coverage. Indeed, opponents will probably try to delay decisions by insisting that all definitional issues be resolved before anything else can be done.[10]

Specifying exactly what constitutes trade, right of establishment, and national treatment for services is particularly difficult, but these definitions will continue to change and cannot be allowed to delay reaching an agreement. To start, it may be useful to accept the working definition of trade in services put forward

Table 9–2. The Four Key Issues in the Service Negotiations.

I. Definition and coverage
  A. All services that can be traded
  B. Fast closure
  C. De facto agreement on investment
    1. Fair market access may require investment.
    2. When the domestic regulatory system requires investment as a condition for doing business, right of establishment and access to local distribution network are trade issues.
    3. Discrimination against foreign firms is inappropriate.
  D. National treatment more important for services.
    1. Grant national treatment unless otherwise specified.
    2. Obligations to foreign firms and individuals may exceed those permitted to domestic firms.

II. International management and national regulation
  A. Will need to rewrite or abolish some national regulations
  B. Stress transparency

III. Development-related issues
  A. Exclude labor and migration issues
  B. Cannot decouple telecommunications services and equipment
  C. Developing countries get time-based preferences.

IV. Enforcement and evolution
  A. Evolve or be out of date
    1. Monthly BIS-like meetings of trade officials
  B. Dispute settlement process imperative

---

by the OECD. The OECD defines traded services as "services essentially produced in one country and paid for by residents of another country."[11]

As noted earlier, defining trade in services is complicated because it is hard to distinguish between trade and investment in services. There is a general consensus that services are becoming more tradable.[12] However, as our case studies showed, separating trade and investment in services is getting harder. Most service providers want new negotiations to assure their right to sell and do business overseas. Skeptics retort that since service firms generally must set up operations in their countries before they can sell their services, this is an investment, not a trade issue, and should not be dealt with in the GATT.

U.S. negotiators have to be clear from the start that *there can be no GATT Agreement on services without de facto treatment of investment*. In order to avoid investment rules per se, however, they will have to be innovative in treating GATT's Rosencrantz and Guildenstern for investment issues: the idea of *fair market access* and the principle of *national treatment* (once admitted, foreign firms are treated like locals).

Fair market access has been a more ambitious attack on investments. The United States has pushed hard to extend market access so that U.S. firms are assured the right to do business in other countries even if this requires investment. The Services Policy Advisory Committee of the U.S. Trade Representative sees market access for services as comprising two elements: "the *right of establishment* for providers of services that require local presence; the *right of access* to distribution systems for services produced in one country and delivered in another" (emphasis added). The OECD is more restrained, seeing fair market access as requiring "the right of foreign firms to sell services in conditions of fair competition. This implies effective access to an adequate distribution network. . . . To sell his services efficiently the foreign provider of services might sometimes need to have direct access to foreign services." Europeans tiptoe around the market access issues more gingerly, but they acknowledge that the market access will have to be addressed even though it raises delicate questions of establishment, direct investment, and intellectual property.[13]

No single rule will handle all of the issues of trade vesus investment. A rule of thumb should be, *When the domestic regulatory system requires a local presence as a condition for doing business, the right of establishment (and access to the local distribution system) should become a negotiable trade issue rather than an investment issue.*[14]

It also is likely that the "principle of national treatment may have to assume greater importance for services than for goods."[15] For goods, tariffs at the borders are the main obstacles to trade. Once goods meet their tariff obligations, national treatment is accorded to the products. But tariffs have less relevance for services. It will be the companies supplying services and requiring a local business presence to do so—not the services themselves—that need national treatment. The concept of national treatment will need to be defined flexibly so that it is adaptable to different situations (such as cross-border trade with no local presence, trade with a local presence; full establishment if this is required by local regulations). As the Canadian case (Chapter 6) illustrates, minimum rights may need to exceed national treatment. In any event, fair, equivalent, or national treatment should be granted depending on the circumstances.

Some deviations from national treatment will be necessary (for example to permit special capital requirements for foreign financial firms operating locally). In addition, since many service sectors including telecommunications are viewed as central to national interests and defense, any international agreement will have to include exceptions. However, U.S. negotiators should endorse the following rule: *National treatment will be extended except when otherwise specified by agreement.*

In addition, outright discrimination against foreign suppliers (in favor of domestic service suppliers) and discrimination between foreign suppliers should be deemed inappropriate. Although the principles on nondiscrimination and national treatment could help identify inappropriate regulations in many service sectors, the prevalence of monopolies in telecommunications could raise important problems for negotiators.

In a major departure from previous trade rounds, negotiators may recognize explicitly that *countries may have minimum obligations to foreign individuals and firms that sometimes exceed those currently permitted to domestic firms.* For example, governments might decide to sustain a domestic monopoly to compete against foreign firms. As stressed repeatedly in this book, the GATT negotiation is implicitly about a reform of domestic regulatory policies. These negotiating premises makes the point clearly. If they are valid, the Uruguay round of the GATT could serve as a short-term instrument for promoting a more efficient and competitive telecommunications market.

International Management and National Regulations

National regulations get in the way of international management. These negotiations will have to confront that problem. Countries and companies that want the benefits of international cooperation will have to pay a price. The fee for admission to this negotiation will be acceptance that some national regulations will have to be rewritten or abolished.

Most countries still regulate services more strictly than goods. In many countries state or provincial authorities also are heavily involved in regulating specific service sectors. Although many of these regulations are designed to promote legitimate national objectives, they often hamper or distort trade flows. Other regulations deliberately restrict trade. Efforts to liberalize trade in services will affect and be affected by these regulations, and these regulations will become the subject of trade discussions. Negotiators will spend much time and effort examining regulations to determine which are "appropriate" and may continue to exist and which are "protectionist" and should be eliminated.

To begin, *negotiators should strive to make national regulations transparent so that their appropriateness can more easily be assessed.* Thus telecommunications regulations should be made transparent and should be notified. Requirements and conditions set on the offer or sale of services (and equipment) should be made public so that foreign as well as domestic enterprises will understand the regulatory limitations and governments will be able to scrutinize each others' administrative decisions. Because telecommunications are often regulated at a sub-national level, governments also should promote coordination and compliance of states, provinces, and municipalities with the need for transparency. Regulations that are designed to restrict trade should not be presented as something else altogether. Without transparency governments and enterprises cannot determine what constitutes an obstacle or negotiate for their removal.

Development-Related Issues

It is important that industrial countries work to assure that the expansion of trade in services promotes development, or key developing countries will persist in their intransigence.[16] But, developing countries cannot expect to get something for nothing. Industrial countries are dubious when countries such as Brazil loudly insist that goods and services are so different that it is inappropriate to address trade in services in the GATT and then, in the same breath, argue that infant industry strategies designed for manufactured products are equally appropriate to telecommunications and information services.

Again, this time, the developing countries will ask for more than they can get. But a broad service agreement makes more sense if developing countries participate. Therefore, developing countries that participate will get preferential treatment, at least for a time.

The developing countries appear to have three main goals. First, they profess to want labor-intensive services (including those requiring labor migration) on the table along with capital-intensive services such as telecommunications. There is certainly some justice in this demand, but the industrial countries will not allow this to happen. Domestic interest groups in the United States and other OECD countries that are already tempted by protectionism would raise such a howl that the negotiations would be stopped in their tracks. (Leaders of many developing countries may also pause when they consider the implications of this demand for flows of workers among developing countries.)

Second, developing countries want to decouple negotiations on services from those on goods. The developing countries hope to win concessions on tropical and other agricultural products, natural resource-based products, and on textiles, apparel, and other manufactured products during the negotiations. They do not want to pay for these victories with concessions on services, but ultimately they are unlikely to be able to keep goods and services apart. As Chapter 6 made clear: *Negotiations on telecommunications services must inevitably be linked to negotiations on telecommunications equipment.* The two are inseparable.

Third, developing countries want some form of special and differential treatment on services.[17] Given their situation, we favor a modified version of preferential treatment for developing countries.

Developed countries, frustrated that developing countries are unwilling to "graduate" and assume their full obligations under the GATT, will not agree to any formulation that provides developing countries with permanent escape clauses. Instead, an *"automatic countdown" strategy* should be employed: *Developing country signatories to either the unbrella agreement or to the sectoral agreement for telecommunications should be granted special treatment for a period of seven years from the date on which the agreements come into force.*[18] (If a country signed on three years later, it would get only four years of special treatment.) As an incentive to late and reluctant signatories, developing countries that signed on more than five years after the agreements came into force would get a two-year period of special treatment while adjusting to its new responsibilities.

More is possible. For example, *non-dominant carriers should for a time be granted differential treatment in their competition with dominant carriers. Service suppliers based in developing countries should be granted similar advantages.* Such differential treatment might allow developing country PTTs and firms to establish a competitive international presence. Firms from industrial countries might be persuaded to transfer technology to developing countries so that they could operate "export platforms."[19]

Enforcement and Evolution

Unless the agreement is dynamic and evolutionary, it will be out of date before it comes into force. And, unless a service agreement contains a satisfactory dispute settlement mechanism, the effort will be wasted because any services agreement must be strong enough to get signatories to abide by its provisions and flexible enough to allow countries to escape, for a time, their obligations when outside events close off other options.[20]

A more evolutionary process is needed to make a dispute settlement process viable. All countries realize that once an agreement is in place it becomes harder to amend it. The more countries involved, the more difficult it is to push through meaningful reforms. Yet, without ongoing reforms, any system of rules quickly runs aground. The challenge is to create a mechanism not unlike a computerized chess program that learns from experience. Over time, expert systems software gets better at performing its task. The same concept needs to be applied to agreements involving trade in services.

The Bank for International Settlements provides a reasonable model. Every month top central bankers meet in Basel, far from the media, to seek agreement and cooperation on international financial issues. Over time trust developed and their effectiveness increased. This model might be applicable to trade disputes, particularly if, as seems likely, future U.S. trade legislation forces the U.S. administration to conduct specialized sectoral review mechanisms. Thus, *after a services agreement is reached, a group of fifteen or so deputy trade ministers (representing all signatories) should meet monthly in Geneva to update the original agreement and to discuss their continuing differences.* This would help build in a bias toward reform at the outset.[21] It would help to rationalize global trends in an international forum, particularly if it simultaneously could discuss bilateral disputes when they arose.

Governments also will need to develop a fair and expeditious system for the settlement of disputes involving trade in services. Injured signatories must be able to obtain redress and compensation from other signatories. If countries nullify or impair the balance of concessions, they should be obligated to restore the balance by providing trade concessions of equivalent value.

Dispute settlement will be trickier for services because barriers to services are more technical and less visible than tariffs. It will be harder to develop a process that proceeds in orderly manner from notification to redress. However, without an appropriate dispute settlement mechanism (as well as protection afforded by exceptions and safeguards) agreement in the GATT is unlikely. The promise of dispute settlement and enforcement is the primary lure of the GATT for industrial countries. Without a dispute settlement process, they might prefer to negotiate bilaterally or in the OECD.[22]

Efforts to improve enforcement usually run aground of the ritualistic division in the GATT between "legalists," who want the rules written down and enforced across the board and the "pragmatists," who prefer to examine disputes on a case-by-case basis. Each side has its merits. The legalists, usually led by the United States, are concerned that without specific rules, the incentives to cheat will be overwhelming and the ability to bring strays back onto the reservation will be minimal. The pragmatists of the EC contend that each problem needs to be treated on its own merits. Otherwise, rules will be applied by rote without precision, understanding or compassion. By launching continuous negotiations, the rules could be strictly enforced even as they evolved to take new problems into account. This would help preserve the discipline of specific rules with the flexibility of case-by-case attention.

The issue of enforcement poses a broader and troubling question for the U.S. government than simply the efficacy of GATT. As we have argued, the GATT agreement should not be the resting point for U.S. efforts to reorganize the world information economy. This means that bilateral efforts by the United States should seek adaptations that go far beyond the GATT agreements. Given the temper of the U.S. Congress concerning telecommunications, U.S. trade negotiators are unlikely to have the luxury to remain at rest. Accordingly, U.S. negotiators should seek language that permits interested countries to push for more expansive agreements beyond the GATT.

The United States should give high priority to formulating and announcing its agenda of long-term demands inside and beyond the GATT. Without a shared understanding of how the system is supposed to work, a stable system for regulating world commerce is impossible. U.S. government efforts to explain the merits of competition are praiseworthy, but the United States still must present its ideas on a common order for the world information economy.

EXTENDING THE GATT TO TELECOMMUNICATIONS SERVICES

Negotiating a sectoral agreement on telecommunications services is important. But telecommunications services also need to occupy a special position within the umbrella agreement, because they are so central to the tradability of all services.[23] Certain general principles and rules governing the management of international telecommunications services need to be included under the umbrella agreement. Extensive details and rules concerning information services probably can be dealt with under a separate sectoral arrangement. Table 9–3 summarizes tele-

Table 9–3. Telecommunications Services under the Umbrella Agreement.

I. Rules governing monopoly behavior to assure fair competition between private firms and public monopolies
- A. Fairness in supplying services to monopolies
  - 1. Strengthen GATT Government Procurement Code
- B. Fairness in buying services from monopolies
  - 1. National treatment for telecom service providers
- C. Fair competition with monopolies
  - 1. Phase out cross-subsidies
  - 2. Provide services through separate subsidiaries
- D. Fair competition with monopolies in third markets
  - 1. Strengthen GATT Subsidies Code
  - 2. Extend Subsidies Code to telecommunications

II. Guaranteed access to and use of public telecommunications systems

III. Free flow of information (TBDF)
- A. As access improves, possible backlash against TBDF
- B. Improved access make restricting TBDF harder
- C. Let TBDF take care of itself

---

communication-related issues that might be part of the umbrella agreement.

What aspects of telecommunications services should go into the umbrella agreement? It is widely recognized that trade negotiators need to develop rules governing transactions between government monopolies and private firms. These rules might resemble those which the GATT applies (inadequately) to state trading enterprises. In addition, U.S. firms represented on the Services Policy Advisory Committee (SPAC) of the U.S. Trade Representative provide a starting point. They recommend that the "General Framework Agreement on trade in services should include two principles relating to telecommunications and information: first, the freedom to move information internationally and; second, the access to and use of public telecommunications services."[24] These two principles are seen as so important to all services operating internationally that they should not be confined to a sectoral code for telecommunications and information. We agree with the sentiment but believe that these proposals will run into some problems.

The Umbrella and Telecommunications

A Code for Monopolies. Differing regulatory approaches threaten to create major trade disputes and distortions. As a start, governments should work to assure that regulations are adopted in the most transparent and least restrictive manner possible. As a beginning, governments might individually review the impact of their regulatory practices on foreign service providers. In addition, new rules need to be devised to handle interactions between public monopolies and private firms.

Government-owned or -controlled firms can enjoy significant competitive advantages vis-à-vis private firms in less regulated markets, in their own markets, and in third countries. Thus, when the United States tried to promote competition through unilateral deregulation, foreign firms gained more access to the U.S. market without providing similar access to their own markets. Some government monopolies also will try to play competing private firms off against one another, using their monopoly position as leverage. Governments will not lightly abandon their regulatory preferences; therefore, *rules need to be negotiated to allow for fair competition between private firms and government-owned and -controlled firms.*

The SPAC identified four generic problems that need attention. First, private firms need assurance that they will receive fair treatment when supplying services to a monopoly. A first step in this direction would be to amend the Government Procurement Code to cover services. Second, the ability of private firms to purchase services from the monopoly must be assured. This involves adapting national treatment to telecommunications services. Third the ability of private firms to compete with monopolies is needed. In areas where foreign firms compete directly against domestic PTTs, PTTs should eliminate cross subsidies from other lines of business. Finally, the ability of private firms to compete in third markets needs protection. Strengthening the GATT Subsidies Code and applying it to telecommunications services would help meet this goal.[25] We suggest as a rule of thumb (elaborated later): *The greater the degree of competition in facilities and facilities services, the more flexible will be the rules concerning pricing, access, and technical standards for facilities and facility services.*

Telecommunications Services and Market Access. There is considerable dispute over how much market access should be assured to what groups under the umbrella. The SPAC call for guaranteed "access to and use of public telecommunication systems" reflects the impossibility of trading many services without such access. At this level of generality, market access must be dealt with under the umbrella. This is a priority. Pressure for guaranteed access comes from major corporate users and from the small but fast growing firms in the value-added realm. Large service companies want to sell to distant markets without "face-to-face" contact. The PTTs are obviously reluctant to grant this right. Moreover, dominant carriers in liberal settings such as AT&T, British Telecom, and Japan's KDD may be less interested in liberalization, particularly of basic services, than other common carriers (such as MCI, US Sprint, and Mercury). However, unlike the PTTs, AT&T, the regional Bell operating companies, and large service providers in countries that permit competition worry that unless they are competitive their main corporate users will bypass them.

Transborder Data Flows under the Umbrella. This book has dwelt throughout more on conduit than content because conduit issues are the key to successful multilateral negotiations. Corporate users, however, are at least as concerned about content—about transborder data flows. The same coalition of users and suppliers that supports guaranteed market access seeks guarantees for the free flow of data across national borders under the umbrella agreement.[26] They want negotiators to try to strengthen the commitment to the free flow of information during the Uruguay round of GATT negotiations by building on the OECD's Data Declaration.

If corporate preferences are accepted, signatories to the umbrella agreement would commit themselves to removing restrictions on the international movement of data, subject only to national security and other explicitly recognized objectives. (For example, signatories might impose reasonable conditions pertaining to the right of privacy and the public regulation of particular services. But, signatories would have an obligation to make such conditions fully transparent and compatible with the right to establish a competitive presence.[27]) In addition, signatories would be obliged not to impose conditions concerning minimum degrees of local data processing or value-added service provision on those using remote data processing and databases. Thus, firms of all signatories would be guaranteed the right to employ remote data processing and to tap foreign databases.

The sentiment is correct, but *guaranteed market access is much more important*. The free flow of information does not merit so high a priority. Most corporate data flows with relative ease between countries and most problems are resolved amicably when they arise. If market access is assured, most information flow problems will take care of themselves. Putting too much emphasis on the free flow of data could overload the talks and cause a backlash against market access.

As barriers that hamper the interconnection of the global telecommunication network are removed, the temptation to regulate, tax, or otherwise impede the free flow of information is likely to increase. However, in the long-term, with the introduction of broadband ISDNs, even those countries wishing to control transborder data flows may find that it becomes more difficult for them to differentiate between sensitive and nonsensitive data that flows over the network and across their borders. Pinpointing which data to restrict will get harder. Countries that hamper the flow of information across their borders will risk isolating themselves from modern technology. So long as international access is assured, in all but exceptional cases it will be far more trouble than it is worth to restrict data flows.

A Sectoral Code for Telecommunications Services

The sectoral agreement for telecommunication and information services will inevitably be more detailed than what is covered in any umbrella accord. Table 9–4 summarizes what might be covered under this type of sectoral code.

Value-Added and Information Services. The highest U.S. priority should be to use GATT and regulatory policies to promote freedom in the promotion and sales of value-added and information services. This will require changes in pricing principles and access to basic networks for enhanced services for user systems, shared-user systems, and noncarrier service providers. The purpose of this initiative is to allow U.S. companies that use or provide enhanced services a chance to operate as freely as possible within all countries and between countries.

The right of access would be promised in the umbrella agreement. It would be spelled out in detail in the sectoral code. The SPAC wants to assure the right of foreign providers of value-added and information services "both to provide their

Table 9–4. Elements of a Sectoral Code for Telecommunications Services.

I. Enhanced services: the key priority
   A. Need to change pricing principles, access to basic networks
   B. Foreign firms must have minimum rights to do business.
      1. If country cannot agree, should not sign Code.
         a. Suppliers can establish enhanced systems.
         b. Establishment for internal systems
         c. As users, enhanced systems get national treatment.
      2. But two broad protections
         a. Some legitimate reasons to restrict establishment
         b. Investment only if needed to trade
      3. PTTs enhanced services through separate subsidiaries

II. Basic services: not a priority this time
   A. PTTs would block/no clamor from most suppliers
   B. Problems being dealt with
   C. If enhanced rules established, will affect basic services

III. Infrastructure and facilities services: promote competition
   A. Greater competition in facilities should give country more freedom on pricing, access, standards
   B. If no facilities competition, then
      1. Nondiscriminatory interconnection
      2. Right to lease circuits
      3. Liberal terms on creating shared use systems

IV. Right to fair network standards
   A. Improve transparency
   B. No tight standards that deny flexibility of design
   C. Promote standardization that does not preempt design
   D. Foster designs that can accommodate designs accepted by a substantial share of the market

V. Pricing obligations: leased circuits, flat rates
   A. Pricing consistent with competitive process
   B. Reflect economies of scale
   C. Nondiscriminatory
   D. Take international practices into account

VI. Link to telecommunications equipment: inevitable
   A. CPE attachments liberalization
   B. Network equipment dealt with more in bilaterals

services from within the host country (right of establishment) and to provide them from remote locations (right of non-establishment)."[28]

The U.S. position must begin with a simple fundamental: *The telecommunications industry should establish certain minimum rights to do business for foreign firms irrespective of the rules governing domestic competition.* If nations will not abide by this rule, they should not sign the code. More specifically, there are three basic implications of this fundamental premise. As suppliers of value-added or information services, signatories to a new GATT Telecommunications Service Code should be guaranteed the right to establish businesses for the provision of value-added and information services (as defined in Chapter 3). Moreover, for purposes of internal provision of services individuals and firms operating within foreign signatory countries should have the right to establish internal systems and networks for value-added and information services for their own use and shared use with related businesses. Signatories also would accept an obligation to work to reduce any tariff or nontariff barriers that impede the establishment or use of these services in their countries, including equal treatment in government procurement. As users of value-added and information services provided by local suppliers in other countries, foreign firms and individuals would be guaranteed national treatment.

But there must be two broad protections that limit the obligations of signatories. First, signatories could introduce limited restrictions on the right to establishment for such official, noncommercial purposes as national security and public safety, or the right of privacy and other reasons recognized as legitimate under a GATT Telecommunications Code. But signatories would be obliged to notify other GATT signatories of such limitations and these limitations would be subject to challenge by other signatories. Second, guaranteeing the right to establishment under the new Telecommunications Code would not imply a right to invest unless investment can be shown to be essential for establishment. (In short, the burden of proving that investment is necessary for establishing a competitive presence would rest with the complainant.)

The provision of enhanced services by the local PTT will be a thorny item for the international negotiations. The United States should not oppose the provision of such services by the PTT. It should urge PTTs to provide such services through separate subsidiaries. The United States should view the establishment of a separate subsidiary as another item contributing to the transparency of regulations and the creation of national treatment. If the PTT establishes a separate subsidiary, the United States might take a more lenient view of its practices on other items.

Basic Services. Except for a few nondominant carriers, most notably US Sprint, there is no public clamor to put basic services competition on the negotiating table this time around. For three reasons, *the negotiators' first priority should be with enhanced, not basic, services*. First, the PTTs are already disturbed by the prospects of trade negotiations. Their profits from international long-distance services are immense. If these earnings are threatened, they will do all in their power to torpedo these negotiations. It would be a mistake for the United States to challenge the monopoly preserve of the PTTs over infrastructure facilities, infrastructure services, and basic services in the short run in the GATT Uruguay round. (Services and facilities are defined in Chapters 3 and 4.) The United States is demanding much but has yet to consider what it will have to give up.

Second, as of October 1987, the only major market that still excludes US Sprint and MCI is Mexico, and it shows signs of relaxing its opposition. It is better to resolve these legitimate problems bilaterally.[29] Third, the most important goal is to establish new principles and rules for telecommunications services. As distinctions that separate basic and enhanced services continue to erode, the impact of these principles and rules for value-added and information services will spill over to basic services. (See the analysis of the Canadian case.) Using this approach, market access for basic services will be guaranteed, but through the back door. However, nothing done on enhanced services should be perceived as precluding progress on basic services. Indeed, interested countries might insert a clause into the GATT Telecommunications Code that explicitly sanctions negotiations among countries wishing to consider bilateral agreements on basic services.

Infrastructure Facilities and Services. No matter how firmly the general principle of the right to do business is established in the umbrella agreement, to guarantee competition will require developing detailed obligations about specific prerequisites for competition in the sectoral code. The United States should use regulatory policy in the short run and consider using GATT policy in the long run to challenge selective aspects of policies for infrastructure facilities services (and indirectly for basic services). The best way to do so is for the U.S. government to announce a new presumptive standard for judging "fairness" in other countries' rules for value-added and information services: *The greater the degree of competition in the provision of infrastructure and infrastructure services in a country, the more latitude the country should have in setting rules concerning prices, access to the network, and technical standards.* This does not exempt signatories from their basic Code obligations; it provides a standard for evaluating complex evidence.

Competition in facilities introduces incentives for efficient pricing and use of facilities. Many of the specific safeguards being sought by the U.S. government to protect American firms in other countries are sometimes arbitrary and inefficient, but they are the best that can be done when there is no competition in facilities. The U.S. government should adopt a negotiating stance that rewards facilities competition. Again, this presumptive standard should not excuse a country from its GATT obligations, but it would serve as a guideline for interpreting often complex cases.[30]

Still, most countries will forbid extensive competition in infrastructure facilities or infrastructure services. Therefore a need exists for extensive procedural safeguards. The United States should seek the following items.

First, all individuals and firms operating in a foreign country would have the right to interconnect with the public network on reasonable and nondiscriminatory terms. What is critical is that *signatories to the Telecommunications Code would be obligated to provide all competitors with access to infrastructure facilities and infrastructure services on terms consistent with the right to establishment and national treatment.* Foreign firms should not be required to use only the public data network (PTT provided value-added and enhanced services).[31]

Second, any meaningful negotiation will need to reaffirm the right of foreign firms to lease circuits. As noted in the case studies, extending these guarantees to permit the shared use and resale of leased circuits is far more controversial. Many companies do not need the capacity provided by a single circuit, but the same circuit could serve several companies. PTTs often object to this practice, fearing that resale among companies would be a back door for foreign firms trying to create and sell enhanced services and that even shared use (without resale) would encourage more extensive use of leased circuits. Nonetheless, the PTTs are more willing to compromise on shared user systems than on resale to third parties.

Third, because the PTTs could be susceptible to compromise on shared use, the United States should insist on liberal terms for the creation of shared-use systems. A positive sign is that the International Communications Association has joined the British Office of Telecommunications (Oftel) in urging swift approval by the U.S. government of the U.S.-U.K. bilateral agreement to permit shared use and resale of leased circuits between the two countries (legal under CCITT arrangements as a bilateral arrangement).[32] (This would also open the way for the corporate alliance model suggested in Chapter 8.) U.S. negotiators might respond to objections to resale with a simple bargaining point: *No meaningful right to establish value-added and enhanced services in international competition is possible without the right to share and resell circuit capacity.* The minimum objective of this negotiation is to establish international free trade in value-added and information services. Therefore, shared use and resale is indispensable.

Right to Fair Network Standards. Most work on standards will remain in the CCITT. But GATT negotiators must develop a set of understandings that clarify when standard setting creates inappropriate nontariff barriers.

Extensive precedents exist showing how to enhance transparency when setting technical standards while at the same time providing foreign interests with fair representation. Usually this involves some combination of public notification and hearings. Using intense pressure on Japan, the United States also secured representation for U.S. firms on committees that set certain Japanese telecommunications standards.

The United States also seeks to establish comprehensive standards related to the provision of new services and to the interconnection of various families of computing and communications equipment. But all interested parties cannot agree on tight detailed standards on many key items. Even if they could, the United States chafes about these standards, because tight standards deny flexible design of customized networks and work against users' interest. Tight standards also undermine the U.S. advantage in highly customized equipment and for very large installed bases of customers' equipment.

Accordingly, the United States seeks to promote standardization, but not standards that preempt the network designs of major users or equipment suppliers. One way to achieve this end could be to agree that the right to network architecture be guided by a simple rule: *Signatory countries shall foster network designs that can accommodate services or equipment that conform to technical standards accepted in a substantial share of the world market.*[33] This rule would still obligate foreign suppliers to pay for development and adaptation work needed to meet local conditions, but a pattern of unreasonable special requirements or a network design intolerant of foreign specialized architectures would be in violation of the GATT Telecommunications Code.

The right to network architecture is intended to stimulate a general burden of good faith with regard to network design rather than to focus on narrow debates about specific technical obligations. It pushes national networks to be broadly tolerant of different specialized service architectures and equipment designs and to build in the capacity for dynamic configuration. The U.S.-supported Open Network Architecture qualifies in principle, and new proposals for a single broad architecture for Europe that allows freedom of competition in enhanced services might also.[34]

A standard of a "substantial share of the market" is desirable because networks cannot be infinitely flexible. If a trade dispute arises, market share data for the specific technology would be submitted as evidence to those adjudicating the claim. However, in fairness, market share should not be determined almost entirely from a producer's home market. For example, a firm supplying only the United States, a market with numerous design peculiarities, would not be entitled to be automatically accommodated in other countries.[35] However, a firm supplying, for example, cellular pagers used widely in North America and Japan should probably be accommodated in Europe.

The dynamics discussed in Chapter 7 also suggest that this rule will not lead to hopeless technological anarchy because equipment designers and service providers have an incentive to conform with prevailing standards. The rule's main advantage is that winning significant acceptance in two of the three critical regional industrial country markets would translate into a presumptive right to be tolerated. This would push national networks toward harmonization and stimulate innovation in evolving technologies.

Pricing Obligations. If pricing indeed affects the creation of service options, then, as a rule of thumb, *there should be leased circuits available at reasonable flat rates.* Although writing more complicated pricing rules into a GATT Telecommunications Code will be difficult, as a start negotiators could adopt four ideas that together might promote cost-based pricing, create stronger precedents for competition in international operations, and help assure foreign firms equal footing with local PTTs in the provision of enhanced services.

First, the Telecommunications Code should guarantee all firms the right to pricing arrangements consistent with the right to establish a competitive presence. Second, signatories should accept an obligation to reflect economies of scale in use and other cost related factors in their pricing systems. Third, each signatory should adhere to the principle of nondiscrimination in pricing, by making channels available to foreign firms on terms no worse than are made available to its domestic public carriers and their subsidiaries. Fourth, challenges to the reasonableness of national pricing arrangements could be compared with prevailing past and current international pricing practices.

Alone these four principles will not override the political pressures for cross-subsidies for local consumers. Therefore the United States might initiate an international discussion about appropriate principles governing access fees. Moreover, the FCC's 1987 proposal of an access fee for enhanced service networks in the United States was ill considered and may slow progress. Even if the FCC reverses itself, the idea is now on the international table.[36]

The Link to Telecommunications Equipment. Any GATT Telecommunications Code must ultimately cover equipment for two reasons. First, unless the Telecommunications Code takes into account the ways in which services can open up the equipment markets, manufacturers' interests will be poorly served. Second, if the equipment market is closed, many services also will be closed de facto.

Chapter 2 noted that most industrial countries are liberalizing rules governing attachment of customer premises equipment to the network. The Telecommunications Code should reinforce this trend, perhaps by creating an obligation for signatories to design and operate their networks so that all customer premises equipment needed to provide value-added and information services could be freely attached. Equipment manufacturers would only need certify that their product would not harm the network. Signatories would permit manufacturers to approve and register such equipment by type for use outside their home markets.

The outlook for ever achieving free competition in network equipment is far more pessimistic. The United States can be expected ultimately to rely on bilateral trade talks to bolster competition in network equipment. The GATT Procurement Code should be strengthened and the general negotiations on goods used to boost liberalization in this area. The only likely application to network equipment under the Telecommunications Code is that providers of specialized services should be urged to buy more switches (and other network equipment) for their internal operations. During the negotiations, it should be stressed that such uses of network equipment should be legitimate under the Telecommunications Code as long as it does not provide an alternative to the local network facilities.

INTERNATIONAL TELECOMMUNICATIONS INNOVATION

The United States and other countries also can act unilaterally outside the GATT exercise to promote telecommunications competition. Table 9–5 summarizes suggestions.

Expanding International Competition

Inevitably, a GATT agreement will depend on the broader framework of telecommunications regulations. Although the GATT should be dealt certain trump cards for dealing with these regulations, most work on these regulations will come from the

Table 9–5. International Telecommunications Innovations.

I.	Pro-competitive opportunities	
	A.	Structural reforms
		1. Divide post from telecommunications authorities
		2. Divide regulatory and carrier responsibilities
		3. PTT enhanced services provided by separate subsidiaries
	B.	Encourage creation of new international facilities
	C.	More internationally recognized private operating agencies
	D.	Phase out balanced loading rules
	E.	Special treatment for nondominant carriers
	F.	Do not extend whipsaw rule to enhanced services
II.	International data zones	
III.	An international carrier model	

FCC and its counterparts. Certain changes in national regulatory approaches and FCC policies (outlined below) would foster competition and freer trade. These regulations also might advance the international alliance model discussed in Chapter 8.

Break Down the PTT Monoliths. GATT negotiations cannot force countries to change their domestic regulatory structures or the way they provide telecommunications services, but pressure is building in many countries to consider change. Ultimately, only a few more countries may choose to abandon the monopoly provision of basic services in their domestic markets, but many others may decide to promote efficiency in the provision of services. Three structural changes already evident in some countries are particularly desirable. First, countries that have not yet done so, should separate their post and telecommunications services and reduce or eliminate cross-subsidies to the postal services as rapidly as possible. Second, telecommunications regulators should be separated from the PTTs. The temptation for self-regulated service providers to discriminate against would-be competitors is too great. Third, those PTTs that choose to provide value-added and information services should do so through separate subsidiaries. These subsidiaries should be operated at arm's length and be treated identically to domestic and foreign competitors. Without resorting to privatization, these three changes, if widely adopted, would encourage greater efficiency in domestic service provision and promote fairer competition and freer trade.

The Creation of New International Facilities. Although beyond the scope of the GATT negotiations, a second useful goal is for countries to encourage the creation of new international facilities. The United States is actively promoting international satellite systems (see Chapter 5). So far these new systems are solely owned by U.S. investors, but the U.S. government also should allow foreign nationals to be joint owners of these new systems (perhaps requiring that U.S. equipment be used at the core of the system). This approach is consistent with the international alliance model.

Ownership of present and proposed international transmission cables is already spread among many countries. The U.S. goal should be to promote systems of property rights that encourage competition.[37] The FCC should review its policies that influence the ownership and indefeasible right of use on cables and assess the feasibility of creating something close to an international auction market for ownership.[38]

Internationally Recognized Private Operating Agencies (RPOAs). The ITU recognizes the right of RPOAs (such as the traditional international record carriers) to share and resell the use of circuits. The United States recently expanded the number of service providers which will qualify for this designation. This will help enhanced service enter the international market.[39] Japan is considering a similar move. This innovation should be encouraged. Indeed, the United States should consider imposing new reporting requirements on RPOAs from countries that do not go along with this initiative.

To encourage cooperation, the United States might relax its procedures for granting RPOA status to entities from countries that demonstrate that their new service met a significant international need. This obligation could be satisfied by identifying services, prices, or (most important) specific partners that would use the service. The United States could informally encourage foreign equity participation in such service providers.

Phasing Out Balanced Loading Requirements. The greatest promise for competition in facilities is the expected period of surplus transmission capacity. The United States should encourage aggressive bargaining in this market. One way to accomplish this is to permit AT&T more latitude than it enjoys under the current balanced loading rule (see Chapter 5). The balanced loading rule could be phased out over the next five to ten years. It would be counterproductive to tie AT&T's hands just at the time when it is most critical to push more competitive deals in facilities. The FCC appears to agree.

Special Treatment for Nondominant Carriers. The FCC treats AT&T and all foreign carriers serving the United States as dominant carriers that have greater responsibilities in filing tariffs and receiving regulatory approvals. The FCC's idea of a waiver for foreign countries under certain circumstances deserves praise. Two conditions could be set. Countries that permit U.S. carriers extensive service rights in their home and international markets would be eligible for a waiver. In addition, developing countries that sign the GATT Telecommunications Code and operate services in partnership with U.S. carriers might receive a waiver during the automatic countdown period of their special preferences. This incentive might encourage developing countries to cooperate with the GATT process.

Do Not Extend the Whipsaw Rule. Finally, there is a bad idea that should be dropped. The United States has rules that require all of its carriers to have identical accounting and settlement rates with foreign countries (see Chapter 4). Recently the FCC announced its intention to extend the rule to enhanced services to protect U.S. firms from being played off against one another. We believe this is a mistake.

The whipsaw rule should not be extended to enhanced service providers precisely because it will legitimize the idea that PTTs can regulate enhanced service providers.[40] In the absence of extensive evidence of whipsawing this rule poses too great of a risk for broader U.S. objectives. More generally, the newer U.S. service providers need some flexibility in their efforts to build international connections. And AT&T deserves to benefit from its strong ties in its pursuit of better financial terms. (It would, however, be appropriate for the FCC to maintain a standby power over basic services to protect against cases of flagrant abuse.)

International Data Zones

To the extent that negotiations liberalize market access for enhanced service providers, some backlash against the free flow of information is likely. This may require new ways to assure that information flows are maintained. To fill this gap we propose the creation of international data zones. Then we look at a model that might be adopted to promote international competition even if national regulations block market access and the services negotiations stumble.

If achieving freer flows of international information proves difficult, incentives will be needed to make restrictions on data flows unattractive to individual countries. Eventually, such incentives might open up the system.

Users argue that their global operations require special accommodations that routine domestic rules often do not handle. Suppliers of data services argue that they need to be able to guarantee secure access to data and reasonable rules governing confidentiality. Both users and suppliers worry about important data becoming entangled with local rules and about local content, confidentiality, national security, and the dangers of new forms of taxation on data flows.[41] Their problems resemble those that for many years plagued international banking markets.

The United States should explore a remedy similar to international banking zones. These might be called international data zones. Data zones could be granted several special guarantees. Foreign companies could be allowed the right to operate in international data zones in countries that otherwise restrict their operations. Countries could still impose data restrictions outside of the data zones. Countries also might agree that all data moving in and out of an international data zone would be free from taxation, and not subject to local content rules. Variations on normal rules covering obligations related to national security and privacy might, in some cases, be negotiated.

This proposal would be particularly appropriate if no agreement to establish an ambitious multilateral agreement guaranteeing the free flow of information is reached. International data zones would provide a clear model for countries wishing to profit from new commercial opportunities by accommodating transborder data flows. The United States might recognize these zones under its bilateral commerce treaties, or it might promote an OECD model code for them. Even better would be a campaign to convince developing countries with strong interests in international markets to devise model codes. As countries become convinced that blocking international information flows is impractical or counterproductive, they might embrace greater liberalization.

Moving to the International Carrier Model

If GATT negotiations do not produce an adequate Telecommunications Code, the United States might eventually promote a competitive model for telecommunications that resembles the airline carrier model more closely than the free trade model.[42] The anti-competitive coalition in telecommunications is built on two important interest groups. In some countries the electronics industry views the telecommunications network as a powerful source of cross-subsidy and a potential ally of the computer industry. All countries also have a substantial interest group that supports maintaining cross-subsidies for small residential and business customers. These two coalition partners are often supported by groups concerned that competition will not produce sophisticated new value-added services for medium-sized firms.

Even though the carrier model recognizes the validity of these concerns, the benefits of competition for internationally oriented users are too great to ignore. This model would enable countries to regulate basic and enhanced services as they chose, as long as they did not obstruct or undermine new rules regarding international telecommunications services.

This model would consider international telecommunications as communications facilities and all communications services between countries. The flows of all forms of facilities and services between signatory countries would be covered by international rules. The model would also cover the right to pick up and deliver communications traffic between "ports of entry" inside of signatory countries.

To illustrate, a U.S. international carrier such as AT&T could carry a conference call (or any form of phone or computer service) from New York to Tokyo. Parties in Osaka and Kyoto could be added to the conference call, and later parties in London could be connected as well. Under this model AT&T could run the conference call entirely over its own facilities without local partners, so long as traffic moved only between points in the United States and "ports of entry" in other signatory countries. However, to interconnect the call to a nonport, say Kobe, AT&T would need to use a local partner. The local Japanese carrier would have to offer AT&T comparable terms to those afforded Japanese international carriers on the connection to Kobe. That would be Japan's only international obligation.

Signatories to such an agreement would negotiate how many carriers from each country that could service the other, bargain over specific ports of entry, and agree to pricing rules. Nations would be obligated to provide local interconnection for international carriers on reasonable, nondiscriminatory terms. Conceivably, signatories might agree to allow foreign carriers (subject to a review process) to establish in a country infrastructure facilities necessary to deliver their services. And, importantly, foreign carriers would pay the equivalent to an "access fee" for using the local national network. In short, these rules closely resemble the ones evolving in the international airline market.

This model has three advantages. First, if a country so desires, the bulk of the local monopoly remains untouched. The reform could be almost invisible because international services are little used by most consumers. Second, this model targets large users, international service providers, and large electronic firms that are the center of the telecommunications reform coalition. Specifically, this model would make it possible to more cheaply and innovatively provide large international users with services and equipment. And, later the lessons learned internationally could be applied domestically. Third, this arrangement allows the PTTs to retain most of their traditional subsidy for the average user and the less powerful electronics firms. Access fees from international carriers and continued national control (to the degree desired) over the domestic market would provide ample room for cross-subsidies.

This ambitious plan could start small. The logical participants would be the United States, the United Kingdom, and Japan because they permit domestic competition in all services. All three countries also have more than one competitor licensed to provide basic and enhanced services internationally. The logical starting point would be with rules governing dominant and nondominant carriers and the uniform settlements policy.

Initially, the United States might propose two changes. First, the United States could offer to amend the traditional rule that splits the accounting rates for international services 50-50. The FCC has discussed offering variations on a "winner takes all" approach to international services revenues. (In other words, the international services carrier selected by a customer would receive all the revenue.) Second, subject to increased regulatory oversight, the FCC could relax the rules that make all foreign carriers "dominant" by U.S. standards for countries that agreed to accept some version of this model. The FCC also could use its discretionary powers to permit foreign carriers from participating countries controlling interest in domestic facilities. For regulatory purposes they would be treated similarly to small domestic carriers of long-distances services that sell mainly in a national market.

These first two steps could start the evolution of a more systematic carrier model. Two other steps might attract additional support. First, some countries might be allowed to apply this model only to infrastructure facilities and enhanced sevices (and the necessary infrastructure to support them). Second, some form of alliance ownership structure for the new international carriers could be introduced. Diverse users and providers of services would be allowed to band together to operate carriers. If the FCC insisted on majority ownership by U.S. interests, it still could encourage foreign interests to take significant minority shares. These would not replicate "jointly provided services" which served as a mask for cartel arrangements between national monopolies.

If this model gained favor, an appropriate multilateral framework might be developed by combining elements of a GATT Telecommunications Code with a significant reworking of the rules governing RPOAs. It is not likely that this model will be popular in most countries anytime in the near future, but it does attack the central political economic issue involving international telecommunications more cleanly than other options.

CONCLUSION

You have reached the end of this voyage through the politics, economics, and technology of the communication and information revolution. If we are right that major economic and technological changes have made the current system for managing the world economy insupportable, then the future of a critical part of the world economic and cultural system is at stake.

Three diverging paths lie before us. The first is the path of least resistance. If nobody acts decisively, the world economy will sail along on its own. Perhaps we will thrive, but history is not very reassuring. Or the world economy may just vastly underperform its potential. In the worst instance, the world economy could collapse into disarray. Second, the large global firms could reorganize the world economy themselves, ignoring the bickering governments and making the GATT irrelevant. Some free market economists may prefer to saunter in this direction. Prosperity is possible if the foreign investment or international corporate alliance models prove to be dynamic and durable. Governments could even reinforce these developments by removing existing restrictions that hamper the globalization of capital. The triumph of this model, however, would radically alter the way the world works. In failure, the world economy would slip back to the first path.

The third path is uphill too. It demands that governments reach important agreements that at least gradually shift responsibility for the management of the world economy to the international level. These agreements will have important consequences for domestic regulation. Some national autonomy will be lost by all. In the past, governments and their leaders have not succeeded in such bold initiatives very often. But we think its worth a try. (Failure would still leave the possibility of going in either of the other directions.)

It is in this context that we consider the current trade negotiations. These negotiations have their own narrow rules and internal logic that will inevitably affect technological choices in important ways. But the challenges facing negotiators so outrun traditional ideas about the roles of national regulation and international commerce that many existing trade concepts will need to be reworked in fundamental ways.

The challenge and the choice are before us. Human genius for technological innovation has made the old rules and instruments for managing world commerce antiquated. Traditional trade diplomacy simply is not equipped to cope with current changes in international power and opportunity and or with the struggles for dominance in the domestic arena. We have tried to explore the issues, broad and narrow. We have proposed some first ideas about reform as well as some more ambitious alternatives. The ball is now squarely in the court of the diplomats and politicians. They can continue to complain about the difficulty and complexity of their task, thus abdicating their responsibilities. They can place their faith in large firms, mostly from industrial countries. Or they can demonstrate their creativity and imagination by shaping a competitive, fair, and prosperous new order.

NOTES

1. These goals were spelled out from the U.S. perspective in the *U.S. National Study on Trade in Services* (Washington, D.C.: U.S. Government Printing Office, 1984) prepared for the GATT. Also see James R. Basche, "Eliminating Barriers to International Trade and Investment in Services," The Conference Board Research Bulletin, No. 200 (New York: The Conference Board, 1986) a much earlier effort is Ronald Kent Shelp, *Beyond Industrialization: Ascendancy of the Global Service Economy* (New York: Praeger, 1981).

2. The United Nations Conference on Trade and Development (UNCTAD) has considerable experience in dealing with several service sectors, including shipping and insurance. For example, the UNCTAD Liner Code, a far from free-trade oriented agreement, established UNCTAD's visibility in the shipping arena. Industrial countries, however, refused to let services negotiations take place in UNCTAD. Industrial countries preferred the GATT to the OECD because of its wider membership and greater potential for dispute settlement.

3. Arguments raged over details of language such as the meaning of "offered to the public" or "any entity" or "underlying international telecommunications transport service" because these could have important implications later. *Telecommunication Reports*, May 4, 1987, pp. 19–20. Trade officials take the lead in GATT negotiations, PTT and communication officials tend to dominate ITU discussion, Transportation officials populate IMO and ICAO meetings, and finance ministries tend to control IMF and World Bank gatherings. When turf battles are lost at home, losing ministries will often try to regain their position in international negotiations.

4. Care will need to be exercised to minimize the politicization of technical issues and not to overload the GATT.

5. If the GATT process fails to produce a services agreement, then interested countries might develop a "GATT-Plus," or a "super-GATT," which would go further than any GATT agreement but would have fewer signatories. This would constitute the central nucleus of an alternative, more liberal service trade regime and generate strong pressure on developing countries to accede to a services agreement. (Only those countries that participated in the agreement would benefit from liberalization extended by it. Other countries might later join this sort of agreement if and when it became clear that there were real benefits to be gained from competing in the larger, more open markets that the agreement would create.)

6. Some suggest that it would be better to treat the sectors in long annotations to the umbrella agreement, as was done in the U.S.-Israeli agreement. We disagree. We fear an umbrella would quickly get so complicated that it would sink into oblivion. Irrespective of whether the sectors are handled by codes or annotation, we favor the U.S. delegation pushing for an understanding that signing the umbrella means a country has at least

some obligations in regard to applying the umbrella to all sectors to which it does not make a formal exception. Obviously, these obligations would be smaller than those mandated by the detailed sector codes.

7. The dangers of compartmentalization and fragmentation in this approach are spelled out in Robert O. Keohane, "Reciprocity in International Relations," *International Organization* 41, no. 1 (Winter 1986):1–27.

8. We expect some trade-offs among service sectors during the negotiations. At the final sessions top leaders may choose to disregard constraints that decoupled goods and services during preliminary negotiations and put everything on the table.

9. John B. Richardson, "Negotiating on Services—the Central Issues," paper for the Centre for Applied Studies in International Negotiation, February 12, 1987, mimeo. An abridged version appeared in *Transnational Data and Communications Reports*, March 1987.

10. Predictably, Brazil and India are insisting on definitional rigor prior to substantive negotiations. See "Trade in Services: Brazilian View of the Negotiating Process," Statement Made at the General Debate in the Group of Negotiations on Services by Ambassador Paulo Nogueira Batista, MTN.GNS/W/3 (Geneva: GATT, March 11, 1987) and the "Statement of India at the Group of Negotiations on Services Meeting on 23 February 1987," MTN.GNS/W/4 (Geneva: GATT, March 11, 1987).

11. OECD Working Party of the Trade Committee, "The Elements of a Conceptual Framework for Trade in Services," 1C/WP(85)79 (Paris: OECD, December 1985), p. 4. For a more detailed discussion see Jonathan David Aronson and Peter F. Cowhey, *Trade in Services: A Case for Open Markets* (Washington, D.C.: American Enterprise Institute, 1984).

12. See for example, Raymond J. Krommenacker, "The Impact of Information Technology on Trade Interdependence," *Journal of World Trade Law* 20, no. 4 (July/August 1986):389–393.

13. Services Policy Advisory Committee to USTR, "Telecommunications and Information Services in the Trade in Services Negotiations: An Industry View," March 20, 1987, mimeo (hereafter SPAC), p. 15; OECD, "Elements of a Conceptual Framework for Trade in Services," p. 5; European Community Services Group, "The European Service Sector's View on the Liberalization of

Trade in Services," a paper by the ECSG for the European Commission, April 14, 1987, mimeo, p. 6.

14. John Richardson, "Negotiating on Services," distinguishes nine, not necessarily exhaustive categories running from one that covers clear cases of pure cross-frontier trade (e.g., remote data processing) to one that covers pure investment (e.g., a licensing or franchising agreement to set up a hotel). The problem is drawing the line. Every country will try to draw the line so it gains advantage. For a discussion of the market access problem see Brian Hindley, "Introducing Services into the GATT," January 30, 1987, mimeo.

15. European Community Services Group, "The European Service Sector's View on the Liberalization of Trade in Services," p. 11.

16. Jagdish Bhagwati, "International Trade in Services and Its Relevance for Economic Development," in Orio Giarini, ed., *The Emerging Service Economy* (Geneva: Pergamon Press for Services World Forum, 1986), pp. 3–34 and Dorothy I. Riddle, *Service-Led Growth: The Role of the Service Sector in World Development* (New York: Praeger, 1986) provide overviews of the role of services and trade in services in development.

17. There is now significant doubt about whether earlier preferential treatment boosted development, and some scholars suggest that such treatment may actually have reduced the bargaining power of developing countries. See John McMillan, "International Trade Negotiations: A Game-Theoretic View," paper for the Ford Foundation Project on Trade Policy and the Developing World, March 1987, mimeo.

18. The exact nature and time period of this special treatment would be negotiated along with the agreements.

19. Alternatively, GATT negotiators could examine whether certain forms of trade (e.g., establishing a commercial presence) are preferable to others (e.g., trade across borders) in terms of transferring technology and promoting development. They could encourage the more growth-promoting forms. Special efforts could be made to assure that opening markets to large foreign suppliers promotes competition rather than precluding it. If foreign service suppliers abuse their dominant positions and technological superiority, developing countries are unlikely to permit significant liberalization. Richardson, "Negotiating on Services," pp.11–12.

20. One reason that the GATT was chosen as the forum for negotiations was the existence of its dispute settlement mechanism. The OECD, in contrast, requires unanimous decisions and cannot penalize member states that do not abide by its decisions.

21. If the "culture" of a firm or a working arrangement is flexible and forward-looking, then positive reform is easy to introduce. The problem is akin to rolling a boulder down a mountain. At rest at the peak, it takes just a small push to start it rolling in any direction. But once it begins to pick up momentum, major course corrections are almost impossible. The trick is to start the boulder (or the services agreement) rolling in the right direction.

22. We agree with the OECD proposal to restrict participation in dispute settlement panels to contracting parties that are signatories of the sectoral code relevant to a dispute.

23. Only the financial sector has the potential to compete with telecommunications for center stage in a services negotiation. See Ingo Walter, *Global Competition in Financial Services: Market Structure, Protection, and Trade Liberalization* (Cambridge, Mass.: Ballinger, forthcoming) in this series. We question how central financial services can be, however, for two reasons. First, in most countries finance ministries are more powerful than trade ministries and are unlikely to cede much authority over domestic or international monetary policy to trade officials. Second, the internationalization of financial markets is built on telecommunications breakthroughs and not the other way around.

24. SPAC, "An Industry View," p. 1.

25. These four points are cited in elaborated form in C. Michael Aho and Jonathan D. Aronson, *Trade Talks: America Better Listen!* (New York: Council on Foreign Relations, 1985), pp. 147–48. They seem to be generally accepted in USTR and the U.S. service sector.

26. SPAC, "An Industry View," European Community Services Group, "The European Service Sector's View on the Liberalization of Trade in Services," p. 16.

27. Firms want to avoid the Dresser industry fiasco in which the U.S. government ordered an American firm to stop providing data to its French subsidiary during the Reagan administration's unsuccessful effort to block the construction of the Soviet gas pipeline in 1982–1983. The pipeline was built, but the reputation for reliability of the U.S. government and U.S. firms was undermined.

28. The SPAC sees opening access to telecommunications services as an evolutionary process in which value-added and information

services should be a key goal of the sectoral code. It worries that the PTT will use its control of the distribution system to discriminate against foreign firms. SPAC to USTR, "An Industry View," p. 13. US Sprint dissented from this view because the newer international phone companies want a greater emphasis on the right of U.S. companies to be interconnected with foreign PTTs.

29. US Sprint, however, has aggressively urged the United States government, including the USTR, to work to assure international competition in the provision of basic services. (See Telemation Associates, "Addressing International Long-Distance Telecommunications Services in Trade-Related Negotiations," for US Sprint, Bank of America, and Manufacturers Hanover Trust, April 22, 1986, mimeo.) US Sprint's tactic of threatening to push basic services onto the agenda of the GATT round unless it gains access to key overseas markets is an inspired piece of leverage. The arguments against including basic services are practical and political, not technical or economic. It is easier for the United States and West Germany to buy off Sprint and MCI than to risk having to discuss basic services during the GATT negotiations. This strategy helped Sprint gain access to Canada in 1986. As of October 1987 US Sprint and MCI were still working to get direct access to Mexico but an agreement with the Bundespost was almost finalized.

30. As Chapter 4 noted, Japan introduced a plan for liberalizing competition for facilities and basic services that initially seemed to discriminate against foreign competitors. The U.S. government vigorously protested the rules. However, since the rules were modified, the competition in facilities has made the Japanese "opening" in enhanced services a more meaningful opportunity for foreign companies.

31. There are two other concerns related to access to leased circuits. First, unless the quality of available leased circuits is adequate, all efforts to assure access are quixotic. The United States should stress that systematic discrimination in the availability of high-quality infrastructure services constitutes a breach. Second, as the number of enhanced services increases, the importance of listings in public directories on a fair basis grows. More subtly, the numbering system used in the management of networks contains numerous opportunities for abuse. Countries have to construct

their numbering systems in ways that permit multiple providers for enhanced services.

32. At present a third-party individual or firm may provide the management and part of the capital for a shared end user system. Previously the International Communications Association opposed FCC efforts in this direction, fearing that unilateral U.S. action might trigger usage-sensitive tariffs in retaliation. *Telecommunications Reports* July 27, 1987, pp. 16–17.

33. Negotiations would determine the meaning of "accepted in a substantial share of the world market."

34. European Commission, *Towards a Dynamic European Economy*, Green Paper on the Development of the Common Market for Telecommunications Services and Equipment, June 1987.

35. This rule could be a problem for a small, new firm. It might be asked to show that its products fit the technological standards set by products with larger market shares. This is the natural strategy for such firms, so it should not impose undue hardships.

36. The European Community considered a proposal to allow any carrier dedicated to universal services to charge a lower rate to its subsidiaries offering enhanced services. This lower rate would have constituted a reward for the losses entailed by universal service. It would have been tied to permission for competition in both basic and enhanced services (but not in facilities or facilities services). This idea was a slightly different twist on an access charge. The proposal died before being raised officially.

37. More competition on property rights presupposes a real effort to diversify the choice of facilities, thereby making private fiber optic cable more important.

38. US Sprint opposed market pricing for indefeasible right-of-use, fearing that foreign PTTs might require it to use a cable owned jointly with AT&T. This would make US Sprint vulnerable. We still favor market pricing, but it should be tied to competition in facilities.

39. "In the Matter of Regulatory Policies and International Telecommunications: Notice of Inquiry and Proposed Rule-making" Before the F.C.C.. Docket No. 86-491. Adopted December 23, 1986, p. 17. "Japan-U.S. VAN Liberalization May Trigger Local Upheaval," *Japan Economic Journal* (March 21, 1987):22.

40. In early 1987 the FCC clarified its uniform settlements policy to make clear that "indirect" traffic agreements that newer entrants rely on to win friends overseas do not have to have equal sharing

of revenues so long as they are equitable. *Telecommunication Reports*, February 23, 1987. pp. 12–13.

41. The U.S. government is as much a sinner in restricting data flows as any country because of its national security rules.

42. We are working out the implications of adopting Model 4 in Chapter 8 to the world economy. We will explore this theme in depth in Jonathan D. Aronson and Peter F. Cowhey, *International Corporate Alliances* (Cambridge, Mass.: Ballinger, forthcoming).

Index

Accounting services, 4, 6
Aeronautical Radio, Inc. (ARINC), 134, 149, 227–228
Africa, 42
Agriculture, 35, 38
Airlines, 225, 228; reservations service, 7, 79, 106 n. 4, 134; telecommunications costs, 52
Alberta, Canada, 174 n. 12
Alcatel, 81 n. 16, 180, 207 n. 16, 228
Algeria, 120
American Airlines, 7
American Express, 36, 145, 222
American International Group (AIG), 36, 37, 56 n. 16
American Satellites, 127
Ameritech, 54 n. 8, 167, 175 n. 26, 204
Amstar, 131
Animation services, 6–7
Apple Computers, 159, 200
Arabsat, 59 n. 30, 120
Argentina, 42
Assembly of Parties, 126, 129, 132
AT&T, 92, 219, 224–225, 263; and balanced loading, 262; and cables, 74–75, 114, 145; and Canada, 22, 156, 158, 160, 165, 175 n. 24; and computers, 28, 54 n. 9; and conference calls, 265–266; and cross-subsidies, 107 n. 17; and deregulation, 26–27, 28, 30–31, 72–73, 124; and digital switches, 67–68; and equipment suppliers, 29, 31; and Global Information Movement and Management, 203; international long-distance profits, 103 n. 5, 104 n. 8; international transmission, 74–75,

104 n. 7, 114; and Japan, 141, 144, 145, 172–173 n. 2, 200, 228; and leased circuits, 84 n. 16; and local area networks, 196; and leased circuits, 84 n. 16; and market access, 249–250; and market share, 30; and packet switching, 94; and PTTs, 90; rates, 78, 84 n. 16, 90; and satellites, 114, 123, 126, 133–134; System V, 209 n. 24; and telex and telegrams, 105 n. 12; Unix, 209; and value-added services, 84 n. 21, 96; and West Germany, 180
AT&T Long Line, 104 n. 8
AT&T Technologies, 31
Atlanta, 7
Australia, 19, 20, 89, 104 ns. 7 and 8
Austria, 99, 184
Automatic Data Processing, 106 n. 15
AVSAT system, 134

Baker Plan, 43
Balanced loading, 74–75, 114, 146 n. 1, 262
Baldrige, Malcolm, 129
Bank of America, 145
Bank for International Settlement, 245
Bank of Tokyo, 143
Banks, 79, 100, 168–169, 176 n. 30
Barbados, 7
Bardi of Venice, 17 n. 9
Basic telecommunications services, 85–91; and GATT, 254–255; market, 86–87, 249–250
Bavaria, 182
Bearer services, 106 n. 16
Belgium, 69, 81 n. 6, 186, 187, 212 n. 42

ABOUT THE AUTHORS

Jonathan D. Aronson is an associate professor in the School of International Relations and in the Annenberg School of Communications at the University of Southern California. His publications include *Trade Talks: America Better Listen!* (with Michael Aho); *Trade in Services: The Case for Open Markets* (with Peter Cowhey); *Profit and the Pursuit of Energy: Markets and Regulation* (co-edited with Peter Cowhey); *Debt and the Less Developed Countries* (edited); and *Money and Power: Banks and the World Monetary System.* Aronson was a Council on Foreign Relations International Affairs Fellow in the Office of the United States Trade Representative in 1982–1983. He was one of the principal authors of the U.S. National Study on Trade in Services submitted to the GATT in 1983. He received a B.A. in government from Harvard University, an M.A. in applied economics from Stanford University and a Ph.D. in political science from Stanford University.

Peter F. Cowhey is an associate professor in the Department of Political Science and in the Graduate School of International Relations and Pacific Studies at the University of California, San Diego. His publications include *The Problems of Plenty: Energy Policy and International Politics; Trade in Services: The Case for Open Markets* (with Jonathan Aronson); and *Profit and the Pursuit of Energy: Markets and Regulations* (co-edited with Jonathan Aronson). Cowhey received a Rockefeller Foundation International Affairs Fellowship for 1984–1986 and, as a Council on Foreign Relations International Affairs Fellow in 1984–1985, served as a market planner and consultant at AT&T International and AT&T Communications International. He received his

B.S.F.S. in foreign service from Georgetown University and his Ph.D. in political science from the University of California, Berkeley.